How Our Laws Are Made

The Legislative Process, Introducing a Bill or Resolution, Parliamentary Reference Sources, Committee of the Whole, Committee Markup, Amendment Tree, Amendments Between the Houses, and the Committee System

TheCapitol.Net

For over 30 years, TheCapitol.Net and its predecessor, Congressional Quarterly Executive Conferences, have been training professionals from government, military, business, and NGOs on the dynamics and operations of the legislative and executive branches and how to work with them.

Our training and publications include congressional operations, legislative and budget process, communication and advocacy, media and public relations, research, business etiquette, and more.

TheCapitol.Net is a non-partisan firm.

Our publications and courses, written and taught by *current* Washington insiders who are all independent subject matter experts, show how Washington works.™ Our products and services can be found on our web site at *<www.TheCapitol.Net>*.

Additional copies of *How Our Laws Are Made* can be ordered online: *<www.GovernmentSeries.com>*.

Design and production by Zaccarine Design, Inc., Evanston, IL; 847-864-3994.

∞ The paper used in this publication exceeds the requirements of the American National Standard for Information Sciences—Permanence of Paper for Printed Library Materials, ANSI Z39.48-1992.

v 1.1

How Our Laws Are Made, softbound:
ISBN: 158733-125-X
ISBN 13: 978-1-58733-125-1

Summary Table of Contents

Table of Contents

703-739-3790 **xi**

Commit, Recommit, Refer

    Commit

    Recommit

    Recommit with Instructions

    Refer

Resolving Differences

    Concur in the Senate Amendment(s), Concur in the Senate Amendment(s) with an Amendment

    Disagree to the Senate Amendment(s)

    Insist on House Amendment(s)

    Instruct Conferees

    Recede and Concur, Recede and Concur with an Amendment

    Recede from House Amendment(s)

Chapter 18:

Chapter 19:

108TH CONGRESS 1st Session	HOUSE OF REPRESENTATIVES	DOCUMENT 108–93

HOW OUR LAWS ARE MADE

Revised and Updated

By Charles W. Johnson, Parliamentarian,
U.S. House of Representatives

Presented by Mr. Ney

June 20, 2003.—Ordered to be printed

U.S. GOVERNMENT PRINTING OFFICE

87–101   WASHINGTON : 2003

For sale by the Superintendent of Documents, U.S. Government Printing Office
Internet: bookstore.gpo.gov   Phone: toll free (866) 512–1800; DC area (202) 512–1800
Fax: (202) 512–2250   Mail: Stop SSOP, Washington, DC 20402–0001

H. Con. Res. 139   Agreed to June 20, 2003

One Hundred Eighth Congress
of the
United States of America

AT THE FIRST SESSION

Begun and held at the City of Washington on Tuesday, the seventh day of January, two thousand and three

Concurrent Resolution

Resolved by the House of Representative (the Senate concurring),

SECTION 1. HOW OUR LAWS ARE MADE.

(a) IN GENERAL.—An edition of the brochure entitled "How Our Laws Are Made", as revised under the direction of the Parliamentarian of the House of Representatives in consultation with the Parliamentarian of the Senate, shall be printed as a House document under the direction of the Joint Committee on Printing.

(b) ADDITIONAL COPIES.—In addition to the usual number, there shall be printed the lesser of—

> (1) 550,000 copies of the document, of which 440,000 copies shall be for the use of the House of Representatives, 100,000 copies shall be for the use of the Senate, and 10,000 copies shall be for the use of the Joint Committee on Printing; or

> (2) such number of copies of the document as does not exceed a total production and printing cost of $220,794, with distribution to be allocated in the same proportion as described in paragraph (1), except that in no case shall the number of copies be less than 1 per Member of Congress.

Attest:

JEFF TRANDAHL,
Clerk of the House of Representatives.

Attest:

EMILY J. REYNOLDS
Secretary of the Senate.

(II)

2

EARLIER PRINTINGS

Document	Number of copies
1953, H. Doc. 210, 83d Cong. (H. Res. 251 by Mr. Reed)	36,771
1953, H. Doc. 210, 83d Cong. (H. Res. 251 by Mr. Reed)	122,732
1955, H. Doc. 210, 83d Cong. (H. Con. Res. 93 by Mr. Willis)	167,728
1956, H. Doc. 451, 84th Cong. (H. Con. Res. 251 by Mr. Willis)	30,385
1956, S. Doc. 152, 84th Cong. (S. Res. 293 by Senator Kennedy)	182,358
1959, H. Doc. 156, 86th Cong. (H. Con. Res. 95 by Mr. Lesinski)	228,591
1961, H. Doc. 136, 87th Cong. (H. Con. Res. 81 by Mr. Willis)	211,797
1963, H. Doc. 103, 88th Cong. (H. Con. Res. 108 by Mr. Willis)	14,000
1965, H. Doc. 103, 88th Cong. (S. Res. 9 by Senator Mansfield)	196,414
1965, H. Doc. 164, 89th Cong. (H. Con. Res. 165 by Mr. Willis)	319,766
1967, H. Doc. 125, 90th Cong. (H. Con. Res. 221 by Mr. Willis)	324,821
1969, H. Doc. 127, 91st Cong. (H. Con. Res. 192 by Mr. Celler)	174,500
1971, H. Doc. 144, 92d Cong. (H. Con. Res. 206 by Mr. Celler)	292,000
1972, H. Doc. 323, 92d Cong. (H. Con. Res. 530 by Mr. Celler)	292,500
1974, H. Doc. 377, 93d Cong. (H. Con. Res. 201 by Mr. Rodino)	246,000
1976, H. Doc. 509, 94th Cong. (H. Con. Res. 540 by Mr. Rodino)	282,400
1978, H. Doc. 259, 95th Cong. (H. Con. Res. 190 by Mr. Rodino)	298,000
1980, H. Doc. 352, 96th Cong. (H. Con. Res. 95 by Mr. Rodino)	298,000
1981, H. Doc. 120, 97th Cong. (H. Con. Res. 106 by Mr. Rodino)	298,000
1985, H. Doc. 158, 99th Cong. (H. Con. Res. 203 by Mr. Rodino)	298,000

(III)

IV

FOREWORD

First published in 1953 by the Committee on the Judiciary of the House of Representatives, this 23rd edition of "How Our Laws Are Made" reflects changes in congressional procedures since the 22nd edition, which was revised and updated in 2000. This fiftieth anniversary edition was prepared by the Office of the Parliamentarian of the U.S. House of Representatives in consultation with the Office of the Parliamentarian of the U.S. Senate.

The framers of our Constitution created a strong federal government resting on the concept of "separation of powers."

In Article I, Section 1, of the Constitution, the Legislative Branch is created by the following language: "All legislative Powers herein granted shall be vested in a Congress of the United States, which shall consist of a Senate and House of Representatives." Article I, Section 5, of the Constitution provides that: "Each House may determine the Rules of its Proceedings, . . .".

Upon this elegant, yet simple, grant of legislative powers and rulemaking authority has grown an exceedingly complex and evolving legislative process—much of it unique to each House of Congress. To aid the public's understanding of the legislative process, we have revised this popular brochure. For more detailed information on how our laws are made and for the text of the laws themselves, the reader should refer to government internet sites or pertinent House and Senate publications available from the Superintendent of Documents, U.S. Government Printing Office, Washington, D.C. 20402.

CHARLES W. JOHNSON.

(V)

TABLE OF CONTENTS

(VII)

VIII

7

HOW OUR LAWS ARE MADE

I. INTRODUCTION

This brochure is intended to provide a basic outline of the numerous steps of our federal lawmaking process from the source of an idea for a legislative proposal through its publication as a statute. The legislative process is a matter about which every person should be well informed in order to understand and appreciate the work of Congress.

It is hoped that this guide will enable readers to gain a greater understanding of the federal legislative process and its role as one of the foundations of our representative system. One of the most practical safeguards of the American democratic way of life is this legislative process with its emphasis on the protection of the minority, allowing ample opportunity to all sides to be heard and make their views known. The fact that a proposal cannot become a law without consideration and approval by both Houses of Congress is an outstanding virtue of our bicameral legislative system. The open and full discussion provided under the Constitution often results in the notable improvement of a bill by amendment before it becomes law or in the eventual defeat of an inadvisable proposal.

As the majority of laws originate in the House of Representatives, this discussion will focus principally on the procedure in that body.

II. THE CONGRESS

Article I, Section 1, of the United States Constitution, provides that:

> All legislative Powers herein granted shall be vested in a Congress of the United States, which shall consist of a Senate and House of Representatives.

The Senate is composed of 100 Members—two from each state, regardless of population or area—elected by the people in accordance with the 17th Amendment to the Constitution. The 17th Amendment changed the former constitutional method under which Senators were chosen by the respective state legislatures. A Senator must be at least 30 years of age, have been a citizen of the United States for nine years, and, when elected, be a resident of the state for which the Senator is chosen. The term of office is six years and one-third of the total membership of the Senate is elect-

(1)

2

ed every second year. The terms of both Senators from a particular state are arranged so that they do not terminate at the same time. Of the two Senators from a state serving at the same time the one who was elected first—or if both were elected at the same time, the one elected for a full term—is referred to as the "senior" Senator from that state. The other is referred to as the "junior" Senator. If a Senator dies or resigns during the term, the governor of the state must call a special election unless the state legislature has authorized the governor to appoint a successor until the next election, at which time a successor is elected for the balance of the term. Most of the state legislatures have granted their governors the power of appointment.

Each Senator has one vote.

As constituted in the 108th Congress, the House of Representatives is composed of 435 Members elected every two years from among the 50 states, apportioned to their total populations. The permanent number of 435 was established by federal law following the Thirteenth Decennial Census in 1910, in accordance with Article I, Section 2, of the Constitution. This number was increased temporarily to 437 for the 87th Congress to provide for one Representative each for Alaska and Hawaii. The Constitution limits the number of Representatives to not more than one for every 30,000 of population. Under a former apportionment in one state, a particular Representative represented more than 900,000 constituents, while another in the same state was elected from a district having a population of only 175,000. The Supreme Court has since held unconstitutional a Missouri statute permitting a maximum population variance of 3.1 percent from mathematical equality. The Court ruled in *Kirkpatrick* v. *Preisler*, 394 U.S. 526 (1969), that the variances among the districts were not unavoidable and, therefore, were invalid. That decision was an interpretation of the Court's earlier ruling in *Wesberry* v. *Sanders*, 376 U.S. 1 (1964), that the Constitution requires that "as nearly as is practicable one man's vote in a congressional election is to be worth as much as another's".

A law enacted in 1967 abolished all "at-large" elections except in those less populous states entitled to only one Representative. An "at-large" election is one in which a Representative is elected by the voters of the entire state rather than by the voters in a congressional district within the state.

A Representative must be at least 25 years of age, have been a citizen of the United States for seven years, and, when elected, be a resident of the state in which the Representative is chosen. Unlike the Senate where a successor may be appointed by a governor when a vacancy occurs during a term, if a Representative dies or

9

3

resigns during the term, the executive authority of the state must call a special election pursuant to state law for the choosing of a successor to serve for the unexpired portion of the term.

Each Representative has one vote.

In addition to the Representatives from each of the States, a Resident Commissioner from the Commonwealth of Puerto Rico and Delegates from the District of Columbia, American Samoa, Guam, and the Virgin Islands are elected pursuant to federal law. The Resident Commissioner, elected for a four-year term, and the Delegates, elected for two-year terms, have most of the prerogatives of Representatives including the right to vote in committees to which they are elected. However, the Resident Commissioner and the Delegates do not have the right to vote on matters before the House.

Under the provisions of Section 2 of the 20th Amendment to the Constitution, Congress must assemble at least once every year, at noon on the third day of January, unless by law they appoint a different day.

A Congress lasts for two years, commencing in January of the year following the biennial election of Members. A Congress is divided into two sessions.

The Constitution authorizes each House to determine the rules of its proceedings. Pursuant to that authority, the House of Representatives adopts its rules on the opening day of each Congress. The Senate considers itself a continuing body and operates under continuous standing rules that it amends from time to time.

Unlike some other parliamentary bodies, both the Senate and the House of Representatives have equal legislative functions and powers with certain exceptions. For example, the Constitution provides that only the House of Representatives originate revenue bills. By tradition, the House also originates appropriation bills. As both bodies have equal legislative powers, the designation of one as the "upper" House and the other as the "lower" House is not appropriate.

The chief function of Congress is the making of laws. In addition, the Senate has the function of advising and consenting to treaties and to certain nominations by the President. However under the 25th Amendment to the Constitution, both Houses confirm the President's nomination for Vice-President when there is a vacancy in that office. In the matter of impeachments, the House of Representatives presents the charges—a function similar to that of a grand jury—and the Senate sits as a court to try the impeachment. No impeached person may be removed without a two-thirds vote of the Senate. The Congress under the Constitution and by statute also plays a role in presidential elections. Both Houses meet in

4

joint session on the sixth day of January, following a presidential election, unless by law they appoint a different day, to count the electoral votes. If no candidate receives a majority of the total electoral votes, the House of Representatives, each state delegation having one vote, chooses the President from among the three candidates having the largest number of electoral votes. The Senate, each Senator having one vote, chooses the Vice President from the two candidates having the largest number of votes for that office.

III. SOURCES OF LEGISLATION

Sources of ideas for legislation are unlimited and proposed drafts of bills originate in many diverse quarters. Primary among these is the idea and draft conceived by a Member. This may emanate from the election campaign during which the Member had promised, if elected, to introduce legislation on a particular subject. The Member may have also become aware after taking office of the need for amendment to or repeal of an existing law or the enactment of a statute in an entirely new field.

In addition, the Member's constituents, either as individuals or through citizen groups, may avail themselves of the right to petition and transmit their proposals to the Member. The right to petition is guaranteed by the First Amendment to the Constitution. Many excellent laws have originated in this way, as some organizations, because of their vital concern with various areas of legislation, have considerable knowledge regarding the laws affecting their interests and have the services of legislative draftspersons for this purpose. Similarly, state legislatures may "memorialize" Congress to enact specified federal laws by passing resolutions to be transmitted to the House and Senate as memorials. If favorably impressed by the idea, a Member may introduce the proposal in the form in which it has been submitted or may redraft it. In any event, a Member may consult with the Legislative Counsel of the House or the Senate to frame the ideas in suitable legislative language and form.

In modern times, the "executive communication" has become a prolific source of legislative proposals. The communication is usually in the form of a message or letter from a member of the President's Cabinet, the head of an independent agency, or the President himself, transmitting a draft of a proposed bill to the Speaker of the House of Representatives and the President of the Senate. Despite the structure of separation of powers, Article II, Section 3, of the Constitution imposes an obligation on the President to report to Congress from time to time on the "State of the Union" and to recommend for consideration such measures as the President considers necessary and expedient. Many of these executive commu-

5

nications follow on the President's message to Congress on the state of the Union. The communication is then referred to the standing committee or committees having jurisdiction of the subject matter of the proposal. The chairman or the ranking minority member of the relevant committee usually introduces the bill promptly either in the form in which it was received or with desired changes. This practice is usually followed even when the majority of the House and the President are not of the same political party, although there is no constitutional or statutory requirement that a bill be introduced to effectuate the recommendations. The committee or one of its subcommittees may also decide to examine the communication to determine whether a bill should be introduced. The most important of the regular executive communications is the annual message from the President transmitting the proposed budget to Congress. The President's budget proposal, together with testimony by officials of the various branches of the government before the Appropriations Committees of the House and Senate, is the basis of the several appropriation bills that are drafted by the Committee on Appropriations of the House.

Many of the executive departments and independent agencies employ legislative counsels who are charged with the drafting of bills. These legislative proposals are forwarded to Congress with a request for their enactment.

The drafting of statutes is an art that requires great skill, knowledge, and experience. In some instances, a draft is the result of a study covering a period of a year or more by a commission or committee designated by the President or a member of the Cabinet. The Administrative Procedure Act and the Uniform Code of Military Justice are two examples of enactments resulting from such studies. In addition, congressional committees sometimes draft bills after studies and hearings covering periods of a year or more.

IV. FORMS OF CONGRESSIONAL ACTION

The work of Congress is initiated by the introduction of a proposal in one of four forms: the bill, the joint resolution, the concurrent resolution, and the simple resolution. The most customary form used in both Houses is the bill. During the 107th Congress (2001–2002), 8,948 bills and 178 joint resolutions were introduced in both Houses. Of the total number introduced, 5,767 bills and 125 joint resolutions originated in the House of Representatives.

For the purpose of simplicity, this discussion will be confined generally to the procedure on a House of Representatives bill, with brief comment on each of the forms.

6

BILLS

A bill is the form used for most legislation, whether permanent or temporary, general or special, public or private.

The form of a House bill is as follows:

A BILL

For the establishment, etc. [as the title may be].

Be it enacted by the Senate and House of Representatives of the United States of America in Congress assembled, That, etc.

The enacting clause was prescribed by law in 1871 and is identical in all bills, whether they originate in the House of Representatives or in the Senate.

Bills may originate in either the House of Representatives or the Senate with one notable exception provided for in the Constitution. Article I, Section 7, of the Constitution provides that all bills for raising revenue shall originate in the House of Representatives but that the Senate may propose or concur with amendments. By tradition, general appropriation bills also originate in the House of Representatives.

There are two types of bills—public and private. A public bill is one that affects the public generally. A bill that affects a specified individual or a private entity rather than the population at large is called a private bill. A typical private bill is used for relief in matters such as immigration and naturalization and claims against the United States.

A bill originating in the House of Representatives is designated by the letters "H.R." followed by a number that it retains throughout all its parliamentary stages. The letters signify "House of Representatives" and not, as is sometimes incorrectly assumed, "House resolution". A Senate bill is designated by the letter "S." followed by its number. The term "companion bill" is used to describe a bill introduced in one House of Congress that is similar or identical to a bill introduced in the other House of Congress.

A bill that has been agreed to in identical form by both bodies becomes the law of the land only after—

(1) Presidential approval; or

(2) failure by the President to return it with objections to the House in which it originated within 10 days (Sundays excepted) while Congress is in session; or

(3) the overriding of a presidential veto by a two-thirds vote in each House.

It does not become law without the President's signature if Congress by their final adjournment prevent its return with objections.

7

This is known as a "pocket veto". For a discussion of presidential action on legislation, see Part XVIII.

JOINT RESOLUTIONS

Joint resolutions may originate either in the House of Representatives or in the Senate—not, as is sometimes incorrectly assumed, jointly in both Houses. There is little practical difference between a bill and a joint resolution and the two forms are often used interchangeably. One difference in form is that a joint resolution may include a preamble preceding the resolving clause. Statutes that have been initiated as bills have later been amended by a joint resolution and vice versa. Both are subject to the same procedure except for a joint resolution proposing an amendment to the Constitution. When a joint resolution amending the Constitution is approved by two-thirds of both Houses, it is not presented to the President for approval. Following congressional approval, a joint resolution to amend the Constitution is sent directly to the Archivist of the United States for submission to the several states where ratification by the legislatures of three-fourths of the states within the period of time prescribed in the joint resolution is necessary for the amendment to become part of the Constitution.

The form of a House joint resolution is as follows:

JOINT RESOLUTION

Authorizing, etc. [as the title may be].

Resolved by the Senate and House of Representatives of the United States of America in Congress assembled, That all, etc.

The resolving clause is identical in both House and Senate joint resolutions as prescribed by statute in 1871. It is frequently preceded by a preamble consisting of one or more "whereas" clauses indicating the necessity for or the desirability of the joint resolution.

A joint resolution originating in the House of Representatives is designated "H.J. Res." followed by its individual number which it retains throughout all its parliamentary stages. One originating in the Senate is designated "S.J. Res." followed by its number.

Joint resolutions, with the exception of proposed amendments to the Constitution, become law in the same manner as bills.

CONCURRENT RESOLUTIONS

A matter affecting the operations of both Houses is usually initiated by a concurrent resolution. In modern practice, and as determined by the Supreme Court in *INS* v. *Chadha,* 462 U.S. 919 (1983), concurrent and simple resolutions normally are not legislative in character since not "presented" to the President for ap-

8

proval, but are used merely for expressing facts, principles, opinions, and purposes of the two Houses. A concurrent resolution is not equivalent to a bill and its use is narrowly limited within these bounds. The term "concurrent", like "joint", does not signify simultaneous introduction and consideration in both Houses.

A concurrent resolution originating in the House of Representatives is designated "H. Con. Res." followed by its individual number, while a Senate concurrent resolution is designated "S. Con. Res." together with its number. On approval by both Houses, they are signed by the Clerk of the House and the Secretary of the Senate and transmitted to the Archivist of the United States for publication in a special part of the Statutes at Large volume covering that session of Congress.

SIMPLE RESOLUTIONS

A matter concerning the rules, the operation, or the opinion of either House alone is initiated by a simple resolution. A resolution affecting the House of Representatives is designated "H. Res." followed by its number, while a Senate resolution is designated "S. Res." together with its number. Simple resolutions are considered only by the body in which they were introduced. Upon adoption, simple resolutions are attested to by the Clerk of the House of Representatives or the Secretary of the Senate and are published in the Congressional Record.

V. INTRODUCTION AND REFERRAL TO COMMITTEE

Any Member, Delegate or the Resident Commissioner from Puerto Rico in the House of Representatives may introduce a bill at any time while the House is in session by simply placing it in the "hopper", a wooden box provided for that purpose located on the side of the rostrum in the House Chamber. Permission is not required to introduce the measure. The Member introducing the bill is known as the primary sponsor. An unlimited number of Members may cosponsor a bill. To prevent the possibility that a bill might be introduced in the House on behalf of a Member without that Member's prior approval, the primary sponsor's signature must appear on the bill before it is accepted for introduction. Members who cosponsor a bill upon its date of introduction are original cosponsors. Members who cosponsor a bill after its introduction are additional cosponsors. Cosponsors are not required to sign the bill. A Member may not be added or deleted as a cosponsor after the bill has been reported by the last committee authorized to consider it, but the Speaker may not entertain a request to delete the name of the primary sponsor at any time. Cosponsors names may be deleted by their own unanimous consent request or that of the pri-

9

mary sponsor. In the Senate, unlimited multiple sponsorship of a bill is permitted. Occasionally, a Member may insert the words "by request" after the Member's name to indicate that the introduction of the measure is at the suggestion of some other person or group—usually the President or a member of his Cabinet.

In the Senate, a Senator usually introduces a bill or resolution by presenting it to one of the clerks at the Presiding Officer's desk, without commenting on it from the floor of the Senate. However, a Senator may use a more formal procedure by rising and introducing the bill or resolution from the floor. A Senator usually makes a statement about the measure when introducing it on the floor. Frequently, Senators obtain consent to have the bill or resolution printed in the Congressional Record following their formal statement.

If any Senator objects to the introduction of a bill or resolution, the introduction of the bill or resolution is postponed until the next day. If there is no objection, the bill is read by title and referred to the appropriate committee. If there is an objection, the bill is placed on the Calendar.

In the House of Representatives, it is no longer the custom to read bills—even by title—at the time of introduction. The title is entered in the Journal and printed in the Congressional Record, thus preserving the purpose of the custom. The bill is assigned its legislative number by the Clerk. The bill is then referred as required by the rules of the House to the appropriate committee or committees by the Speaker, the Member elected by the Members to be the Presiding Officer of the House, with the assistance of the Parliamentarian. The bill number and committee referral appear in the next issue of the Congressional Record. It is then sent to the Government Printing Office where it is printed in its introduced form and printed copies are made available in the document rooms of both Houses. Printed and electronic versions of the bill are also made available to the public.

Copies of the bill are sent to the office of the chairman of the committee to which it has been referred. The clerk of the committee enters it on the committee's Legislative Calendar.

Perhaps the most important phase of the legislative process is the action by committees. The committees provide the most intensive consideration to a proposed measure as well as the forum where the public is given their opportunity to be heard. A tremendous volume of work, often overlooked by the public, is done by the Members in this phase. There are, at present, 19 standing committees in the House and 16 in the Senate as well as several select committees. In addition, there are four standing joint committees of the two Houses, with oversight responsibilities but no legislative

10

jurisdiction. The House may also create select committees or task forces to study specific issues and report on them to the House. A task force may be established formally through a resolution passed by the House or informally through organization of interested Members by the House leadership.

Each committee's jurisdiction is divided into certain subject matters under the rules of each House and all measures affecting a particular area of the law are referred to the committee with jurisdiction over that particular subject matter. For example, the Committee on the Judiciary in the House has jurisdiction over measures relating to judicial proceedings generally, and 17 other categories, including constitutional amendments, immigration and naturalization, bankruptcy, patents, copyrights, and trademarks. In total, the rules of the House and of the Senate each provide for over 200 different classifications of measures to be referred to committees. Until 1975, the Speaker of the House could refer a bill to only one committee. In modern practice, the Speaker may refer an introduced bill to multiple committees for consideration of those provisions of the bill within the jurisdiction of each committee concerned. Except in extraordinary circumstances, the Speaker must designate a primary committee of jurisdiction on bills referred to multiple committees. The Speaker may place time limits on the consideration of bills by all committees, but usually time limits are placed only on additional committees. Additional committees are committees other than the primary committee to which a bill has been referred, either initially on its introduction or sequentially following the report of the primary committee. A time limit is placed on an additional committee only when the primary committee has reported its version to the House.

Membership on the various committees is divided between the two major political parties. The proportion of the Members of the minority party to the Members of the majority party is determined by the majority party, except that half of the members on the Committee on Standards of Official Conduct are from the majority party and half from the minority party. The respective party caucuses nominate Members of the caucus to be elected to each standing committee at the beginning of each Congress. Membership on a standing committee during the course of a Congress is contingent on continuing membership in the party caucus that nominated a Member for election to the committee. If a Member ceases to be a Member of the party caucus, a Member automatically ceases to be a member of the standing committee.

Members of the House may serve on only two committees and four subcommittees with certain exceptions. However, the rules of the caucus of the majority party in the House provide that a Mem-

11

ber may be chairman of only one subcommittee of a committee or select committee with legislative jurisdiction, except for certain committees performing housekeeping functions and joint committees.

A Member usually seeks election to the committee that has jurisdiction over a field in which the Member is most qualified and interested. For example, the Committee on the Judiciary traditionally is composed almost entirely of lawyers. Many Members are nationally recognized experts in the specialty of their particular committee or subcommittee.

Members rank in seniority in accordance with the order of their appointment to the full committee and the ranking majority member with the most continuous service is usually elected chairman. The rules of the House require that committee chairmen be elected from nominations submitted by the majority party caucus at the commencement of each Congress. In the 108th Congress, no Member of the House may serve as chairman of the same standing committee or of the same subcommittee thereof for more than three consecutive Congresses.

The rules of the House prohibit a committee that maintains a subcommittee on oversight from having more than six subcommittees with the exception of the Committee on Appropriations and the Committee on Government Reform.

Each committee is provided with a professional staff to assist it in the innumerable administrative details involved in the consideration of bills and its oversight responsibilities. For standing committees, the professional staff is limited to 30 persons appointed by a vote of the committee. Two-thirds of the committee staff are selected by a majority vote of the majority committee members and one-third of the committee staff are selected by a majority vote of minority committee members. All staff appointments are made without regard to race, creed, sex, or age. Minority staff requirements do not apply to the Committee on Standards of Official Conduct because of its bipartisan nature. The Committee on Appropriations has special authority under the rules of the House for appointment of staff for the minority.

VI. CONSIDERATION BY COMMITTEE

One of the first actions taken by a committee is to seek the input of the relevant departments and agencies about a bill. Frequently, the bill is also submitted to the General Accounting Office with a request for an official report of views on the necessity or desirability of enacting the bill into law. Normally, ample time is given for the submission of the reports and they are accorded serious consideration. However, these reports are not binding on the com-

12

mittee in determining whether or not to act favorably on the bill. Reports of the departments and agencies in the executive branch are submitted first to the Office of Management and Budget to determine whether they are consistent with the program of the President. Many committees adopt rules requiring referral of measures to the appropriate subcommittee unless the full committee votes to retain the measure at the full committee.

COMMITTEE MEETINGS

Standing committees are required to have regular meeting days at least once a month. The chairman of the committee may also call and convene additional meetings. Three or more members of a standing committee may file with the committee a written request that the chairman call a special meeting. The request must specify the measure or matter to be considered. If the chairman does not call the requested special meeting within three calendar days after the filing of the request, to be held within seven calendar days after the filing of the request, a majority of the members of the committee may call the special meeting by filing with the committee written notice specifying the date, hour, and the measure or matter to be considered at the meeting. In the Senate, the Chair may still control the agenda of the special meeting through the power of recognition. Committee meetings may be held for various purposes including the "markup" of legislation, authorizing subpoenas, or internal budget and personnel matters.

A subpoena may be authorized and issued at a meeting by a vote of a committee or subcommittee with a majority of members present. The power to authorize and issue subpoenas also may be delegated to the chairman of the committee. A subpoena may require both testimonial and documentary evidence to be furnished to the committee. A subpoena is signed by the chairman of the committee or by a member designated by the committee.

All meetings for the transaction of business of standing committees or subcommittees, except the Committee on Standards of Official Conduct, must be open to the public, except when the committee or subcommittee, in open session with a majority present, determines by record vote that all or part of the remainder of the meeting on that day shall be closed to the public. Members of the committee may authorize congressional staff and departmental representatives to be present at any meeting that has been closed to the public. Open committee meetings may be covered by the media. Permission to cover hearings and meetings is granted under detailed conditions as provided in the rules of the House.

The rules of the House provide that House committees may not meet during a joint session of the House and Senate or during a

13

recess when a joint meeting of the House and Senate is in progress. Committees may meet at other times during an adjournment or recess up to the expiration of the constitutional term.

PUBLIC HEARINGS

If the bill is of sufficient importance, the committee may set a date for public hearings. The chairman of each committee, except for the Committee on Rules, is required to make public announcement of the date, place, and subject matter of any hearing at least one week before the commencement of that hearing, unless the committee chairman with the concurrence of the ranking minority member or the committee by majority vote determines that there is good cause to begin the hearing at an earlier date. If that determination is made, the chairman must make a public announcement to that effect at the earliest possible date. Public announcements are published in the Daily Digest portion of the Congressional Record as soon as possible after an announcement is made and are often noted by the media. Personal notice of the hearing, usually in the form of a letter, is sometimes sent to relevant individuals, organizations, and government departments and agencies.

Each hearing by a committee or subcommittee, except the Committee on Standards of Official Conduct, is required to be open to the public except when the committee or subcommittee, in open session and with a majority present, determines by record vote that all or part of the remainder of the hearing on that day shall be closed to the public because disclosure of testimony, evidence, or other matters to be considered would endanger national security, would compromise sensitive law enforcement information, or would violate a law or a rule of the House. The committee or subcommittee may by the same procedure vote to close one subsequent day of hearing, except that the Committees on Appropriations, Armed Services, and the Permanent Select Committee on Intelligence, and subcommittees thereof, may vote to close up to five additional, consecutive days of hearings. When a quorum for taking testimony is present, a majority of the members present may close a hearing to discuss whether the evidence or testimony to be received would endanger national security or would tend to defame, degrade, or incriminate any person. A committee or subcommittee may vote to release or make public matters originally received in a closed hearing or meeting. Open committee hearings may be covered by the media. Permission to cover hearings and meetings is granted under detailed conditions as provided in the rules of the House.

Hearings on the Budget are required to be held by the Committee on Appropriations in open session within 30 days after its

14

transmittal to Congress, except when the committee, in open session and with a quorum present, determines by record vote that the testimony to be taken at that hearing on that day may be related to a matter of national security. The committee may by the same procedure close one subsequent day of hearing.

On the day set for a public hearing in a committee or subcommittee, an official reporter is present to record the testimony. After a brief introductory statement by the chairman and often by the ranking minority member or other committee member, the first witness is called. Members or Senators who wish to be heard sometimes testify first out of courtesy and due to the limitations on their time. Cabinet officers and high-ranking government officials, as well as interested private individuals, testify either voluntarily or by subpoena.

So far as practicable, committees require that witnesses who appear before it file a written statement of their proposed testimony in advance of their appearance and limit their oral presentations to a brief summary of their arguments. In the case of a witness appearing in a nongovernmental capacity, a written statement of proposed testimony shall include a curriculum vitae and a disclosure of certain federal grants and contracts.

Minority party members of the committee are entitled to call witnesses of their own to testify on a measure during at least one additional day of a hearing.

Each member of the committee is provided only five minutes in the interrogation of each witness until each member of the committee who desires to question a witness has had an opportunity to do so. In addition, a committee may adopt a rule or motion to permit committee members to question a witness for a specified period not longer than one hour. Committee staff may also be permitted to question a witness for a specified period not longer than one hour.

A transcript of the testimony taken at a public hearing is made available for inspection in the office of the clerk of the committee. Frequently, the complete transcript is printed and distributed widely by the committee.

MARKUP

After hearings are completed, the subcommittee usually will consider the bill in a session that is popularly known as the "markup" session. The views of both sides are studied in detail and at the conclusion of deliberation a vote is taken to determine the action of the subcommittee. It may decide to report the bill favorably to the full committee, with or without amendment, or unfavorably, or without recommendation. The subcommittee may also suggest that

15

the committee "table" it or postpone action indefinitely. Each member of the subcommittee, regardless of party affiliation, has one vote. Proxy voting is no longer permitted in House committees.

FINAL COMMITTEE ACTION

At full committee meetings, reports on bills may be made by subcommittees. Bills are read for amendment in committees by section and members may offer germane amendments. Committee amendments are only proposals to change the bill as introduced and are subject to acceptance or rejection by the House itself. A vote of committee members is taken to determine whether the full committee will report the bill favorably, adversely, or without recommendation. If the committee votes to report the bill favorably to the House, it may report the bill without amendments or may introduce and report a "clean bill". Committees may authorize the chairman to postpone votes in certain circumstances. If the committee has approved extensive amendments, the committee may decide to report the original bill with one "amendment in the nature of a substitute" consisting of all the amendments previously adopted, or may report a new bill incorporating those amendments, commonly known as a clean bill. The new bill is introduced (usually by the chairman of the committee), and, after referral back to the committee, is reported favorably to the House by the committee. A committee may table a bill or not take action on it, thereby preventing further action on a bill. This makes adverse reports or reports without recommendation to the House by a committee unusual. The House also has the ability to discharge a bill from committee. For a discussion of the motion to discharge, see Part X.

Generally, a majority of the committee or subcommittee constitutes a quorum. A quorum is the number of members who must be present in order for the committee to report. This ensures participation by both sides in the action taken. However, a committee may vary the number of members necessary for a quorum for certain actions. For example, a committee may fix the number of its members, but not less than two, necessary for a quorum for taking testimony and receiving evidence. Except for the Committees on Appropriations, the Budget, and Ways and Means, a committee may fix the number of its members, but not less than one-third, necessary for a quorum for taking certain other actions. The absence of a quorum is subject to a point of order, an objection that the proceedings are in violation of a rule of the committee or of the House, because the required number of members are not present.

16

POINTS OF ORDER WITH RESPECT TO COMMITTEE HEARING
PROCEDURE

A point of order in the House does not lie with respect to a measure reported by a committee on the ground that hearings on the measure were not conducted in accordance with required committee procedure. However, certain points of order may be made by a member of the committee that reported the measure if, in the committee hearing on that measure, that point of order was (1) timely made and (2) improperly disposed of.

VII. REPORTED BILLS

If the committee votes to report the bill to the House, the committee staff writes a committee report. The report describes the purpose and scope of the bill and the reasons for its recommended approval. Generally, a section-by-section analysis is set forth explaining precisely what each section is intended to accomplish. All changes in existing law must be indicated in the report and the text of laws being repealed must be set out. This requirement is known as the "Ramseyer" rule. A similar rule in the Senate is known as the "Cordon" rule. Committee amendments also must be set out at the beginning of the report and explanations of them are included. Executive communications regarding the bill may be referenced in the report.

If at the time of approval of a bill by a committee, except for the Committee on Rules, a member of the committee gives notice of an intention to file supplemental, minority, or additional views, that member is entitled to not less than two additional calendar days after the day of such notice (excluding Saturdays, Sundays, and legal holidays unless the House is in session on those days) in which to file those views with the clerk of the committee. Those views that are timely filed must be included in the report on the bill. Committee reports must be filed while the House is in session unless unanimous consent is obtained from the House to file at a later time or the committee is awaiting additional views.

The report is assigned a report number upon its filing and is sent to the Government Printing Office for printing. House reports are given a prefix-designator that indicates the number of the Congress. For example, the first House report in the 108th Congress was numbered 108–1.

In the printed report, committee amendments are indicated by showing new matter in italics and deleted matter in line-through type. The report number is printed on the bill and the calendar number is shown on both the first and back pages of the bill. However, in the case of a bill that was referred to two or more committees for consideration in sequence, the calendar number is printed

17

only on the bill as reported by the last committee to consider it. For a discussion of House calendars, see Part IX.

Committee reports are perhaps the most valuable single element of the legislative history of a law. They are used by the courts, executive departments, and the public as a source of information regarding the purpose and meaning of the law.

CONTENTS OF REPORTS

The report of a committee on a measure that has been approved by the committee must include: (1) the committee's oversight findings and recommendations; (2) a statement required by the Congressional Budget Act of 1974, if the measure is a bill or joint resolution providing new budget authority (other than continuing appropriations) or an increase or decrease in revenues or tax expenditures; (3) a cost estimate and comparison prepared by the Director of the Congressional Budget Office whenever the Director has submitted that estimate and comparison to the committee prior to the filing of the report; and (4) a statement of general performance goals and objectives, including outcome-related goals and objectives, for which the measure authorizes funding. Each report accompanying a bill or joint resolution relating to employment or access to public services or accommodations must describe the manner in which the provisions apply to the legislative branch. Each of these items are set out separately and clearly identified in the report.

With respect to each record vote by a committee, the total number of votes cast for, and the total number of votes cast against any public measure or matter or amendment thereto and the names of those voting for and against, must be included in the committee report.

In addition, each report of a committee on a public bill or public joint resolution must contain a statement citing the specific powers granted to Congress in the Constitution to enact the law proposed by the bill or joint resolution. Committee reports that accompany bills or resolutions that contain federal unfunded mandates are also required to include an estimate prepared by the Congressional Budget Office on the cost of the mandates on state, local, and tribal governments. If an estimate is not available at the time a report is filed, committees are required to publish the estimate in the Congressional Record. Each report also must contain an estimate, made by the committee, of the costs which would be incurred in carrying out that bill or joint resolution in the fiscal year reported and in each of the five fiscal years thereafter or for the duration of the program authorized if less than five years. The report must include a comparison of the estimates of those costs with any esti-

24

18

mate made by any Government agency and submitted to that committee. The Committees on Appropriations, House Administration, Rules, and Standards of Official Conduct are not required to include cost estimates in their reports. In addition, the committee's own cost estimates are not required to be included in reports when a cost estimate and comparison prepared by the Director of the Congressional Budget Office has been submitted prior to the filing of the report and included in the report.

FILING OF REPORTS

Measures approved by a committee must be reported by the Chairman promptly after approval. If not, a majority of the members of the committee may file a written request with the clerk of the committee for the reporting of the measure. When the request is filed, the clerk must immediately notify the chairman of the committee of the filing of the request, and the report on the measure must be filed within seven calendar days (excluding days on which the House is not in session) after the day on which the request is filed. This does not apply to a report of the Committee on Rules with respect to a rule, joint rule, or order of business of the House or to the reporting of a resolution of inquiry addressed to the head of an executive department.

AVAILABILITY OF REPORTS AND HEARINGS

A measure or matter reported by a committee (except the Committee on Rules in the case of a resolution providing a rule, joint rule, or order of business) may not be considered in the House until the third calendar day (excluding Saturdays, Sundays, and legal holidays unless the House is in session on those days) on which the report of that committee on that measure has been available to the Members of the House. This rule is subject to certain exceptions including resolutions providing for certain privileged matters and measures declaring war or other national emergency. However, it is in order to consider a report from the Committee on Rules on the same day it is reported that proposes only to waive this availability requirement. If hearings were held on a measure or matter so reported, the committee is required to make every reasonable effort to have those hearings printed and available for distribution to the Members of the House prior to the consideration of the measure in the House. Committees are also required, to the maximum extent feasible, to make their publications available in electronic form. A general appropriation bill reported by the Committee on Appropriations may not be considered until printed committee hearings and a committee report thereon have been available to the Members of the House for at least three calendar days (exclud-

19

ing Saturdays, Sundays, and legal holidays unless the House is in session on those days).

VIII. LEGISLATIVE OVERSIGHT BY STANDING COMMITTEES

Each standing committee, other than the Committees on Appropriations and on the Budget, is required to review and study, on a continuing basis, the application, administration, execution, and effectiveness of the laws dealing with the subject matter over which the committee has jurisdiction and the organization and operation of federal agencies and entities having responsibility for the administration and evaluation of those laws.

The purpose of the review and study is to determine whether laws and the programs created by Congress are being implemented and carried out in accordance with the intent of Congress and whether those programs should be continued, curtailed, or eliminated. In addition, each committee having oversight responsibility is required to review and study any conditions or circumstances that may indicate the necessity or desirability of enacting new or additional legislation within the jurisdiction of that committee, and must undertake, on a continuing basis, future research and forecasting on matters within the jurisdiction of that committee. Each standing committee also has the function of reviewing and studying, on a continuing basis, the impact or probable impact of tax policies on subjects within its jurisdiction.

The rules of the House provide for special treatment of an investigative or oversight report of a committee. Committees are allowed to file joint investigative reports and to file investigative and activities reports after the House has completed its final session of a Congress. In addition, several of the standing committees have special oversight responsibilities. The details of those responsibilities are set forth in the rules of the House.

IX. CALENDARS

The House of Representatives has five calendars of business: the Union Calendar, the House Calendar, the Private Calendar, the Corrections Calendar, and the Calendar of Motions to Discharge Committees. The calendars are compiled in one publication printed each day the House is in session. This publication also contains a history of Senate-passed bills, House bills reported out of committee, bills on which the House has acted, and other useful information.

When a public bill is favorably reported by all committees to which referred, it is assigned a calendar number on either the Union Calendar or the House Calendar, the two principal calendars

20

of business. The calendar number is printed on the first page of the bill and, in certain instances, is printed also on the back page. In the case of a bill that was referred to multiple committees for consideration in sequence, the calendar number is printed only on the bill as reported by the last committee to consider it.

UNION CALENDAR

The rules of the House provide that there shall be:

A Calendar of the Committee of the Whole House on the state of the Union, to which shall be referred public bills and public resolutions raising revenue, involving a tax or charge on the people, directly or indirectly making appropriations of money or property or requiring such appropriations to be made, authorizing payments out of appropriations already made, releasing any liability to the United States for money or property, or referring a claim to the Court of Claims.

The large majority of public bills and resolutions reported to the House are placed on the Union Calendar. For a discussion of the Committee of the Whole House, see Part XI.

HOUSE CALENDAR

The rules further provide that there shall be:

A House Calendar, to which shall be referred all public bills and public resolutions not requiring referral to the Calendar of the Committee of the Whole House on the state of the Union.

Bills not involving a cost to the government and resolutions providing special orders of business are examples of bills and resolutions placed on the House Calendar.

PRIVATE CALENDAR

The rules also provide that there shall be:

A Private Calendar, . . . to which shall be referred all private bills and private resolutions.

All private bills reported to the House are placed on the Private Calendar. The Private Calendar is called on the first and third Tuesdays of each month. If two or more Members object to the consideration of any measure called, it is recommitted to the committee that reported it. There are six official objectors, three on the majority side and three on the minority side, who make a careful study of each bill or resolution on the Private Calendar. The official objectors' role is to object to a measure that does not conform to the requirements for that calendar and prevent the passage without debate of nonmeritorious bills and resolutions. Private bills that have been reported from committee are only considered under the private calendar procedure. Alternative procedures reserved for public bills are not applicable for reported private bills.

21

CORRECTIONS CALENDAR

If a measure pending on either the House or Union Calendar is of a noncontroversial nature, it may be placed on the Corrections Calendar. The Corrections Calendar was created to address specific problems with federal rules, regulations, or court decisions that bipartisan and narrowly targeted bills could expeditiously correct. After a bill has been favorably reported and is on either the House or Union Calendar, the Speaker may, after consultation with the Minority Leader, file with the Clerk a notice requesting that such bill also be placed upon a special calendar known as the Corrections Calendar. On the second and fourth Tuesdays of each month, the Speaker directs the Clerk to call any bill that has been printed on the Corrections Calendar. A three-fifths vote of the Members voting is required to pass any bill called from the Corrections Calendar. A failure to adopt a bill from the Corrections Calendar does not necessarily mean the final defeat of the bill because it may then be brought up for consideration in the same way as any other bill on the House or Union Calendar.

CALENDAR OF MOTIONS TO DISCHARGE COMMITTEES

When a majority of the Members of the House sign a motion to discharge a committee from consideration of a public bill or resolution, that motion is referred to the Calendar of Motions to Discharge Committees. For a discussion of the motion to discharge, see Part X.

X. OBTAINING CONSIDERATION OF MEASURES

Certain measures, either pending on the House and Union Calendars or unreported and pending in committee, are more important and urgent than others and a system permitting their consideration ahead of those that do not require immediate action is necessary. If the calendar numbers alone were the determining factor, the bill reported most recently would be the last to be taken up as all measures are placed on the House and Union Calendars in the order reported.

UNANIMOUS CONSENT

The House occasionally employs the practice of allowing reported or unreported measures to be considered by the unanimous agreement of all Members in the House Chamber. The power to recognize Members for a unanimous consent request is ultimately in the discretion of the Chair but recent Speakers have issued strict guidelines on when such a request is to be entertained. Most unanimous consent requests for consideration of measures may only be

28

22

entertained by the Chair when assured that the majority and minority floor and committee leaderships have no objection.

SPECIAL RESOLUTION OR "RULE"

To avoid delays and to allow selectivity in the consideration of public measures, it is possible to have them taken up out of their order on their respective calendar or to have them discharged from the committee or committees to which referred by obtaining from the Committee on Rules a special resolution or "rule" for their consideration. The Committee on Rules, which is composed of majority and minority members but with a larger proportion of majority members than other committees, is specifically granted jurisdiction over resolutions relating to the order of business of the House. Typically, the chairman of the committee that has favorably reported the bill requests the Committee on Rules to originate a resolution that will provide for its immediate or subsequent consideration. Under some circumstances, the Committee on Rules may originate a resolution providing for the "discharge" and consideration of a measure that has not been reported by the legislative committee or committees of jurisdiction. If the Committee on Rules has determined that the measure should be taken up, it may report a resolution reading substantially as follows with respect to a bill on the Union Calendar or an unreported bill:

Resolved, That upon the adoption of this resolution the Speaker declares pursuant to rule XVIII that the House resolve itself into the Committee of the Whole House on the State of the Union for the consideration of the bill (H.R._____) entitled, etc., and the first reading of the bill shall be dispensed with. After general debate, which shall be confined to the bill and shall continue not to exceed _____ hours, to be equally divided and controlled by the chairman and ranking minority member of the Committee on _____, the bill shall be read for amendment under the five-minute rule. At the conclusion of the consideration of the bill for amendment, the Committee shall rise and report the bill to the House with such amendments as may have been adopted, and the previous question shall be considered as ordered on the bill and amendments thereto to final passage without intervening motion except one motion to recommit with or without instructions.

If the measure is on the House Calendar or the recommendation is to avoid consideration in the Committee of the Whole, the resolution reads substantially as follows:

Resolved, That upon the adoption of this resolution it shall be in order to consider the bill (H.R. _____) entitled, etc., in the House.

The resolution may waive points of order against the bill. A point of order is an objection that a pending matter or proceeding is in violation of a rule of the House. The bill may be susceptible to various points of order that may be made against its consideration, including an assertion that the bill carries a retroactive federal income tax increase, contains a federal unfunded mandate, or has not

23

been reported from committee properly. At times, the rule may "self-execute" changes to the bill, that is, incorporate the changes in the bill upon adoption of the rule. The rule may also make a specified "manager's amendment" in order prior to any other amendment or may make a "compromise substitute" amendment in order as original text to replace the version reported from committee. When a rule limits or prevents floor amendments, it is popularly known as a "closed rule" or "modified closed rule." However, a rule may not deny the minority party the right to offer a motion to recommit the bill with proper amendatory or general instructions. For a discussion of the motion to recommit, see Part XI.

CONSIDERATION OF MEASURES MADE IN ORDER BY RULE REPORTED FROM THE COMMITTEE ON RULES

When a rule has been reported to the House, it is referred to the calendar and if it is to be considered immediately on the same legislative day reported, it requires a two-thirds vote for its consideration. Normally, however, the rule is on the calendar for at least one legislative day and if not called up for consideration by the Member who filed the report within seven legislative days thereafter, any member of the Committee on Rules may call it up as a privileged matter, after having given one calendar day notice of the Member's intention to do so. The Speaker will recognize any member of the committee seeking recognition for that purpose.

If the House has adopted a resolution making in order a motion to consider a bill, and such a motion has not been offered within seven calendar days thereafter, such a motion shall be privileged if offered by direction of all reporting committees having initial jurisdiction of the bill.

There are several other methods of obtaining consideration of bills that either have not been reported by a committee or, if reported, for which a rule has not been granted. Two of those methods, a motion to discharge a committee and a motion to suspend the rules, are discussed below.

MOTION TO DISCHARGE COMMITTEE

A Member may present to the Clerk a motion in writing to discharge a committee from the consideration of a public bill or resolution that has been referred to it 30 legislative days prior thereto. A Member also may file a motion to discharge the Committee on Rules from further consideration of a resolution providing a special rule for the consideration of a public bill or resolution reported by a standing committee, or a special rule for the consideration of a public bill or resolution that has been referred to a standing committee for 30 legislative days. This motion to discharge the Com-

24

mittee on Rules may be made only when the resolution has been referred to that committee at least seven legislative days prior to the filing of the motion to discharge. The motion may not permit consideration of nongermane amendments. The motion is placed in the custody of the Journal Clerk, where Members may sign it at the House rostrum only when the House is in session. The names of Members who have signed a discharge motion are made available electronically and published in the Congressional Record on a weekly basis. When a majority of the total membership of the House (218 Members) have signed the motion, it is entered in the Journal, printed with all the signatures thereto in the Congressional Record, and referred to the Calendar of Motions to Discharge Committees.

On the second and fourth Mondays of each month, except during the last six days of a session, a Member who has signed a motion to discharge that has been on the calendar at least seven legislative days may seek recognition and be recognized for the purpose of calling up the motion. The motion to discharge is debated for 20 minutes, one-half in favor of the proposition and one-half in opposition.

If the motion to discharge the Committee on Rules from a resolution prevails, the House shall immediately consider such resolution. If the resolution is adopted, the House proceeds to its execution. This is the modern practice for utilization of the discharge rule.

If the motion to discharge a standing committee of the House from a public bill or resolution pending before the committee prevails, a Member who signed the motion may move that the House proceed to the immediate consideration of the bill or resolution. If the motion is agreed to, the bill or resolution is considered immediately under the general rules of the House. If the House votes against the motion for immediate consideration, the bill or resolution is referred to its proper calendar with the same status as if reported by a standing committee.

MOTION TO SUSPEND THE RULES

On Monday and Tuesday of each week and during the last six days of a session, the Speaker may entertain a motion to suspend the rules of the House and pass a public bill or resolution. Sometimes the motion is allowed on days other than Monday and Tuesday by unanimous consent or a rule from the Committee on Rules. For example, the House by rule from the Committee on Rules provided for the motion on Wednesdays for the remainder of the 108th Congress. Members need to arrange in advance with the Speaker to be recognized to offer such a motion. The Speaker usually recognizes only a majority member of the committee that has reported

25

or has primary jurisdiction over the bill. The motion to suspend the rules and pass the bill is debatable for 40 minutes, one-half of the time in favor of the proposition and one-half in opposition. The motion may not be separately amended but may be amended in the form of a manager's amendment included in the motion when it is offered. Because the rules may be suspended and the bill passed only by affirmative vote of two-thirds of the Members voting, a quorum being present, this procedure is usually used only for expedited consideration of relatively noncontroversial public measures.

The Speaker may postpone all recorded and yea-nay votes on certain questions before the House, including a motion to suspend the rules and on passage of bills and resolutions, until a specified time or times on that legislative day or the next two legislative days. At these times, the House disposes of the postponed votes consecutively without further debate. After an initial fifteen-minute vote is taken, the Speaker may reduce to not less than five minutes the time period for subsequent votes. Eliminating intermittent recorded votes on suspensions reduces interruptions of committee activity and allows more efficient scheduling of voting.

CALENDAR WEDNESDAY

On Wednesday of each week, unless dispensed with by unanimous consent or by affirmative vote of two-thirds of the Members voting, a quorum being present, the standing committees are called in alphabetical order. A committee when named may call up for consideration any bill reported by it on a previous day and pending on either the House or Union Calendar. The report on the bill must have been available for three days and must not be privileged under the rules of the House. General debate is limited to two hours on any Calendar Wednesday measure and must be confined to the subject matter of the measure, the time being equally divided between those for and those against. An affirmative vote of a simple majority of the Members present is sufficient to pass the measure. The purpose of this rarely utilized procedure is to provide an alternative method of consideration when the Committee on Rules has not reported a rule for a specific bill.

DISTRICT OF COLUMBIA BUSINESS

On the second and fourth Mondays of each month, after the disposition of motions to discharge committees and after the disposal of business on the Speaker's table requiring only referral to committee, the Committee on Government Reform may call up for consideration any District of Columbia business reported from that committee. This procedure is rarely utilized in the modern House.

26

QUESTIONS OF PRIVILEGE

House rules provide special privilege to questions of privilege. Questions of privilege are classified as those questions: (1) affecting the rights of the House collectively, its safety, dignity, and the integrity of its proceedings; and (2) affecting the rights, reputations, and conduct of Members, individually, in their representative capacity. A question of privilege has been held to take precedence over all questions except the motion to adjourn. Questions of the privileges of the House, those concerning the rights of the House collectively, take the form of a resolution which may be called up by any Member after proper notice. A question of personal privilege, affecting the rights, reputation, and conduct of individual Members, may be raised from the floor without formal notice. Debate on a question of privilege proceeds under the hour rule, with debate on a question of the privileges of the House divided between the proponent and the leader of the opposing party or a designee.

PRIVILEGED MATTERS

Under the rules of the House, certain matters are regarded as privileged matters and may interrupt the order of business. Conference reports, veto messages from the President, and certain amendments to measures by the Senate after the stage of disagreement between the two Houses are examples of privileged matters. Certain reports from House committees are also privileged, including reports from the Committee on Rules, reports from the Committee on Appropriations on general appropriation bills, printing and committee funding resolutions reported from the Committee on House Administration, and reports on Member's conduct from the Committee on Standards of Official Conduct. Bills, joint resolutions, and motions may also take on privileged status as a result of special procedures written into statute. The Member in charge of such a matter may call it up at practically any time for immediate consideration when no other business is pending. Usually, this is done after consultation with both the majority and minority floor leaders so that the Members of both parties will have advance notice.

At any time after the reading of the Journal, a Member, by direction of the Committee on Appropriations, may move that the House resolve itself into the Committee of the Whole House on the state of the Union for the purpose of considering a general appropriation bill. A general appropriation bill may not be considered in the House until three calendar days (excluding Saturdays, Sundays, and legal holidays unless the House is in session on those days) after printed committee reports and hearings on the bill have been available to the Members. The limit on general debate on such a

27

bill is generally fixed by a rule reported from the Committee on Rules.

XI. CONSIDERATION AND DEBATE

Our democratic tradition demands that bills be given consideration by the entire membership usually with adequate opportunity for debate and the proposing of amendments.

COMMITTEE OF THE WHOLE

In order to expedite the consideration of bills and resolutions, the rules of the House provide for a parliamentary mechanism, known as the Committee of the Whole House on the state of the Union, that enables the House to act with a quorum of less than the requisite majority of 218. A quorum in the Committee of the Whole is 100 members. All measures on the Union Calendar—those involving a tax, making appropriations, authorizing payments out of appropriations already made, or disposing of property—must be first considered in the Committee of the Whole.

The Committee on Rules reports a rule allowing for immediate consideration of a measure by the Committee of the Whole. After adoption of the rule by the House, the Speaker may declare the House resolved into the Committee of the Whole. When the House resolves into the Committee of the Whole, the Speaker leaves the chair after appointing a Chairman to preside.

The rule referred to in the preceding paragraph also fixes the length of the debate in the Committee of the Whole. This may vary according to the importance of the measure. As provided in the rule, the control of the time is usually divided equally between the chairman and the ranking minority member of the relevant committee. Members seeking to speak for or against the measure may arrange in advance with the Member in control of the time on their respective side to be allowed a certain amount of time in the debate. Members may also ask the Member speaking at the time to yield to them for a question or a brief statement. A transcript of the proceedings in the House and the Senate is printed daily in the Congressional Record. Frequently, permission is granted a Member by unanimous consent to revise and extend his remarks in the Congressional Record if sufficient time to make a lengthy oral statement is not available during actual debate. These revisions and extensions are printed in a distinctive type and cannot substantively alter the verbatim transcript.

The conduct of the debate is governed principally by the rules of the House that are adopted at the opening of each Congress. In the 106th Congress, the rules were recodified for simplification and clarity. *Jefferson's Manual,* prepared by Thomas Jefferson for his

34

28

own guidance as President of the Senate from 1797 to 1801, is another recognized authority. The House has a long-standing rule that the provisions of *Jefferson's Manual* should govern the House in all applicable cases and where they are not inconsistent with the rules of the House. The House also relies on an 11-volume compilation of parliamentary precedents, entitled *Hinds' Precedents and Cannon's Precedents of the House of Representatives,* dating from 1789 to 1935, to guide its action. A later compilation, *Deschler-Brown Precedents of the House of Representatives,* spans 16 volumes and covers 1936 to date. In addition, a summary of the House precedents prior to 1959 can be found in a single volume entitled *Cannon's Procedure in the House of Representatives. Procedure in the U.S. House of Representatives,* fourth edition, as supplemented, and *House Practice,* first published in 1996 and updated in 2003, are more recent compilations of the precedents of the House, in summary form, together with other useful related material. Also, various rulings of the Chair are set out as notes in the current *House Rules and Manual.* Most parliamentary questions arising during the course of debate are responded to by a ruling based on a precedent of action in a similar situation. The Parliamentarian of the House is present in the House Chamber in order to assist the Speaker or the Chairman in making a correct ruling on parliamentary questions.

SECOND READING

During general debate on a bill, an accurate account of the time used on both sides is kept and the Chairman terminates the debate when all the time allowed under the rule has been consumed. After general debate, the second reading of the bill begins. The second reading is a section-by-section reading during which time germane amendments may be offered to a section when it is read. Under many special "modified closed" rules adopted by the House, certain bills are considered as read and open only to prescribed amendments under limited time allocations. Under the normal "open" amendment process, a Member is permitted five minutes to explain the proposed amendment, after which the Member who is first recognized by the Chair is allowed to speak for five minutes in opposition to it. There is technically no further debate on that amendment, thereby effectively preventing filibuster-like tactics. This is known as the "five-minute rule". However, Members may offer an amendment to the amendment, for separate five-minute debate, or may offer a pro forma amendment—"to strike out the last word"—which does not change the language of the amendment but allows the Member five minutes for debate. Each substantive amendment and amendment thereto is put to the Committee of the Whole for

29

adoption unless the House has adopted a special rule "self-executing" the adoption of certain amendments in the Committee of the Whole. The House may, after initially adopting an open rule, later alter that rule by unanimous consent to establish a "universe" or list of amendments to a bill. This procedure is most commonly used on general appropriation bills because of the volume of amendments.

At any time after debate has begun on proposed amendments to a section or paragraph of a bill under the five-minute rule, the Committee of the Whole may by majority vote of the Members present close debate on the amendment or the pending section or paragraph. However, if debate is closed on a section or paragraph before there has been debate on an amendment that a Member has caused to be printed in the Congressional Record at least one day prior to floor consideration of the amendment, the Member who caused the amendment to be printed in the Record is given five minutes in which to explain the amendment. Five minutes is also given to speak in opposition to the amendment and no further debate on the amendment is allowed. Amendments placed in the Congressional Record must indicate the full text of the proposed amendment, the name of the Member proposing it, the number of the bill or amendment to which it will be offered, and the point in the bill or amendment thereto where the amendment is intended to be offered. These amendments appear in the portion of the Record designated for that purpose.

AMENDMENTS AND THE GERMANENESS RULE

The rules of the House prohibit amendments of a subject matter different from the text under consideration. This rule, commonly known as the germaneness rule, is considered the single most important rule of the House of Representatives because of the obvious need to keep the focus of a body the size of the House on a predictable subject matter. The germaneness rule applies to the proceedings in the House, the Committee of the Whole, and the standing committees. There are hundreds of prior rulings or "precedents" on germaneness available to guide the Chair.

THE COMMITTEE "RISES"

At the conclusion of the consideration of a bill for amendment, the Committee of the Whole "rises" and reports the bill to the House with any amendments that have been adopted. In rising, the Committee of the Whole reverts back to the House and the Chairman of the Committee is replaced in the chair by the Speaker of the House. The House then acts on the bill and any amendments adopted by the Committee of the Whole. If the Committee of the

30

Whole rises on motion prior to the conclusion of consideration of amendments, the bill must return to the Committee of the Whole for subsequent consideration. Thus, the simple motion to rise may be used to immediately halt consideration of a bill similar to a motion to adjourn in the House.

HOUSE ACTION

Debate on a bill in the House is cut off by moving and ordering "the previous question". All debate is cut off on the bill if this motion is carried by a majority of the Members voting, a quorum being present, or by a special rule ordering the previous question upon the rising of the Committee of the Whole. The Speaker then puts the question: "Shall the bill be engrossed and read a third time?" If this question is decided in the affirmative, the bill is read a third time by title only and voted on for passage.

If the previous question has been ordered by the terms of the rule on a bill reported by the Committee of the Whole, the House immediately votes on whatever amendments have been reported by the Committee in the order in which they appear in the bill unless voted on en bloc. After completion of voting on the amendments, the House immediately votes on the passage of the bill with the amendments it has adopted. However, a motion to recommit, as described in the next section, may be offered and voted on prior to the vote on passage.

The Speaker may postpone a recorded vote on final passage of a bill or resolution or agreement to a conference report for up to two legislative days.

Measures that do not have to be considered in the Committee of the Whole are considered in the House in accordance with the terms of the rule limiting debate on the measure or under the "hour rule". The hour rule limits the amount of time that a Member may occupy in debate on a pending question to 60 minutes. Generally, the opportunity for debate may also be curtailed when the Speaker makes the rare determination that a motion is dilatory.

After passage or rejection of the bill by the House, a pro forma motion to reconsider it is automatically made and laid on the table. The motion to reconsider is tabled to prohibit this motion from being made at a later date because the vote of the House on a proposition is not final and conclusive until there has been an opportunity to reconsider it.

MOTION TO RECOMMIT

After the previous question has been ordered on the passage of a bill or joint resolution, it is in order to offer one motion to recom-

31

mit the bill or joint resolution to a committee and the Speaker is required to give preference in recognition for that purpose to a minority party Member who is opposed to the bill or joint resolution. This motion is normally not subject to debate. However, a motion to recommit with instructions offered after the previous question has been ordered is debatable for 10 minutes, except that the majority floor manager may demand that the debate be extended to one hour. Whatever time is allotted for debate is divided equally between the proponent and opponent of the motion. Instructions in the motion to recommit normally take the form of germane amendments proposed by the minority to immediately change the final form of the bill prior to passage. Instructions may also be "general," consisting of nonbinding instructions to the committee to take specified actions such as to "promptly" review the bill with a particular political viewpoint or to hold further hearings. Such instructions may not contain argument.

QUORUM CALLS AND ROLLCALLS

Article I, Section 5, of the Constitution provides that a majority of each House constitutes a quorum to do business and authorizes a smaller number than a quorum to compel the attendance of absent Members. In order to fulfill this constitutional responsibility, the rules of the House provide alternative procedures for quorum calls in the House and the Committee of the Whole.

In the absence of a quorum, 15 Members may initiate a call of the House to compel the attendance of absent Members. Such a call of the House must be ordered by a majority vote. A call of the House is then ordered and the call is taken by electronic device or by response to the alphabetical call of the roll of Members. Absent Members have a minimum of 15 minutes from the ordering of the call of the House by electronic device to have their presence recorded. If sufficient excuse is not offered for their absence, they may be sent for by the Sergeant-at-Arms and their attendance secured and retained. The House then determines the conditions on which they may be discharged. Members who voluntarily appear are, unless the House otherwise directs, immediately admitted to the Hall of the House and must report their names to the Clerk to be entered on the Journal as present. Compulsory attendance or arrest of Members has been rare in modern practice.

The rules of the House provide special authority for the Speaker to recognize a Member of the Speaker's choice to move a call of the House at any time.

When a question is put to a vote by the Speaker and a quorum fails to vote on such question, if a quorum is not present and objection is made for that reason, there is a call of the House unless the

32

House adjourns. The call is taken by electronic device and the Sergeant-at-Arms may bring in absent Members. The yeas and nays on the pending question are at the same time considered as ordered and an "automatic" recorded vote is taken. The Clerk utilizes the electronic system or calls the roll and each Member who is present may vote on the pending question. If those voting on the question and those who are present and decline to vote together make a majority of the House, the Speaker declares that a quorum is constituted and the pending question is decided as the majority of those voting have determined.

The rules of the House prohibit points of order of no quorum unless the Speaker has put a question to a vote.

The rules for quorum calls are different in some respects in the Committee of the Whole. The first time the Committee of the Whole finds itself without a quorum during a day the Chairman is required to order the roll to be called by electronic device, unless the Chairman orders a call of the Committee. However, the Chairman may refuse to entertain a point of order of no quorum during general debate. If on a call, a quorum (100 Members) appears, the Committee continues its business. If a quorum does not appear, the Committee rises and the Chairman reports the names of the absentees to the House. The rules provide for the expeditious conduct of quorum calls in the Committee of the Whole. The Chairman may suspend a quorum call after 100 Members have recorded their presence. Under such a short quorum call, the Committee will not rise and proceedings under the quorum call are vacated. In that case, a recorded vote, if ordered immediately following the termination of the short quorum call, is a minimum of 15 minutes. In the alternative, the Chair may choose to permit a full 15 minute quorum call, wherein all Members are recorded as present or absent, to be followed by a five-minute record vote on the pending question. Once a quorum of the Committee of the Whole has been established for a day, a quorum call in the Committee is only in order when the Committee is operating under the five-minute rule and the Chairman has put the pending question to a vote. The rules prohibit a point of order of no quorum against a vote in which the Committee of the Whole agrees to rise. However, an appropriate point of no quorum would be permitted against a vote defeating a motion to rise.

VOTING

There are three methods of voting in the Committee of the Whole that are also employed in the House. These are the voice vote, the division, and the recorded vote. The yea-and-nay vote is an additional method used only in the House, which may be automatic if

33

a Member objects to the vote on the ground that a quorum is not present.

To conduct a voice vote the Chair puts the question: "As many as are in favor (as the question may be) say 'Aye'. As many as are opposed, say 'No'". The Chair determines the result on a comparison of the volume of ayes and noes. This is the form in which the vote is ordinarily taken in the first instance.

If it is difficult to determine the result of a voice vote, a division may be demanded by a Member or initiated by the Chair. The Chair then states: "As many as are in favor will rise and stand until counted". After counting those in favor he calls on those opposed to stand and be counted, thereby determining the number in favor of and those opposed to the question.

If any Member requests a recorded vote and that request is supported by at least one-fifth of a quorum of the House (44 Members), or 25 Members in the Committee of the Whole, the vote is taken by electronic device. After the recorded vote is concluded, the names of those voting and those not voting are entered in the Journal. Members have a minimum of 15 minutes to be counted from the time the record vote is ordered. The Speaker may reduce the period for voting to five minutes on subsequent votes in certain situations where there has been no intervening debate or business. The Speaker is not required to vote unless the Speaker's vote would be decisive.

The modern practice in the Committee of the Whole is to postpone and cluster votes on amendments to maximize efficient scheduling of voting. The rules of the House provide the Chairman of the Committee of the Whole discretionary authority to postpone votes on amendments and to reduce the time for voting on amendments to five minutes following a 15-minute vote on the first amendment in a series. The Chairman is not allowed to postpone votes on matters other than amendments and is mindful not to postpone votes where the outcome could be prejudicial to the offering of another amendment.

In the House, if the yeas and nays are demanded, the Speaker directs those in favor of taking the vote by that method to stand and be counted. The support of one-fifth of the Members present is necessary for ordering the yeas and nays. When the yeas and nays are ordered or a point of order is made that a quorum is not present, the Speaker states: "As many as are in favor of the proposition will vote 'Aye'." "As many as are opposed will vote 'No'." The Clerk activates the electronic system or calls the roll and reports the result to the Speaker, who announces it to the House.

The rules of the House require a three-fifths vote to pass a bill, joint resolution, amendment, or conference report that contains a

34

specified type of federal income tax rate increase. The rules of the House also provide for automatic yeas and nays on votes on passage of certain fiscal measures including a concurrent resolution on the budget or a general appropriation bill.

The rules prohibit a Member from: (1) casting another Member's vote or recording another Member's presence in the House or the Committee of the Whole; or (2) authorizing another individual to cast a vote or record the Member's presence in the House or the Committee of the Whole.

ELECTRONIC VOTING

Recorded votes are usually taken by electronic device, except when the Speaker orders the vote to be recorded by other methods prescribed by the rules of the House, or in the failure of the electronic device to function. In addition, quorum calls are generally taken by electronic device. The electronic system works as follows: A number of vote stations are attached to selected chairs in the Chamber. Each station is equipped with a vote card slot and four indicators, marked "yea", "nay", "present", and "open" that are lit when a vote is in progress and the system is ready to accept votes. Each Member is provided with an encyrpted Vote-ID Card. A Member votes by inserting the voting card into any one of the vote stations and depressing the appropriate button to indicate the Member's choice. If a Member is without a Vote-ID Card or wishes to change his vote during the last five minutes of a vote, the Member may be recorded by handing a paper ballot to the Tally Clerk, who then records the vote electronically according to the indicated preference of the Member. The paper ballots are green for "yea", red for "nay", and amber for "present". The voting machine records the votes and reports the result when the vote is completed.

PAIRING OF MEMBERS

The former system of pairing of Members, where a Member could arrange in advance to be recorded as being either in favor of or opposed to the question by being "paired" with another absent Member who holds contrary views on the question, has largely been eliminated. The rules still allow for "live pairs". A live pair is where a Member votes as if not paired, subsequently withdraws that vote, and then asks to be marked "present" to protect the other Member. The most common practice is for absent Members to submit statements for the Record stating how they would have voted if present on specific votes.

SYSTEM OF LIGHTS AND BELLS

Due to the diverse nature of daily tasks that they have to perform, it is not practicable for Members to be present in the House

35

or Senate Chamber at every minute that the body is in session. Furthermore, many of the routine matters do not require the personal attendance of all the Members. A system consisting of electric lights and bells or buzzers located in various parts of the Capitol Building and House and Senate Office Buildings alerts Members to certain occurrences in the House and Senate Chambers.

In the House, the Speaker has ordered that the bells and lights comprising the system be utilized as follows:

1 long ring followed by a pause and then 3 rings and 3 lights on the left—Start or continuation of a notice or short quorum call in the Committee of the Whole that will be vacated if and when 100 Members appear on the floor. Bells are repeated every five minutes unless the call is vacated or the call is converted into a regular quorum call.

1 long ring and extinguishing of 3 lights on the left—Short or notice quorum call vacated.

2 rings and 2 lights on the left—15 minute recorded vote, yea-and-nay vote or automatic rollcall vote by electronic device. The bells are repeated five minutes after the first ring.

2 rings and 2 lights on the left followed by a pause and then 2 more rings—Automatic rollcall vote or yea-and-nay vote taken by a call of the roll in the House. The bells are repeated when the Clerk reaches the R's in the first call of the roll.

2 rings followed by a pause and then 5 rings—First vote on clustered votes. Two bells are repeated five minutes after the first ring. The first vote will take 15 minutes with successive votes at intervals of not less than five minutes. Each successive vote is signaled by five rings.

3 rings and 3 lights on the left—15 minute quorum call in either the House or in the Committee of the Whole by electronic device. The bells are repeated five minutes after the first ring.

3 rings followed by a pause and then 3 more rings—15 minute quorum call by a call of the roll. The bells are repeated when the Clerk reaches the R's in the first call of the roll.

3 rings followed by a pause and then 5 more rings—Quorum call in the Committee of the Whole that may be followed immediately by a five-minute recorded vote.

4 rings and 4 lights on the left—Adjournment of the House.

5 rings and 5 lights on the left—Any five-minute vote.

6 rings and 6 lights on the left—Recess of the House.

12 rings at 2-second intervals with 6 lights on the left—Civil Defense Warning.

The 7th light indicates that the House is in session.

RECESS AUTHORITY

The House may by vote authorize the Speaker to declare a recess under the rules of the House. The Speaker also has the authority to declare the House in recess for a short time when no question is pending before the House or in the case of an emergency.

LIVE COVERAGE OF FLOOR PROCEEDINGS

The rules of the House provide for unedited radio and television broadcasting and recording of proceedings on the floor of the House. However, the rules prohibit the use of these broadcasts and recordings for any political purpose or in any commercial advertisement. The rules of the Senate also provide for broadcasting and recording of proceedings in the Senate Chamber with similar restrictions.

36

XII. CONGRESSIONAL BUDGET PROCESS

The Congressional Budget and Impoundment Control Act of 1974, as amended, provides Congress with a procedure establishing appropriate spending and revenue levels for each year. The congressional budget process, as set out in the 1974 Budget Act, is designed to coordinate decisions on sources and levels of revenues and on objects and levels of expenditures. Its basic method is to prescribe the overall size of the fiscal pie and the particular sizes of its various pieces. Each year the Congress adopts a concurrent resolution imposing overall constraints on revenues and spending and distributing the overall constraint on spending among groups of programs and activities.

Congress aims to complete action on a concurrent resolution on the budget for the next fiscal year by April 15. Congress may adopt a later budget resolution that revises the most recently adopted budget resolution. One of the mechanisms Congress uses to implement the constraints on revenue and spending is called the reconciliation process. Reconciliation is a multiple-step process designed to bring existing law in conformity with the most recently adopted concurrent resolution on the budget. The first step in the reconciliation process is the language found in a concurrent resolution on the budget instructing House and Senate committees to determine and recommend changes in laws or bills that will achieve the constraints established in the concurrent resolution on the budget. The instructions to a committee specify the amount of spending reductions or revenue changes a committee must attain and leave to the discretion of the committee the specific changes to laws or bills that must be made. The subsequent steps involve the combination of the various instructed committees' recommendations into an omnibus reconciliation bill or bills which are reported by the Committee on the Budget or by the one committee instructed, if only one committee has been instructed, and considered by the whole House. In the Senate, reconciliation bills reported from committee are entitled to expedited consideration, permitting a majority of Senators, rather than sixty, to assure consideration of the bill with limited time for amendments.

The Budget Act maintains that reconciliation provisions must be related to reconciling the budget. This principle is codified in section 313 of the Budget Act, the so-called Byrd Rule, named after Senator Robert C. Byrd of West Virginia. Section 313 provides a point of order in the Senate against extraneous matter in reconciliation bills. Determining what is extraneous is a difficult task for the Senate's Presiding Officer. The Byrd Rule may only be waived in the Senate by a three-fifths vote and sixty votes are required to overturn the presiding officer's ruling.

37

Congress aims to complete action on a reconciliation bill or resolution by a specified date of each year. After Congress has completed action on a concurrent resolution on the budget for a fiscal year, it is generally not in order to consider legislation that does not conform to the constraints on spending and revenue set out in the resolution.

The Unfunded Mandates Reform Act of 1995, through an amendment to the Congressional Budget Act, established requirements on committees with respect to measures containing unfunded intergovernmental mandates. An unfunded intergovernmental mandate is the imposition of a substantial financial requirement or obligation on a state, local, or tribal government. The Act also established a unique point of order to enforce the requirements of the Act with respect to intergovernmental mandates in excess of fifty million dollars annually. In the House, an unfunded mandate point of order is not disposed of by a ruling of the Chair but by the Chair putting the question of consideration to the body. The House or the Committee of the Whole then decides by vote whether or not to proceed with the measure with the alleged mandate contained therein.

XIII. ENGROSSMENT AND MESSAGE TO SENATE

The preparation of a copy of the bill in the form in which it has passed the House can be a detailed and complicated process because of the large number and complexity of amendments to some bills adopted by the House. Frequently, these amendments are offered during a spirited debate with little or no prior formal preparation. The amendment may be for the purpose of inserting new language, substituting different words for those set out in the bill, or deleting portions of the bill. It is not unusual to have more than 100 amendments adopted, including those proposed by the committee at the time the bill is reported and those offered from the floor during the consideration of the bill in the Chamber. In some cases, amendments offered from the floor are written in longhand. Each amendment must be inserted in precisely the proper place in the bill, with the spelling and punctuation exactly as it was adopted by the House. It is extremely important that the Senate receive a copy of the bill in the precise form in which it has passed the House. The preparation of such a copy is the function of the enrolling clerk.

In the House, the enrolling clerk is under the Clerk of the House. In the Senate, the enrolling clerk is under the Secretary of the Senate. The enrolling clerk receives all the papers relating to the bill, including the official Clerk's copy of the bill as reported by the standing committee and each amendment adopted by the House.

38

From this material, the enrolling clerk prepares the engrossed copy of the bill as passed, containing all the amendments agreed to by the House. At this point, the measure ceases technically to be called a bill and is termed "An Act" signifying that it is the act of one body of the Congress, although it is still popularly referred to as a bill. The engrossed bill is printed on blue paper and is signed by the Clerk of the House. Bills may also originate in the Senate with certain exceptions. For a discussion of bills originating in the Senate, see Part XVI.

XIV. SENATE ACTION

The Parliamentarian, in the name of the Vice President, as the President of the Senate, refers the engrossed bill to the appropriate standing committee of the Senate in conformity with the rules of the Senate. The bill is reprinted immediately and copies are made available in the document rooms of both Houses. This printing is known as the "Act print" or the "Senate referred print".

COMMITTEE CONSIDERATION

Senate committees give the bill the same detailed consideration as it received in the House and may report it with or without amendment. A committee member who wishes to express an individual view or a group of Members who wish to file a minority report may do so by giving notice, at the time of the approval of a report on the measure, of an intention to file supplemental, minority, or additional views. These views may be filed within three days with the clerk of the committee and become a part of the report. When a committee reports a bill, it is reprinted with the committee amendments indicated by showing new matter in italics and deleted matter in line-through type. The calendar number and report number are indicated on the first and back pages, together with the name of the Senator making the report. The committee report and any minority or individual views accompanying the bill also are printed at the same time.

All committee meetings, including those to conduct hearings, must be open to the public. However, a majority of the members of a committee or subcommittee may, after discussion in closed session, vote in open session to close a meeting or series of meetings on the same subject for no longer than 14 days if it is determined that the matters to be discussed or testimony to be taken will disclose matters necessary to be kept secret in the interests of national defense or the confidential conduct of the foreign relations of the United States; will relate solely to internal committee staff management or procedure; will tend to charge an individual with a crime or misconduct, to disgrace or injure the professional stand-

39

ing of an individual, or otherwise to expose an individual to public contempt, or will represent a clearly unwarranted invasion of the privacy of an individual; will disclose law enforcement information that is required to be kept secret; will disclose certain information regarding certain trade secrets; or may disclose matters required to be kept confidential under other provisions of law or government regulation.

CHAMBER PROCEDURE

The rules of procedure in the Senate differ to a large extent from those in the House. The Senate relies heavily on the practice of obtaining unanimous consent for actions to be taken. For example, at the time that a bill is reported, the Majority Leader may ask unanimous consent for the immediate consideration of the bill. If the bill is of a noncontroversial nature and there is no objection, the Senate may pass the bill with little or no debate and with only a brief explanation of its purpose and effect. Even in this instance, the bill is subject to amendment by any Senator. A simple majority vote is necessary to carry an amendment as well as to pass the bill. If there is any objection, the report must lie over one legislative day and the bill is placed on the calendar.

Measures reported by standing committees of the Senate may not be considered unless the report of that committee has been available to Senate Members for at least two days (excluding Sundays and legal holidays) prior to consideration of the measure in the Senate. This requirement, however, may be waived by agreement of the Majority and Minority leaders and does not apply in certain emergency situations.

In the Senate, measures are brought up for consideration by a simple unanimous consent request, by a complex unanimous consent agreement, or by a motion to proceed to the consideration of a measure on the calendar. A unanimous consent agreement, sometimes referred to as a "time agreement", makes the consideration of a measure in order and often limits the amount of debate that will take place on the measure and lists the amendments that will be considered. The offering of a unanimous consent request to consider a measure or the offering of a motion to proceed to the consideration of a measure is reserved, by tradition, to the Majority Leader.

Usually a motion to consider a measure on the calendar is made only when unanimous consent to consider the measure cannot be obtained. There are two calendars in the Senate, the Calendar of Business and the Executive Calendar. All legislation is placed on the Calendar of Business and treaties and nominations are placed on the Executive Calendar. Unlike the House, there is no differen-

40

tiation on the Calendar of Business between the treatment of: (1) bills raising revenue, general appropriation bills, and bills of a public character appropriating money or property; and (2) other bills of a public character not appropriating money or property.

The rules of the Senate provide that at the conclusion of the morning business for each "legislative day" the Senate proceeds to the consideration of the calendar. In the Senate, the term "legislative day" means the period of time from when the Senate adjourns until the next time the Senate adjourns. Because the Senate often "recesses" rather than "adjourns" at the end of a daily session, the legislative day usually does not correspond to the 24-hour period comprising a calendar day. Thus, a legislative day may cover a long period of time—from days to weeks, or even months. Because of this and the modern practice of waiving the call of the calendar by unanimous consent at the start of a new legislative day, it is rare to have a call of the calendar. When the calendar is called, bills that are not objected to are taken up in their order, and each Senator is entitled to speak once and for five minutes only on any question. Objection may be interposed at any stage of the proceedings, but on motion the Senate may continue consideration after the call of the calendar is completed, and the limitations on debate then do not apply.

On any day (other than a Monday that begins a new legislative day), following the announcement of the close of morning business, any Senator, usually the Majority Leader, obtaining recognition may move to take up any bill out of its regular order on the calendar. The five-minute limitation on debate does not apply to the consideration of a bill taken up in this manner, and debate may continue until the hour when the Presiding Officer of the Senate "lays down" the unfinished business of the day. At that point consideration of the bill is discontinued and the measure reverts back to the Calendar of Business and may again be called up at another time under the same conditions.

When a bill has been objected to and passed over on the call of the calendar it is not necessarily lost. The Majority Leader, after consulting the Minority Leader, determines the time at which the bill will be considered. At that time, a motion is made to consider the bill. The motion is debatable if made after the morning hour.

Once a Senator is recognized by the Presiding Officer, the Senator may speak for as long as the Senator wishes and loses the floor only when the Senator yields it or takes certain parliamentary actions that forfeit the Senator's right to the floor. However, a Senator may not speak more than twice on any one question in debate on the same legislative day without leave of the Senate. Debate ends when a Senator yields the floor and no other Senator seeks

41

recognition, or when a unanimous consent agreement limiting the time of debate is operating.

On occasion, Senators opposed to a measure may extend debate by making lengthy speeches or a number of speeches at various stages of consideration intended to prevent or defeat action on the measure. This is the tactic known as "filibustering". Debate, however, may be closed if 16 Senators sign a motion to that effect and the motion is carried by three-fifths of the Senators duly chosen and sworn. Such a motion is voted on one hour after the Senate convenes, following a quorum call on the next day after a day of session has intervened. This procedure is called "invoking cloture". In 1986, the Senate amended its rules to limit "post-cloture" consideration to 30 hours. A Senator may speak for not more than one hour and may yield all or a part of that time to the majority or minority floor managers of the bill under consideration or to the Majority or Minority leader. The Senate may increase the time for "post-cloture" debate by a vote of three-fifths of the Senators duly chosen and sworn. After the time for debate has expired, the Senate may consider only amendments actually pending before voting on the bill.

While a measure is being considered it is subject to amendment and each amendment, including those proposed by the committee that reported the bill, is considered separately. Generally, there is no requirement that proposed amendments be germane to the subject matter of the bill except in the case of general appropriation bills or where "cloture" has been invoked. Under the rules, a "rider", an amendment proposing substantive legislation to an appropriation bill, is prohibited. However, this prohibition may be suspended by two-thirds vote on a motion to permit consideration of such an amendment on one day's notice in writing. Debate must be germane during the first three hours after business is laid down unless determined to the contrary by unanimous consent or on motion without debate. After final action on the amendments the bill is ready for engrossment and the third reading, which is by title only. The Presiding Officer then puts the question on the passage and a voice vote is usually taken although a yea-and-nay vote is in order if demanded by one-fifth of the Senators present. A simple majority is necessary for passage. Before an amended measure is cleared for its return to the House of Representatives, or an unamended measure is cleared for enrollment, a Senator who voted with the prevailing side, or who abstained from voting, may make a motion within the next two days to reconsider the action. If the measure was passed without a recorded vote, any Senator may make the motion to reconsider. That motion is usually tabled and its tabling constitutes a final determination. If, however, the mo-

42

tion is granted, the Senate, by majority vote, may either affirm its action, which then becomes final, or reverse it.

The original engrossed House bill, together with the engrossed Senate amendments, if any, or the original engrossed Senate bill, as the case may be, is then returned to the House with a message stating the action taken by the Senate. Where the Senate has adopted amendments, the message requests that the House concur in them.

For a more detailed discussion of Senate procedure, see *Enactment of a Law*, by Robert B. Dove, former Parliamentarian of the Senate.

XV. FINAL ACTION ON AMENDED BILL

On their return to the House, the official papers relating to the amended measure are placed on the Speaker's table to await House action on the Senate amendments. Although rarely exercised, the Speaker has the authority to refer Senate amendments to the appropriate committee or committees with or without time limits on their consideration. If the amendments are of a minor or non-controversial nature, any Member, usually the chairman of a committee that reported the bill, may, at the direction of the committee, ask unanimous consent to take the bill with the amendments from the Speaker's table and agree to the Senate amendments. At this point, the Clerk reads the title of the bill and the Senate amendments. If there is no objection, the amendments are then declared to be agreed to, and the bill is ready to be enrolled for presentation to the President. If unanimous consent is not obtainable, the few bills that do not require consideration in the Committee of the Whole are privileged and may be called up from the Speaker's table by motion for immediate consideration of the amendments. A simple majority is necessary to carry the motion and thereby complete floor action on the measure. A Senate amendment to a House bill is subject to a point of order that it must first be considered in the Committee of the Whole, if, originating in the House, it would be subject to that point of order. Most Senate amendments require consideration in the Committee of the Whole and this procedure by privileged motion is seldom utilized.

REQUEST FOR A CONFERENCE

The mere fact that each House may have separately passed its own bill on a subject is not sufficient to make either bill eligible for conference. One House must first take the additional step of amending and then passing the bill of the other House to form the basis for a conference. If the amendments of the Senate are sub-

43

stantial or controversial, a Member, usually the chairman of the committee of jurisdiction, may request unanimous consent to take the House bill with the Senate amendments from the Speaker's table, disagree to the amendments and request or agree to a conference with the Senate to resolve the disagreeing votes of the two Houses. In the case of a Senate bill with House amendments, the House may insist on the House amendments and request a conference. For a discussion of bills originating in the Senate, see Part XVI. If there is objection, the Speaker may recognize a Member for a motion, if offered by the direction of the primary committee and of all reporting committees that had initial referral of the bill, to: (1) disagree to the Senate amendments and ask for or agree to a conference; or (2) insist on the House amendments to a Senate bill and request or agree to a conference. This may also be accomplished by a motion to suspend the rules with a two-thirds vote or by a rule from the Committee on Rules. If there is no objection to the request, or if the motion is carried, a motion to instruct the managers of the conference would be in order. This initial motion to instruct is the prerogative of the minority party. The instructions to conferees usually urge the managers to accept or reject a particular Senate or House provision or to take a more generally described political position to the extent possible within the scope of the conference. However, such instructions may not contain argument and are not binding on House or Senate conferees. After the motion to instruct is disposed of, the Speaker then appoints the managers, informally known as conferees, on the part of the House and a message is sent to the Senate advising it of the House action. A majority of the Members appointed to be conferees must have been supporters of the House position, as determined by the Speaker. The Speaker must appoint Members primarily responsible for the legislation and must include, to the fullest extent feasible, the principal proponents of the major provisions of the bill as it passed the House. The Speaker usually follows the suggestion of the committee chairman in designating the conferees on the part of the House from among the members of the committee with jurisdiction over the House or Senate provisions. Occasionally, the Speaker appoints conferees from more than one committee and may specify the portions of the House and Senate versions to which they are assigned. The number is fixed by the Speaker and majority party representation generally reflects the ratio for the full House committee, but may be greater on important bills. The Speaker also has the authority to name substitute conferees on specific provisions and add or remove conferees after his original appointment. Representation of both major parties is an important attribute of all our parliamentary procedures but, in the case of conference

44

committees, it is important that the views of the House on matters in conference be properly represented.

If the Senate agrees to the request for a conference, a similar committee is appointed by unanimous consent by the Presiding Officer of the Senate. Both political parties may be represented on the Senate conference committee. The Senate and House committees need not be the same size but each House has one vote in conference as determined by a majority within each set or subset of conferees.

The request for a conference may only be made by the body in possession of the official papers. Occasionally, the Senate, anticipating that the House will not concur in its amendments, votes to insist on its amendments and requests a conference on passage of the bill prior to returning the bill to the House. This practice serves to expedite the matter because time may be saved by the designation of the Senate conferees before returning the bill to the House. The matter of which body requests the conference is not without significance because the body asking for the conference normally acts last on the report to be submitted by the conferees and a motion to recommit the conference report is not available to the body that acts last.

AUTHORITY OF CONFEREES

The conference committee is sometimes popularly referred to as the "Third House of Congress". Although the managers on the part of each House meet together as one committee they are in effect two separate committees, each of which votes separately and acts by a majority vote. For this reason, the number of managers from each House is largely immaterial.

The House conferees are strictly limited in their consideration to matters in disagreement between the two Houses. Consequently, they may not strike out or amend any portion of the bill that was not amended by the other House. Furthermore, they may not insert new matter that is not germane to or that is beyond the scope of the differences between the two Houses. Where the Senate amendment revises a figure or an amount contained in the bill, the conferees are limited to the difference between the two numbers and may neither increase the greater nor decrease the smaller figure. Neither House may alone, by instructions, empower its managers to make a change in the text to which both Houses have agreed.

When a disagreement to an amendment in the nature of a substitute is committed to a conference committee, managers on the part of the House may propose a substitute that is a germane modification of the matter in disagreement, but the introduction of any language in that substitute presenting specific additional mat-

45

ter not committed to the conference committee by either House is not in order. Moreover, their report may not include matter not committed to the conference committee by either House. The report may not include a modification of any specific matter committed to the conference committee by either or both Houses if that modification is beyond the scope of that specific matter as committed to the conference committee.

Under a recent reassertion of a Senate rule, Senate conferees are bound to consider only those matters that bare a certain relevancy to a House or Senate provision in conference.

The managers on the part of the House are under specific guidelines when in conference on general appropriation bills. An amendment by the Senate to a general appropriation bill which would be in violation of the rules of the House, if such amendment had originated in the House, including an amendment changing existing law, providing appropriations not authorized by law, or providing reappropriations of unexpended balances, or an amendment by the Senate providing for an appropriation on a bill other than a general appropriation bill, may not be agreed to by the managers on the part of the House. However, the House may grant specific authority to agree to such an amendment by a separate vote on a motion to instruct on each specific amendment.

MEETINGS AND ACTION OF CONFEREES

The rules of the House require that one conference meeting be open, unless the House, in open session, determines by a vote of the yeas and nays that a meeting will be closed to the public. When the report of the conference committee is read in the House, a point of order may be made that the conferees failed to comply with the House rule requiring an open conference meeting. If the point of order is sustained, the conference report is considered rejected by the House and a new conference is deemed to have been requested.

There are generally four forms of recommendations available to the conferees when reporting back to their bodies:

(1) The Senate recede from all (or certain of) its amendments.

(2) The House recede from its disagreement to all (or certain of) the Senate amendments and agree thereto.

(3) The House recede from its disagreement to all (or certain of) the Senate amendments and agree thereto with amendments.

(4) The House recede from all (or certain of) its amendments to the Senate amendments or its amendments to Senate bill.

In most instances, the result of the conference is a compromise growing out of the third type of recommendation available to the

46

conferees because one House has originally substituted its own bill to be considered as a single amendment. The complete report may be composed of any one or more of these recommendations with respect to the various amendments where there are numbered amendments. In earlier practice, on general appropriation bills with numbered Senate amendments, because of the special rules preventing House conferees from agreeing to Senate amendments changing existing law or appropriations not authorized by law, the conferees often found themselves, under the rules or in fact, unable to reach an agreement with respect to one or more amendments and reported back a statement of their inability to agree on those particular amendments. These amendments were acted upon separately. This partial disagreement is not practicable where, as in current practice, the Senate strikes out all after the enacting clause and substitutes its own bill that must be considered as a single amendment.

If they are unable to reach any agreement whatsoever, the conferees report that fact to their respective bodies and the amendments may be disposed of by motion. Usually, new conferees may be appointed in either or both Houses. In addition, the Houses may provide a new nonbinding instruction to the conferees as to the position they are to take.

After House conferees on any bill or resolution in conference between the two bodies have been appointed for 20 calendar days and 10 legislative days and have failed to make a report, a motion to instruct the House conferees, or discharge them and appoint new conferees is privileged. The motion can be made only after the Member announces his intention to offer the motion and only at a time designated by the Speaker in the legislative schedule of the following day. Like the initial motion to instruct, the 20-day motion may not contain argument and must remain within the scope of conference. In addition, during the last six days of a session, it is a privileged motion to move to discharge, appoint, or instruct House conferees after House conferees have been appointed 36 hours without having made a report.

CONFERENCE REPORTS

When the conferees, by majority vote of each group, have reached complete agreement or find that they are able to agree with respect to some but not all separately numbered amendments, they make their recommendations in a report made in duplicate that must be signed by a majority of the conferees appointed by each body on each provision to which they are appointed. The minority of the managers have no authority to file a statement of minority views in connection with the conference report. The report is required to

47

be printed in both Houses and must be accompanied by an explanatory statement prepared jointly by the conferees on the part of the House and the conferees on the part of the Senate. The statement must be sufficiently detailed and explicit to inform Congress of the effects of the report on the matters committed to conference. The engrossed bill and amendments and one copy of the report are delivered to the body that is to act first on the report, usually, the body that agreed to the conference requested by the other.

In the Senate, the presentation of a conference report always is in order except when the Journal is being read, a point of order or motion to adjourn is pending, or while the Senate is voting or ascertaining the presence of a quorum. When the report is received, the question of proceeding to the consideration of the report, if raised, is immediately voted on without debate. The report is not subject to amendment in either body and must be accepted or rejected as an entirety. If the time for debate on the adoption of the report is limited, the time allotted must be equally divided between the majority and minority party. The Senate, acting first, prior to voting on agreeing to the report may by majority vote order it recommitted to the conferees. When the Senate agrees to the report, its managers are thereby discharged and it then delivers the original papers to the House with a message advising that body of its action.

A report that contains any recommendations which extend beyond the scope of differences between the two Houses is subject to a point of order in its entirety unless that point of order is waived in the House by unanimous consent, adoption of a rule reported from the Committee on Rules, or the suspension of the rules by a two-thirds vote. In the Senate, a report exceeding the scope of conference is likewise subject to a point of order and the Chair will use a relevancy standard in testing the relationship of a targeted provision to matter in the House or Senate version.

The presentation of a conference report in the House is in order at any time, except during a reading of the Journal or the conduct of a record vote, a vote by division, or a quorum call. The report is considered in the House and may not be sent to the Committee of the Whole on the suggestion that it contains matters ordinarily requiring consideration in that Committee. The report may not be received by the House if the required joint statement does not accompany it.

However, it is not in order to consider either: (1) a conference report; or (2) a motion to dispose of a Senate amendment (including an amendment in the nature of a substitute) reported in disagreement by a conference committee, until the third calendar day (excluding Saturdays, Sundays, and legal holidays unless the

48

House is in session on those days) after the report and accompanying statement have been filed in the House and made available to the Members in the Congressional Record. However, these provisions do not apply during the last six days of the session. It is also not in order to consider a conference report or a motion to dispose of a Senate amendment reported in disagreement unless copies of the report and accompanying statement, together with the text of the amendment, have been available to Members for at least two hours before their consideration. By contrast, it is always in order to call up for consideration a report from the Committee on Rules on the same day reported that proposes only to waive the availability requirements for a conference report or a Senate amendment reported in disagreement. The time allotted for debate on a conference report or motion is one hour, equally divided between the majority party and the minority party. However, if the majority and minority floor managers both support the conference report or motion, one-third of the debate time must be allotted to a Member who is opposed. If the House does not agree to a conference report that the Senate has already agreed to, the report may not be recommitted to conference. In that situation, the Senate conferees are discharged when the Senate agrees to the report. The House may then request a new conference with the Senate and conferees must be reappointed.

If a conference report is called up before the House containing matter which would be in violation of the rules of the House with respect to germaneness if the matter had been offered as an amendment in the House, and which is contained either: (1) in the Senate bill or Senate amendment to the House measure (including a Senate amendment in the nature of a substitute for the text of that measure as passed by the House) and accepted by the House conferees or agreed to by the conference committee with modification; or (2) in a substitute amendment agreed to by the conference committee, a point of order may be made at the beginning of consideration that nongermane matter is contained in the report. The point of order may also be waived by a special rule. If the point of order is sustained, a motion to reject the nongermane matter identified by the point of order is privileged. The motion is debatable for 40 minutes, one-half of the time in favor of, and one-half in opposition to, the motion. Notwithstanding the final disposition of a point of order made with respect to the report, or of a motion to reject nongermane matter, further points of order may be made with respect to the report, and further motions may be made to reject other nongermane matter in the conference report not covered by any previous point of order which has been sustained. If a motion to reject has been adopted, after final disposition of all points

49

of order and motions to reject, the conference report is considered rejected and the question then pending before the House is whether: (1) to recede and concur with an amendment that consists of that portion of the conference report not rejected; or (2) to insist on the House amendment. If all motions to reject are defeated and the House thereby decides to permit the inclusion of the non-germane Senate matter in the conference report, then, after the allocation of time for debate on the conference report, it is in order to move the previous question on the adoption of the conference report.

Similar procedures are available in the House when the Senate proposes an amendment to a measure that would be in violation of the rule against nongermane amendments, and thereafter it is (1) reported in disagreement by a committee of conference or (2) before the House and the stage of disagreement is reached.

The numbered amendments of the Senate reported in disagreement may be voted on separately and may be adopted by a majority vote after the adoption of the conference report itself as though no conference had been had with respect to those amendments. The Senate may recede from all amendments, or from certain of its amendments, insisting on the others with or without a request for a further conference with respect to them. If the House does not accept the amendments insisted on by the Senate, the entire conference process may begin again with respect to them. One House may also further amend an amendment of the other House until the third degree stage of amendment within that House is reached.

CUSTODY OF PAPERS

The custody of the original official papers is important in conference procedure because either body may act on a conference report only when in possession of the papers. The papers are transmitted to the body agreeing to the conference and from that body to the managers of the House that asked for the conference. The latter in turn carry the papers with them to the conference and at its conclusion turn them over to the managers of the House that agreed to the conference. The managers of the House that agreed to the conference deliver them to their own House, that acts first on the report, and then delivers the papers to the other House for final action on the report. However, if the managers on the part of the House agreeing to the conference surrender the papers to the House asking for the conference, the report may be acted on first by the House asking for the conference.

At the conclusion of the conference, each group of conferees retains one copy of the report that has been made in duplicate and signed by a majority of the managers of each body. The House copy

50

is signed first by the House managers and the Senate copy is signed first by its managers.

A bill cannot become a law of the land until it has been approved in identical form by both Houses of Congress. When the bill has finally been approved by both Houses, all the original papers are transmitted to the enrolling clerk of the body in which the bill originated.

XVI. BILL ORIGINATING IN SENATE

The preceding discussion has described the legislative process for bills originating in the House. When a bill originates in the Senate, this process is reversed. When the Senate passes a bill that originated in the Senate, it is sent to the House for consideration unless it is held by unanimous consent to become a vehicle for a similar House bill if and when passed by the House. The Senate bill is referred to the appropriate House committee for consideration or held at the Speaker's table at the Speaker's discretion for possible amendment following action on a companion House bill. If the committee reports the bill to the full House and if the bill is passed by the House without amendment, it is ready for enrollment. If the House passes an amended version of the Senate bill, the bill is returned to the Senate for action on the House amendments. The Senate may agree to the amendments or request a conference to resolve the disagreement over the House amendments or may further amend the House amendments. In accordance with the Constitution, the Senate cannot originate revenue measures. By tradition, the House also originates general appropriation bills. If the Senate does originate a revenue measure either as a Senate bill or an amendment to a non-revenue House bill, it can be returned to the Senate by a vote of the House as an infringement of the constitutional prerogative of the House.

XVII. ENROLLMENT

When the bill has been agreed to in identical form by both bodies—either: (1) without amendment by the Senate; (2) by House concurrence in Senate amendments; (3) by Senate concurrence in House amendments; or (4) by agreement in both bodies to the conference report—a copy of the bill is enrolled for presentation to the President.

The preparation of the enrolled bill is a painstaking and important task because it must reflect precisely the effect of all amendments, either by way of deletion, substitution, or addition, agreed to by both bodies. The enrolling clerk of the House, with respect to bills originating in the House, receives the original engrossed bill, the engrossed Senate amendments, the signed conference re-

51

port, the several messages from the Senate, and a notation of the final action by the House, for the purpose of preparing the enrolled copy. From these documents, the enrolling clerk must meticulously prepare for presentation to the President the final form of the bill as it was agreed to by both Houses. On occasion, as many as 500 amendments have been adopted, each of which must be set out in the enrollment exactly as agreed to, and all punctuation must be in accord with the action taken.

The enrolled bill is printed on parchment paper and certified by the Clerk of the House stating that the bill originated in the House of Representatives. A bill originating in the Senate is examined and certified by the Secretary of the Senate. A House bill is then examined for accuracy by the Clerk. When he is satisfied with the accuracy of the bill, he attaches a slip stating that it finds the bill truly enrolled and sends it to the Speaker of the House for signature. All bills, regardless of the body in which they originated, are signed first by the Speaker and then by the Vice President of the United States, who, under the Constitution, serves as the President of the Senate. The President pro tempore of the Senate may also sign enrolled bills. The Speaker of the House may sign enrolled bills whether or not the House is in session. The President of the Senate may sign bills only while the Senate is actually sitting but advance permission is normally granted to sign during a recess or after adjournment. If the Speaker or the President of the Senate is unable to sign the bill, it may be signed by an authorized Member of the respective House. After both signatures are affixed, a House bill is returned to the Clerk for presentation to the President for action under the Constitution. A Senate bill is presented to the President by the Secretary of the Senate.

XVIII. PRESIDENTIAL ACTION

Article I, Section 7, of the Constitution provides in part that—

Every Bill which shall have passed the House of Representatives and the Senate, shall, before it becomes a Law, be presented to the President of the United States.

In actual practice, the Clerk, or the Secretary of the Senate when the bill originated in that body, delivers the original enrolled bill to a clerk at the White House and obtains a receipt. The fact of the delivery is then reported to the House by the Clerk. Delivery to a White House clerk has customarily been regarded as presentation to the President and as commencing the 10-day constitutional period for presidential action.

Copies of the enrolled bill usually are transmitted by the White House to the various departments interested in the subject matter so that they may advise the President on the issues surrounding the bill.

52

If the President approves the bill, he signs it and usually writes the word "approved" and the date. However, the Constitution requires only that the President sign it.

The bill may become law without the President's signature by virtue of the constitutional provision that if the President does not return a bill with objections within 10 days (excluding Sundays) after it has been presented to the President, it becomes law as if the President had signed it. However, if Congress by their adjournment prevent its return, it does not become law. This is known as a "pocket veto"; that is, the bill does not become law even though the President has not sent his objections to the Congress. The Congress has interpreted the President's ability to pocket veto a bill to be limited to final adjournment "sine die" of a Congress where Congress has finally prevented return by the originating House and not to interim adjournments or first session adjournments where the originating House of Congress through its agents is able to receive a veto message for subsequent reconsideration by that Congress when it reconvenes. The extent of pocket veto authority has not been definitively decided by the courts.

Notice of the signing of a bill by the President is sent by message to the House in which it originated and that House informs the other, although this action is not necessary for the act to be valid. The action is also noted in the Congressional Record.

A bill becomes law on the date of approval or passage over the President's veto, unless it expressly provides a different effective date.

VETO MESSAGE

By the terms of the Constitution, if the President does not approve the bill "he shall return it, with his Objections to that House in which it shall have originated, who shall enter the Objections at large on their Journal, and proceed to reconsider it". A bill returned with the President's objections, need not be voted on at once when laid before the House, since the vetoed bill can be postponed, referred back to committee, or tabled before the question on passage is pending. A vetoed bill is always privileged until directly voted upon, and a motion to take it from the table or from committee is in order at any time.

Once the relevant Member moves the previous question on the question of override, the question is then put by the Speaker as follows: "Will the House on reconsideration agree to pass the bill, the objections of the President to the contrary notwithstanding?" Under the Constitution, a vote by the yeas and nays is required to pass a bill over the President's veto. The Clerk activates the electronic system or calls the roll with those in favor of passing the bill an-

53

swering "Aye", and those opposed "No". If fewer than two-thirds of the Members present vote in the affirmative, a quorum being present, the bill is rejected, and a message is sent to the Senate advising that body of the House action. However, if two-thirds vote in the affirmative, the bill is sent with the President's objections to the Senate, unless that body has acted first, together with a message advising it of the action in the House.

The procedure in the Senate is the same as a two-thirds affirmative vote is also necessary to pass the bill over the President's objections. If the Senate joins the House and votes two-thirds in the affirmative to pass the bill, the measure becomes the law of the land notwithstanding the objections of the President, and it is ready for publication as a binding statute.

LINE ITEM VETO

From 1997 until it was declared unconstitutional in 1998, the Line Item Veto Act provided the President authority to cancel certain individual items contained in a bill or joint resolution that he had signed into law. The law allowed the President to cancel only three types of fiscal items: a dollar amount of discretionary budget authority, an item of new direct spending, and a tax change benefiting a class of 100 or fewer. While the Act has not been repealed, the Supreme Court in *Clinton* v. *City of New York,* 118 S. Ct. 2091 (1998), struck down the Line Item Veto Act as unconstitutional.

XIX. PUBLICATION

One of the important steps in the enactment of a valid law is the requirement that it shall be made known to the people who are to be bound by it. There would be no justice if the state were to hold its people responsible for their conduct before it made known to them the unlawfulness of such behavior. In practice, our laws are published immediately upon their enactment so that the public will be aware of them.

If the President approves a bill, or allows it to become law without signing it, the original enrolled bill is sent from the White House to the Archivist of the United States for publication. If a bill is passed by both Houses over the objections of the President, the body that last overrides the veto transmits it. It is then assigned a public law number, and paginated for the Statutes at Large volume covering that session of Congress. The public and private law numbers run in sequence starting anew at the beginning of each Congress and are prefixed for ready identification by the number of the Congress. For example, the first public law of the 108th Congress is designated Public Law 108–1 and the first private law of

54

the 108th Congress is designated Private Law 108–1. Subsequent laws of this Congress also will contain the same prefix designator.

SLIP LAWS

The first official publication of the statute is in the form generally known as the "slip law". In this form, each law is published separately as an unbound pamphlet. The heading indicates the public or private law number, the date of approval, and the bill number. The heading of a slip law for a public law also indicates the United States Statutes at Large citation. If the statute has been passed over the veto of the President, or has become law without the President's signature because he did not return it with objections, an appropriate statement is inserted instead of the usual notation of approval.

The Office of the Federal Register, National Archives and Records Administration prepares the slip laws and provides marginal editorial notes giving the citations to laws mentioned in the text and other explanatory details. The marginal notes also give the United States Code classifications, enabling the reader immediately to determine where the statute will appear in the Code. Each slip law also includes an informative guide to the legislative history of the law consisting of the committee report number, the name of the committee in each House, as well as the date of consideration and passage in each House, with a reference to the Congressional Record by volume, year, and date. A reference to presidential statements relating to the approval of a bill or the veto of a bill when the veto was overridden and the bill becomes law is included in the legislative history as a citation to the Weekly Compilation of Presidential Documents.

Copies of the slip laws are delivered to the document rooms of both Houses where they are available to officials and the public. They may also be obtained by annual subscription or individual purchase from the Government Printing Office and are available in electronic form. Section 113 of title 1 of the United States Code provides that slip laws are competent evidence in all the federal and state courts, tribunals, and public offices.

STATUTES AT LARGE

The United States Statutes at Large, prepared by the Office of the Federal Register, National Archives and Records Administration, provide a permanent collection of the laws of each session of Congress in bound volumes. The latest volume containing the laws of the first session of the 107th Congress is number 115 in the series. Each volume contains a complete index and a table of contents. A legislative history appears at the end of each law. There

55

are also extensive marginal notes referring to laws in earlier volumes and to earlier and later matters in the same volume.

Under the provisions of a statute originally enacted in 1895, these volumes are legal evidence of the laws contained in them and will be accepted as proof of those laws in any court in the United States.

The Statutes at Large are a chronological arrangement of the laws exactly as they have been enacted. The laws are not arranged according to subject matter and do not reflect the present status of an earlier law that has been amended. The laws are organized in that manner in the code of laws.

UNITED STATES CODE

The United States Code contains a consolidation and codification of the general and permanent laws of the United States arranged according to subject matter under 50 title headings, largely in alphabetical order. It sets out the current status of the laws, as amended, without repeating all the language of the amendatory acts except where necessary. The Code is declared to be prima facie evidence of those laws. Its purpose is to present the laws in a concise and usable form without requiring recourse to the many volumes of the Statutes at Large containing the individual amendments.

The Code is prepared by the Law Revision Counsel of the House of Representatives. New editions are published every six years and cumulative supplements are published after the conclusion of each regular session of the Congress. The Code is also available in electronic format on CD-ROM and the Internet.

Twenty-four of the 50 titles have been revised and enacted into positive law, and one title has been eliminated by consolidation with another title. Titles that have been revised and enacted into positive law are legal evidence of the law and may be updated by direct amendment. Eventually all the titles will be revised and enacted into positive law.

A P P E N D I X

SELECT LIST OF GOVERNMENT PUBLICATIONS

Constitution of the United States of America

Analysis and Interpretation, with annotations of cases decided by the Supreme Court of the United States to June 28, 2002; prepared by Congressional Research Service, Library of Congress, Johnny H. Killian, George A. Costello, Kenneth R. Thomas, co-editors: Senate Document 103–6 (1996); updated Senate Document 107–27 (2002).

House Rules and Manual

Constitution, Jefferson's Manual, and Rules of the House of Representatives of the United States, prepared by Charles W. Johnson, Parliamentarian of the House, House Document 107–284 (2003). New editions are published each Congress.

Senate Manual

Containing the rules, orders, laws, and resolutions affecting the business of the United States Senate; Jefferson's Manual, Declaration of Independence, Articles of Confederation, Constitution of the United States, etc., prepared under the direction of Senate Committee on Rules and Administration. New editions are published each Congress.

Hinds' and Cannon's Precedents of the House of Representatives

Including references to provisions of the Constitution, laws, and decisions of the Senate, by Asher C. Hinds. Vols. 1–5 (1907).

Vols. 6–8 (1935), as compiled by Clarence Cannon, are supplementary to vols. 1–5 and cover the 28-year period from 1907 to 1935, revised up to and including the 73d Congress.

Vols. 9–11 (1941) are index-digest to vols. 1–8.

Deschler-Brown Precedents of the United States House of Representatives

Including references to provisions of the Constitution and laws, and to decisions of the courts, covering the period from 1928 to date, by Lewis Deschler, J.D., D.J., M.P.L., LL.D., Parliamentarian of the House (1928–1974), Wm. Holmes Brown, Parliamentarian of the House (1974–1994).

Vols. 1–16 have been published, additional volumes in preparation.

Cannon's Procedure in the House of Representatives

By Clarence Cannon, A.M., LL.B., LL.D., Member of Congress, sometime Parliamentarian of the House, Speaker pro tempore, Chairman of the Committee of the Whole, Chairman of the Committee on Appropriations, etc.

House Practice, A Guide to the Rules, Precedents and Procedures of the House

By Wm. Holmes Brown, Parliamentarian of the House (1974–1994); updated 2003 by Charles W. Johnson, Parliamentarian of the House (1994-present).

(57)

58

Procedure in the U.S. House of Representatives, Fourth Edition (1982) (1987 Supp.)

By Lewis Deschler, J.D., D.J., M.P.L., LL.D., Parliamentarian of the House (1928–1974), and Wm. Holmes Brown, Parliamentarian of the House (1974–1994).

Senate Procedure

By Floyd M. Riddick, Parliamentarian Emeritus of the Senate, Alan S. Frumin, Parliamentarian of the Senate: Senate Document No. 101–28 (1992).

Calendars of the House of Representatives and History of Legislation

Published each day the House is in session; prepared under the direction of the Clerk of the House of Representatives.

Committee Calendars

Published periodically by most of the standing committees of the House of Representatives and Senate, containing the history of bills and resolutions referred to the particular committee.

Digest of Public General Bills and Resolutions

A brief synopsis of public bills and resolutions, and changes made therein during the legislative process; prepared by American Law Division, Congressional Research Service, Library of Congress.

Congressional Record

Proceedings and debates of the House and Senate, published daily, and bound with an index and history of bills and resolutions at the conclusion of each session of the Congress. The record of debates prior to 1874 was published in the Annals of Congress (1789–1824), The Register of Debates (1824–1837), and the Congressional Globe (1833–1873). Debates from 1774–1873 are available electronically from a website maintained by the Library of Congress.

Journal of the House of Representatives

Official record of the proceedings of the House, published at the conclusion of each session under the direction of the Clerk of the House.

Journal of the United States Senate

Official record of the proceedings of the Senate, published at the conclusion of each session under the direction of the Secretary of the Senate.

United States Statutes at Large

Containing the laws and concurrent resolutions enacted, and reorganization plans and proclamations promulgated during each session of the Congress, published annually under the direction of the Archivist of the United States by the Office of the Federal Register, National Archives and Records Administration, Washington, D.C. 20408.

Supplemental volumes: Tables of Laws Affected, Volumes 70–84 (1956–1970), Volumes 85–89 (1971–1975), containing tables of prior laws amended, repealed, or patently affected by provisions of public laws enacted during that period.

Additional parts, containing treaties and international agreements other than treaties, published annually under the direction of the Secretary of State until 1950.

United States Code

The general and permanent laws of the United States in force on the day preceding the commencement of the session following the last session the legislation of which is included: arranged in 50 titles; prepared under the direction and supervision of the Law Revision Counsel of the House of Representatives. New editions are published every six years and cumulative supplements are published annually.

59

Federal Register

Presidential Proclamations, Executive Orders, and federal agency orders, regulations, and notices, and general documents of public applicability and legal effect, published daily. The regulations therein amend the Code of Federal Regulations. Published by the Office of the Federal Register, National Archives and Records Administration, Washington, D.C. 20408.

Code of Federal Regulations

Cumulates in bound volumes the general and permanent rules and regulations of Federal agencies published in the Federal Register, including Presidential documents. Each volume of the Code is revised at least once each calendar year and issued on a quarterly basis. Published by the Office of the Federal Register, National Archives and Records Administration, Washington, D.C. 20408.

Weekly Compilation of Presidential Documents

Containing statements, messages, and other presidential materials released by the White House during the preceding week, published every Monday by the Office of the Federal Register, National Archives and Records Administration, Washington, D.C. 20408.

History of the United States House of Representatives

Prepared by Congressional Research Service, Library of Congress, House Document 103–324.

The Senate, 1789–1989, Addresses on the History of the United States Senate, Vol. 1

By Senator Robert C. Byrd, Senate Document No. 100–20 (1988).

Historical Almanac of the United States Senate

By Senator Bob Dole, Senate Document No. 100–35 (1989).

○

Chapter Eight

Legislating in Congress:

Legislative Process

Analysis

§ 8.00 Introduction

If an idea or problem attracts the attention of policymakers, opinion leaders, and the public, it might begin to build political momentum. That momentum may lead members of Congress to introduce legislation, committees to hold hearings and markups, chamber leaders to schedule floor time, and the president to approve the resulting legislation. The legislative process is activated by policy proponents attempting to see a policy enacted into law. *(See § 8.01, Legislative Process Flowchart.)*

But, many problems can occur along the way. The framers of the Constitution devised a system that makes legislation difficult to pass—two very different chambers comprising members from fifty states must agree to the identical proposition by majority votes, and the president must then agree with Congress. Each member is concerned with different local, regional, political, personal, and other interests. The rules of the House and the Senate that build on the bare-bones constitutional system further add to the difficulty of making law by ensuring adequate consideration of proposals, allowing the airing of alternative points of view, and establishing procedural stages through which proposals must pass. In addition, each member of Congress is accountable in elections for his or her performance in office. This democratic cornerstone of the Constitution requires that members constantly weigh the sentiments of their constituencies against their own positions on legislation to determine how to cast their votes. *(See § 8.02, House Rules Citations; and § 8.03, Senate Rules Citations.)*

What follows is an analysis of the legislative process in Congress—a distillation and description of both major, well-known stages of the process and more nuanced points that play a critical role in members' ability to advance or impede legislative proposals. The explanations that supplement the text—definitions of specific terminology, examples, and resources—assist in understanding, monitoring, and participating appropriately and effectively in the policymaking process.

Additional, special legislative procedures applicable to budget legislation, the Senate's executive business, and other kinds of legislation and oversight are described in Chapters Nine and Ten. Congressional documents are described in Chapters Eleven and Twelve. Tracking of legislative action is described in § 14.50. A working example of the legislative process is the subject of Chapter Fifteen.

§ 8.01

Legislative Process Flowchart

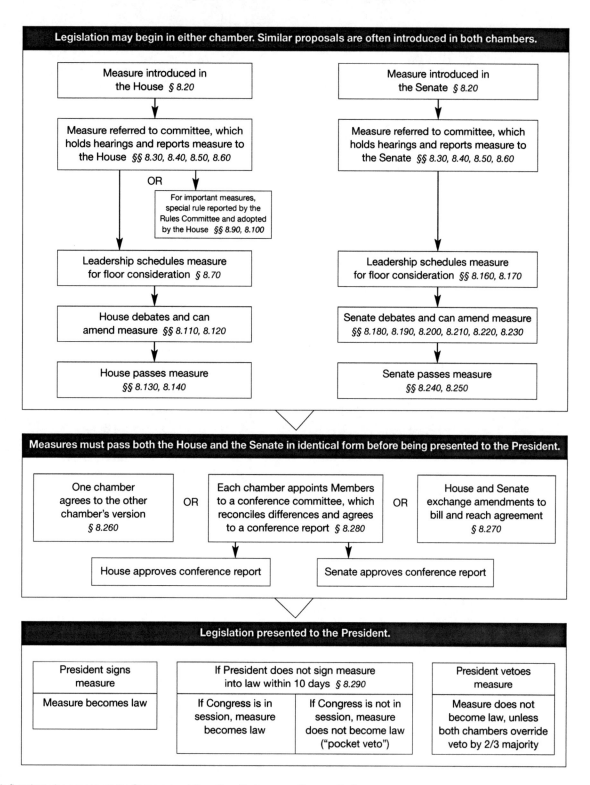

Legislation may begin in either chamber. Similar proposals are often introduced in both chambers.

Measure introduced in the House § 8.20	Measure introduced in the Senate § 8.20
Measure referred to committee, which holds hearings and reports measure to the House §§ 8.30, 8.40, 8.50, 8.60	Measure referred to committee, which holds hearings and reports measure to the Senate §§ 8.30, 8.40, 8.50, 8.60

OR

For important measures, special rule reported by the Rules Committee and adopted by the House §§ 8.90, 8.100

Leadership schedules measure for floor consideration § 8.70	Leadership schedules measure for floor consideration §§ 8.160, 8.170
House debates and can amend measure §§ 8.110, 8.120	Senate debates and can amend measure §§ 8.180, 8.190, 8.200, 8.210, 8.220, 8.230
House passes measure §§ 8.130, 8.140	Senate passes measure §§ 8.240, 8.250

Measures must pass both the House and the Senate in identical form before being presented to the President.

One chamber agrees to the other chamber's version § 8.260	OR	Each chamber appoints Members to a conference committee, which reconciles differences and agrees to a conference report § 8.280	OR	House and Senate exchange amendments to bill and reach agreement § 8.270

House approves conference report   Senate approves conference report

Legislation presented to the President.

President signs measure	If President does not sign measure into law within 10 days § 8.290		President vetoes measure
Measure becomes law	If Congress is in session, measure becomes law	If Congress is not in session, measure does not become law ("pocket veto")	Measure does not become law, unless both chambers override veto by 2/3 majority

This flowchart also appears on the Congressional Operations Poster, <www.CongressPoster.com>.

§ 8.02

House Rules Citations

House Rule Number	Subject Heading	House Rule Number	Subject Heading
I	The Speaker	XV	Business in Order on Special Days
II	Other Officers and Officials	XVI	Motions and Amendments
III	The Members, Delegates, and the Resident Commissioner	XVII	Decorum and Debate
IV	The Hall of the House	XVIII	The Committee of the Whole House on the State of the Union
V	Broadcasting the House	XIX	Motions Following the Amendment Stage
VI	Official Reporters and News Media Galleries	XX	Voting and Quorum Calls
VII	Records of the House	XXI	Restrictions on Certain Bills
VIII	Response to Subpoenas	XXII	House and Senate Relations
IX	Questions of Privilege	XXIII	Code of Official Conduct
X	Organization of Committees	XXIV	Limitations on the Use of Official Funds
XI	Procedures of Committees and Unfinished Business	XXV	Limitations on Outside Earned Income and Acceptance of Gifts
XII	Receipt and Referral of Measures and Matters	XXVI	Financial Disclosure
XIII	Calendars and Committee Reports	XXVII	Statutory Limit on the Public Debt
XIV	Order and Priority of Business	XXVIII	General Provisions

§ 8.03

Senate Rules Citations

Senate Rule Number	Subject Heading
I	Appointment of a Senator to the Chair
II	Presentation of Credentials and Questions of Privilege
III	Oaths
IV	Commencement of Daily Sessions
V	Suspension and Amendment of the Rules
VI	Quorum-Absent Senators May Be Sent For
VII	Morning Business
VIII	Order of Business
IX	Messages
X	Special Orders
XI	Papers-Withdrawal, Printing, Reading of, and Reference
XII	Voting Procedure
XIII	Reconsideration
XIV	Bills, Joint Resolutions, and Preambles Thereto
XV	Amendments and Motions
XVI	Appropriations and Amendments to General Appropriations Bills
XVII	Reference to Committees, Motions to Discharge, Reports of Committees, and Hearings Available
XVIII	Business Continued from Session to Session
XIX	Debate
XX	Questions of Order
XXI	Session with Closed Doors

Senate Rule Number	Subject Heading
XXII	Precedence of Motions
XXIII	Privilege of the Floor
XXIV	Appointment of Conferees
XXV	Standing Committees
XXVI	Committee Procedure
XXVII	Committee Staff
XXVIII	Conference Committees, Reports, Open Meetings
XXIX	Executive Sessions
XXX	Executive Session-Proceedings on Treaties
XXXI	Executive Session-Proceedings on Nominations
XXXII	The President Furnished with Copies of Records of Executive Sessions
XXXIII	Senate Chamber-Senate Wing of the Capitol
XXXIV	Public Financial Disclosure
XXXV	Gifts
XXXVI	Outside Earned Income
XXXVII	Conflict of Interest
XXXVIII	Prohibition of Unofficial Office Accounts
XXXIX	Foreign Travel
XL	Franking Privilege and Radio and Television Studios
XLI	Political Fund Activity, Definitions
XLII	Employment Practices
XLIII	Representation by Members

§ 8.04

Selected Procedures:
House and Senate Rules

Procedure	House Rule Citation	Senate Rule Citation
Amendment Process	XVI	XV
Appropriations Process	XXI	XVI
Committee Jurisdiction	X	XXV
Committee Procedure	XI, XIII	XXVI
Committee Referral	XII	XVII
Conference Committees	XXII	XXIV, XXVIII
Debate	XVII	XIX
Motions	XVI	XV
Order of Business	XIV	VIII
Outside Earned Income	XXVI	XXXVI
Voting	XX	XII

§ 8.10 Types of Measures

Legislation is the form in which policy ideas are translated into a procedural vehicle for consideration by a chamber. There are four types of legislative measures Congress may consider, in addition to the Senate's consideration of treaties and nominations. *(See § 8.11, Legislation Glossary.)*

Bills

A bill is the most commonly used form for legislation. A bill is prefixed with an *H.R.* in the House and with an *S.* in the Senate. A number assigned at the time of introduction signifies the order in which a bill was introduced during a Congress. A bill becomes law only if it is passed with identical language by both houses and signed by the president or passed over his veto. Under certain circumstances, a bill can become law without the president's signature. *(See § 8.290, Presidential Action on Enacted Measures.)* The bill form is used for authorization or reauthorization of federal policies, programs, and activities, among its many lawmaking purposes. *(See § 11.20, Legislation: Bills and Joint Resolutions, and § 9.80, Authorization and Appropriation Processes.)*

74

§ 8.11

Legislation Glossary

Act: Legislation that has passed both houses of Congress and been signed by the president or passed over his veto, thus becoming law. Also, parliamentary term for a measure that has been passed by one chamber and engrossed.

Bill: Measure that becomes law when passed in identical form by both houses and signed by the president or passed over his veto. Designated as *H.R.* or *S. (See also Joint Resolution.)*

Blue-Slip Resolution: House resolution ordering the return to the Senate of a Senate bill or amendment that the House believes violates the constitutional prerogative of the House to originate revenue measures.

By Request: A designation on a measure, which appears next to the sponsor's name, indicating that a member has introduced a measure on behalf of the president, an executive agency, or a private individual or organization.

Christmas-Tree Bill: Jargon for a bill containing many amendments unrelated to the bill's subjects; usually refers to Senate measures.

Clean Bill: A measure reported from a House committee that reflects the revised version of a measure considered in markup and repackaged into a new bill with a new number.

Commemorative Bill: Legislation designating a federal holiday or recognizing a particular issue, such as National Ice Cream Day or National Breast Cancer Awareness Month. Commemorative bills are currently disallowed in the House of Representatives.

Companion Bill: Identical or very similar bills introduced in both houses.

Concurrent Resolution: Used to express the sentiment of both houses on some matter without making law. Also used to carry out the administrative business of both houses. It does not require presidential approval or become law, but requires passage in identical form by both houses to take effect between them. Designated as *H. Con. Res.* or *S. Con. Res.*

Enacting Clause: Phrase at the beginning of a bill that gives it legal force when enacted: "Be it enacted by the Senate and House of Representatives of the United States of America in Congress assembled. . . ."

Engrossed Measure: Official copy of a measure as passed by one chamber, including the text as amended by floor action. Measure is certified by the clerk of the House or the secretary of the Senate.

Enrolled Measure: Final official copy of a measure as passed in identical form by both chambers and then printed on parchment. Measure is certified by the chamber of origin and signed by the Speaker of the House and the president pro tempore of the Senate before it is sent to the president.

Executive Document: A document, usually a treaty, sent by the president to the Senate for its consideration and approval.

Joint Resolution: Similar to a bill, though limited in scope (for example, to change a minor item in existing law). Becomes law when passed in identical form by both houses and signed by the president. It also is the form of legislation used to consider a constitutional amendment. A constitutional amendment requires a two-thirds vote in each house but does not require the president's signature. Designated as *H. J. Res.* or *S. J. Res. (See also Bill.)*

Continued on page 252

75

§ 8.11 (continued)

Law/Public Law/Private Law: Act of Congress signed by the president or passed over his veto.

Official Title: Statement of a measure's subject and purpose that appears above the enacting clause.

Omnibus Bill: A measure that combines the provisions of several disparate subjects into a single measure. Examples include *continuing resolutions* that might contain a number of the annual appropriations bills.

Original Bill: A measure drafted by a committee and introduced by its chair when the committee reports the measure back to its chamber. It is not referred back to the committee after introduction.

Popular Title: The informal, unofficial name or the short title by which a measure is known.

Preamble: Introductory language in a bill preceding the enacting clause. It describes the reasons for and intent of a measure. In a joint resolution, the language appears before the resolving clause. In a concurrent or simple resolution, it appears before the text.

Private Bill: A measure that generally deals with an individual matter, such as a claim against the government, an individual's immigration, or a land title. In the House, a private bill is considered via the Private Calendar on the first and third Tuesdays of each month.

Public Law: Act of Congress that has been signed by the president or passed over his veto. It is designated by the letters *P.L.* and numbers noting the Congress and the numerical sequence in which the measure was signed; for example, P.L. 107-111 was an act of Congress in the 107th Congress and was the 111th measure to become law during the 107th Congress.

Resolution/Simple Resolution: Sentiment of one chamber on an issue, or a measure to carry out the administrative or procedural business of one chamber. It does not become law. Designated as *H. Res.* or *S. Res.*

Resolution of Inquiry: A simple resolution calling on the president or the head of an executive agency to provide specific information or papers to one or both houses.

Resolving Clause: First section of a joint resolution that gives legal force to the measure when enacted: "Resolved by the Senate and House of Representatives of the United States of America in Congress assembled. . . ."

Rider: Term for an amendment unrelated to the subject matter of the measure to which it was attached. Usually associated with policy provisions attached to appropriations measures.

Slip Law: First official publication of a law, published in unbound single sheets or pamphlet form.

Star Print: A reprint of a measure, amendment, or committee report to correct errors in a previous printing. The first page carries a small black star. Rarely used today, with technology mitigating need.

A larger glossary is located at the back of the book.

Joint Resolution

A joint resolution is a legislative measure used for purposes other than general legislation. A joint resolution is designated *H. J. Res.* or *S. J. Res.* in the House and Senate respectively. Like a bill, it has the force of law when passed by both houses and signed by the president or passed over his veto. Joint resolutions are also used for proposing amendments to the Constitution, in which case a joint resolution passed in exactly the same form by a two-thirds vote in both chambers is submitted directly to the states rather than to the president. *(See § 11.20, Legislation: Bills and Joint Resolutions.)*

Concurrent Resolution

A concurrent resolution deals with the internal affairs of both chambers and requires approval by both houses but is not sent to the president. Therefore, it does not have the force of law. A concurrent resolution is designated *H. Con. Res.* or *S. Con. Res.* in the House and Senate respectively. Examples of concurrent resolutions are those providing for the adjournment of Congress or the congressional budget resolution. Nonbinding policy opinions of both chambers, such as "sense of the Congress," are traditionally in the form of concurrent resolutions. *(See § 11.30, Legislation: Simple and Concurrent Resolutions.)*

Resolution (Simple Resolution)

A simple resolution deals with the internal workings of only one chamber or with nonbinding public-policy statements. Designated *H. Res.* or *S. Res.* in the House and Senate respectively, a simple resolution does not require the concurrence of the other chamber or approval by the president. Special rules from the House Rules Committee, the creation of a select and special committee, and funding resolutions for individual committees are in the form of simple resolutions. *(See § 11.30, Legislation: Simple and Concurrent Resolutions.)*

§ 8.20 Drafting and Introducing Legislation
Sources of Legislation

Although legislation can be introduced only by members of Congress, ideas for legislation emanate from many sources. Members and their staffs may develop ideas based on promises made during election campaigns. The media also bring attention to issues that may need legislative solutions. Special-interest groups, and their lobbyists in Washington, often provide detailed ideas for legislation they want to see enacted. Constituents, either as individuals or groups, often suggest legislation to their own members of Congress. The executive branch is a key initiator of legislative proposals. The president in his State of the Union address to Congress outlines his priorities for the year, which may lead to legislation. Executive departments and agencies transmit drafts of legislation to Congress. Foreign governments often ask Congress to take up specific legislation, or seek ratification of certain treaties.

Drafting Legislation

Members and staff seek assistance in drafting legislation from the Office of Legislative Counsel in their respective chamber. The nonpartisan attorneys in these offices provide expert technical assistance in drafting bills, resolutions, and amendments. Legislative counsel are not only proficient in drafting but also knowledgeable about the substance of issues and the legislative process.

The Senate Committee on Rules and Administration has set drafting priorities for the Senate Office of Legislative Counsel. These priorities are measures in conference, measures pending on the floor, measures pending before a committee, and measures to be prepared for individual senators.

The House legislative counsel, as the senior attorney in the office, is appointed by the Speaker of the House. The Senate legislative counsel is appointed by the president pro tempore of the Senate. The staff attorneys are hired by the legislative counsel.

Introducing Legislation

The legislative process formally begins when a measure is introduced. Approximately 10,000 measures are introduced in each two-year Congress. Only a member can introduce legislation. There is no limit on the number of measures a member can introduce or on the issues such measures may address (with a few exceptions such as the House bar on commemorative legislation).

The Constitution stipulates that all revenue measures must originate in the House. House origination is the custom for appropriations bills as well. (When the Senate initiates a measure that the House believes affects revenues and sends it to the House, the measure is returned to the Senate by a so-called *blue-slip resolution*. The Senate may act on revenue measures before the House does, but it must wait for a House revenue measure to be sent to it before it can complete its legislative actions.) All other measures can originate in either the House or the Senate. Many pieces of legislation are introduced in both chambers as *companion bills*.

In the House, a measure is introduced by placing it in the *hopper*, a mahogany box that sits on the rostrum in the House chamber. Measures can be introduced only whenever the House is in session and sitting as the House. (See § 8.110, *Committee of the Whole: Debate.*) In the Senate, measures can technically be introduced only during the *morning business* portion of the *morning hour*. However, in practice they are introduced throughout the day. A senator need only hand a measure to a clerk at the desk in the chamber. In the Senate, a statement is often made on the floor or inserted in the *Congressional Record* when a measure is introduced.

On introduction, a measure is assigned a number by a bill clerk. The numbers are assigned sequentially throughout a Congress. Occasionally, a member will ask to reserve a specific number. For example, H.R. 2020 might be reserved for a measure affecting eye care, or S. 23 might be reserved to honor basketball star Michael Jordan. At the beginning of a new Con-

§ 8.21

House Cosponsorship Form

U.S. House of Representatives

Congress: _____
Session: _____
Date: _____

Pursuant to clause 7 of Rule XII of the Rules of the House Representatives, the following sponsors are hereby added to:

H.R. _____   H.Con. Res. _____
H.J. Res. _____   H.Res. _____

1) _____   21) _____
2) _____   22) _____
3) _____   23) _____
4) _____   24) _____
5) _____   25) _____
6) _____   26) _____
7) _____   27) _____
8) _____   28) _____
9) _____   29) _____
10) _____   30) _____
11) _____   31) _____
12) _____   32) _____
13) _____   33) _____
14) _____   34) _____
15) _____   35) _____
16) _____   36) _____
17) _____   37) _____
18) _____   38) _____
19) _____   39) _____
20) _____   40) _____

Member Signature: _____

§ 8.22

Sample "Dear Colleague" Letter

Congress of the United States
Washington, DC 20515

October 18, 1999

Oppose Unfunded Mandates
Cosponsor the Tiahrt Proposal to Require a 3/5 Majority Vote to Raise the Minimum Wage

Dear Colleague:

Clause 5(a) of rule XXI of the Rules of the House of Representatives provides in part . . . "A bill or joint resolution, amendment, or conference report carrying a Federal income tax rate increase may not be considered as passed or agreed to unless so determined by a vote of not less than three-fifths of the Members voting, a quorum being present. . ." Soon I will be introducing legislation which would add the same three-fifths voting requirement for bills, joint resolutions amendments or conference reports carrying a minimum wage increase, which is an unfunded mandate on small business owners as well as state and local governments.

Each time Congress mandates an increase in the starting wage, state and local governments along with small business owners are forced to make tough decisions about how to deal with this new unfunded mandate that has been imposed on them. This in turn becomes an unfunded mandate on all Americans. Consider the following examples from the restaurant industry in the aftermath of the most recent minimum wage increase:

- *Higher Prices* -- To cope with the increased labor costs, 42% of restaurant operators increased menu prices.

- *Job Elimination* -- As a result of the last increase, more than 146,000 jobs were cut from restaurant payrolls. In addition to existing jobs that were cut, restaurants had to delay expansions, resulting in the postponement of an additional 106,000 jobs.

- *Reduction in Employee Work Hours* -- Restaurants that did not eliminate jobs frequently scaled back on employee hours. More than 28% of operators reported reducing employee hours with the average reduction being 9 hours per week.

I hope you will join with me to support legislation that will make it harder for Congress to impose this unfunded mandate upon small business owners, state and local governments, and the American people. If you have any questions or would like to cosponsor this legislation, please contact me or Sarah Key of my staff at 5-6216.

Best regards,

gress, the first few bill numbers are often reserved for the majority-party leadership to signal their legislative priorities for Congress; the next few bill numbers might be reserved for the minority. Senators, by tradition, rarely introduce legislation until after the president delivers his State of the Union address.

Measures remain active between the two sessions of a Congress. If they are not enacted into law, they die with the adjournment of the Congress in which they were introduced. Treaties, however, which are considered only by the Senate, remain pending from one Congress until they are approved or formally withdrawn by the president, since the Senate is a *continuing body.*

House and Senate rules permit a member to introduce a measure at the request of the president, an executive agency, or a private individual although that member may be opposed to the legislation. The courtesy to introduce legislation on behalf of someone is granted because neither the president nor any person other than a member can introduce legislation. In such a case, "by request" appears on the measure following the name of the sponsor.

Cosponsorship

House and Senate measures may have numerous sponsors in addition to the member who proposes the legislation. It is common in both chambers for the key proponent of a measure to send a *Dear Colleague* letter (in print or electronically) to other members requesting their support for the legislation by cosponsoring its introduction. An original cosponsor signs on and is listed on the legislation when it is introduced. Cosponsors can be added throughout the legislative process until a measure is reported from a committee, or, in the Senate, at any time by unanimous consent. Names of cosponsors added after introduction appear in the *Congressional Record*, and in subsequent printings of a measure. A member can be removed as a cosponsor only by unanimous consent on the House or Senate floor. *(See § 8.21, House Cosponsorship Form; and § 8.22, Sample "Dear Colleague" Letter.)*

§ 8.30 Referral of Legislation to Committee

Once introduced in the House or Senate, or passed by one chamber and sent to the other, the vast majority of measures is referred to committee. Referral to committee occurs so that a committee can scrutinize the legislation by holding hearings and gauging sentiment for its enactment, and, if the committee proceeds to markup, may propose amendments to the parent chamber or write, introduce, and report a new measure.

To which committee(s) a measure is referred can have a significant impact on its fate. Referral of a measure is based on a committee's jurisdiction, which, in turn, is determined by a variety of factors. The principal factor in making a referral is Rule X in the House or Rule XXV in the Senate. Each rule lists the broad subject matter within the purview of each standing committee, although not all issues within a committee's jurisdiction are identified. In addition, these jurisdictional descriptions do not explicitly identify jurisdiction over particular

§ 8.31

Sample Jurisdictional Agreement

Ms. SLAUGHTER. Madam Speaker, I ask unanimous consent to insert in the RECORD a jurisdictional memorandum of understanding between the chairmen-designate from the Committee on Transportation and the Committee on Homeland Security.

The SPEAKER pro tempore. Is there objection to the request of the gentlewoman from New York?

There was no objection.

MEMORANDUM OF UNDERSTANDING BETWEEN THE COMMITTEE ON TRANSPORTATION AND INFRASTRUCTURE AND THE COMMITTEE ON HOMELAND SECURITY

January 4, 2007

On January 4, 2005, the U.S. House of Representatives adopted H. Res. 5, establishing the Rules of the House for the 109th Congress. Section 2(a) established the Committee on Homeland Security as a standing committee of the House of Representatives with specific legislative jurisdiction under House Rule X. A legislative history to accompany the changes to House Rule X was inserted in the Congressional Record on January 4, 2005.

The Committee on Transportation and Infrastructure and the Committee on Homeland Security (hereinafter "Committees") jointly agree to the January 4, 2005 legislative history as the authoritative source of legislative history of section 2(a) of H. Res. 5 with the following two clarifications.

First, with regard to the Federal Emergency Management Agency's, FEMA, emergency preparedness and response programs, the Committee on Homeland Security has jurisdiction over the Department of Homeland Security's responsibilities with regard to emergency preparedness and collective response only as they relate to terrorism. However, in light of the federal emergency management reforms that were enacted as title VI of Public Law 109-

295, a bill amending FEMA's all-hazards emergency preparedness programs that necessarily addresses FEMA's terrorism preparedness programs would be referred to the Committee on Transportation and Infrastructure; in addition, the Committee on Homeland Security would have a jurisdictional interest in such bill. Nothing in this Memorandum of Understanding affects the jurisdiction of the Committee on Transportation and Infrastructure of the Robert T. Stafford Disaster Relief and Emergency Assistance Act and the Federal Fire Prevention and Control Act of 1974.

Second, with regard to port security, the Committee on Homeland Security has jurisdiction over port security, and some Coast Guard responsibilities in that area fall within the jurisdiction of both Committees. A bill addressing the activities, programs, assets, and personnel of the Coast Guard as they relate to port security and non-port security missions would be referred to the Committee on Transportation and Infrastructure; in addition, the Committee on Homeland Security would have a jurisdictional interest in such bill.

This Memorandum of Understanding between the Committee on Transportation and Infrastructure and the Committee on Homeland Security provides further clarification to the January 4, 2005 legislative history of the jurisdiction of the Committees only with regard to these two specific issues. The Memorandum does not address any other issues and does not affect the jurisdiction of other committees.

JAMES L. OBERSTAR,
Chairman-designate, Committee on Transportation & Infrastructure.
BENNIE G. THOMPSON,
Chairman-designate,
Committee on Homeland Security.

Announcement by Rules Committee Chair
Related to a Committee's Jurisdiction

RULES OF THE HOUSE

Ms. SLAUGHTER. Mr. Speaker, I offer a privileged resolution (H. Res. 5) and ask for its immediate consideration.

The Clerk read the resolution, as follows:

H. RES. 5

Resolved, That upon the adoption of this resolution it shall be in order to consider in the House the resolution

(H. Res. 6) adopting the Rules of the House of Representatives for the One Hundred Tenth Congress. The resolution shall be considered as read. The previous question shall be considered as ordered on the resolution to its adoption without intervening motion or demand for division of the question except as specified in sections 2 through 4 of this resolution.

****

Continued on page 259

§ 8.31 *(continued)*

January 4, 2007   CONGRESSIONAL RECORD—HOUSE

Renews the standing order approved during the 109th Congress that prohibits registered lobbyists from using the Members' exercise facilities.

Mr. Speaker, I consider it to be a great honor to have a chance to address our House on the first day of the 110th Congress. That is what serving as a Representative in this body is, an honor.

****

Today, the men and women of America have given us a very special gift. We have the ability to leave our mark on the future of our Nation. It is the only gift Members of Congress should ask for, and one we must cherish for the good of all. Let us begin.

Mr. Speaker, I would like to take this opportunity to reaffirm the jurisdiction of the Committee on Small Business as contained in House Rule X, clause 1(p). The Committee's jurisdiction includes the Small Business Administration and its programs, as well as small business matters related to the Regulatory Flexibility Act and the Paperwork Reduction Act. Its jurisdiction under House Rule X, clause 1(p) also includes other programs and initiatives that address small businesses outside of the confines of those Acts.

This reaffirmation of the jurisdiction of the Committee on Small Business will enable the House to ensure that it is properly considering the consequences of its actions related to small business.

Mr. Speaker, I reserve the balance of my time.

---

measures, executive-branch departments and agencies, or programs operated within those departments. Accordingly, the formal provisions of the rules are supplemented by an intricate series of precedents and informal agreements.

A referral decision is formally the responsibility of the Speaker for the House and the presiding officer for the Senate. In practice, however, the parliamentarian in each chamber advises these officials on an appropriate referral.

House of Representatives

In addition to House Rule X, precedents and agreements affect referral decisions. In general, these precedents dictate that once a measure has been referred to a given committee, the measure's subject matter remains the responsibility of that committee. The precedents further presume that amendments to laws that originated in a committee are within the purview of that committee as well.

Formal agreements, drafted between committees to stipulate their understanding of jurisdictional boundaries, also influence referral decisions. These agreements are usually in the form of an exchange of letters between committee chairs and are often entered in the *Congressional Record* during debate on a measure when it comes to the floor for consideration. The letters are also often kept in committees' so-called *jurisdiction files* and with the parliamentarian. *(See § 8.31, Sample Jurisdictional Agreement.)*

Several other factors may influence the referral of a measure. The committee assignment of the sponsor often serves as a signal that a bill should be referred to a committee on which

§ 8.32

Sample of House Referral

I

110TH CONGRESS
1ST SESSION

H. R. 1064

To amend title 39, United States Code, to extend for 2 years the provisions under which the special postage stamp for breast cancer research is issued.

IN THE HOUSE OF REPRESENTATIVES

FEBRUARY 15, 2007

❶ Sponsor

❶ Mr. BACA (for himself, Mr. MOORE of Kansas, Ms. MCCOLLUM of Minnesota, Mr. VAN HOLLEN, Mr. FARR, Mrs. MALONEY of New York, Mr. FORTUÑO, Mr. MORAN of Virginia, Mr. MCDERMOTT, Mr. CONYERS, Mr. CLEAVER, Mr. DINGELL, Mr. NEAL of Massachusetts, Mrs. MCCARTHY

❷ Original cosponsors

❷ of New York, Mr. ELLISON, Mr. BURTON of Indiana, Mrs. JONES of Ohio, Mr. AL GREEN of Texas, Mr. NADLER, Mr. STARK, Mr. SCOTT of Georgia, Ms. HOOLEY, Mrs. BOYDA of Kansas, Mr. MICHAUD, Mr. KLEIN of Florida, Mr. MCINTYRE, Mr. KILDEE, Mr. GEORGE MILLER of California, Mr. SHAYS, Mr. GRIJALVA, Ms. ROYBAL-ALLARD, Mr. TERRY, Mr. BOSWELL, Mr. GENE GREEN of Texas, Mr. DENT, Mr. HINCHEY, Mr. HINOJOSA, Mr. CHANDLER, Mr. WEINER, Mr. SHIMKUS, Ms. WASSERMAN SCHULTZ, Mr. COOPER, Mr. HONDA, Mr. HOLT, Mr. ORTIZ, Mr. YOUNG of Alaska, Mr. HALL of Texas, Mrs. SCHMIDT, Mr. BERMAN, Mr. PRICE of North Carolina, Mr. DELAHUNT, Ms. KAPTUR, Ms. KIL-PATRICK, Mr. PATRICK J. MURPHY of Pennsylvania, Ms. HIRONO, Mr. ENGEL, Mr. ABERCROMBIE, Ms. BERKLEY, Mr. SHERMAN, Mr. KING of

❸ Explanation of the referral

New York, and Mr. DOGGETT) introduced the following bill; which was

❸ referred to the Committee on Oversight and Government Reform, and in addition to the Committees on Energy and Commerce and Armed Services, for a period to be subsequently determined by the Speaker, in each case for consideration of such provisions as fall within the jurisdiction of the committee concerned

A BILL

To amend title 39, United States Code, to extend for 2 years the provisions under which the special postage stamp for breast cancer research is issued.

the sponsor serves. The timing of a measure's introduction can also influence its referral; for example, introduction following a series of issue hearings held by a committee could signal that the panel wants to legislate on the issue it recently studied.

Under House Rule X, the Speaker usually designates a "primary" committee to receive a referral. If other panels have jurisdictional responsibilities over some of the issues in the measure, they may receive a *sequential* referral. The language of a referral affecting more than one committee would be "to the Committee on XXXX, and in addition, to the Committee on YYYY." The primary panel is always named first. A referral can also designate specific titles or sections of a measure within each committee's responsibility. More common, however, is a referral for "issues within the jurisdiction of the committee." Referral without designation of a primary committee can be made under "exceptional circumstances." A sequential referral may be made after a measure's introduction or after the primary committee reports the measure.

The Speaker has authority to impose a time limit on committees receiving a referral. Sometimes the time limit is determined at the time of referral; sometimes a time limit is imposed after a measure has been referred. *(See § 8.32, Sample of House Referral.)*

Senate

Under Senate Rule XVII, measures are referred to committee based on "the subject matter which predominates" in the legislation, commonly referred to as *predominant jurisdiction*. The Senate generally refers a measure to a single committee based on this rule and the jurisdictions enumerated in Senate Rule XXV.

Predominant jurisdiction allows a measure to be guided to a specific committee, so that the referral predetermines its fate. Many senators, as well as lobbyists, understand that they can influence the legislative agenda by learning how creative drafting of a measure can possibly affect its referral. For example, is tobacco an agricultural issue within the purview of the Agriculture Committee, generally friendly to tobacco? Or, is tobacco a health risk, an issue within the predominant purview of a less friendly Health, Education, Labor, and Pensions Committee? Or, is the issue about tobacco advertising, and thus within the predominant purview of the Commerce, Science, and Transportation Committee? The drafting of a measure on tobacco is not simple if one wants a specific committee to obtain the referral.

The rule further allows a measure to be referred to more than one panel if an issue crosses jurisdictional boundaries or predominance is not clear-cut. Such *multiple referrals* are not common, in part because they are typically made by unanimous consent after negotiations among affected committee chairs. A joint motion made by the majority and minority leader for multiple referrals is also allowed under Senate Rule XVII, but it has never been used.

Finally, under Senate Rule XIV, the majority leader, his designee, or any senator may follow a set of procedures that allow a measure to be placed directly on the Senate's legislative calendar without referral to committee. Placement there, however, does not guarantee that floor action will ever be scheduled. *(See § 8.160, Senate Scheduling.)*

§ 8.40 Committee Hearings

Perhaps the most visible of all congressional actions is the committee hearing. As Woodrow Wilson wrote, "It is not far from the truth to say that Congress in session is Congress on public exhibition, whilst Congress in its committee rooms is Congress at work."

Types of Committee Hearings

Committees and their subcommittees hold hundreds of hearings each year. These hearings are nearly always one of four types.

Legislative Hearings. These hearings typically occur when there is a measure under consideration or when a committee is collecting information so it can draft legislation. Witnesses give their own or their organizations' views on a measure's provisions. They might also express views on competing proposals for legislation that a committee could develop with the input received in hearings and from other sources.

Investigative Hearings. These hearings are not directly connected with legislation, but are called to examine a subject in which a committee has an interest. These hearings are sometimes held when there is possible evidence of wrongdoing or criminal activity by specific individuals.

Oversight Hearings. These hearings are held to ensure that executive agencies are carrying out programs in the manner Congress intended.

Confirmation Hearings. These hearings are held to question presidential appointees when Senate confirmation is required and to investigate nominees' qualifications.

Rules That Govern Hearings

Each committee is required by its respective chamber's rules to adopt and publish rules of procedure. A committee's rules generally apply to its subcommittees, although some rules contain specific procedures for subcommittees. Many committee rules address hearings.

Notice and Scheduling. Under both House and Senate rules, the chair of a committee or subcommittee must publicly announce the date, place, and subject matter of a hearing at least one week in advance in the Daily Digest section of the *Congressional Record*, unless the chair and ranking member—or the committee by majority vote—determines that there is good cause to begin the hearing sooner. *(See § 8.41, Committee Hearings Schedule.)*

Senate committees may not hold a hearing after the Senate has been in session for two hours, or after 2:00 p.m. when the Senate is in session, whichever is earlier. This Senate rule is often waived by unanimous consent on the Senate floor or by agreement between the Senate majority and minority leaders. House hearings can be held at any time, except during a joint session or meeting of the House and Senate. *(See § 8.42, Keeping Up with House and Senate Committee Hearings.)*

Open Hearings. Hearings must be open to the public and the media unless the committee, in open session, decides by record vote to close a hearing. Hearings may be closed if dis-

§ 8.41

Committee Hearings Schedule

HENRY A. WAXMAN, CALIFORNIA
CHAIRMAN

TOM DAVIS, VIRGINIA
RANKING MINORITY MEMBER

ONE HUNDRED TENTH CONGRESS

Congress of the United States

House of Representatives

COMMITTEE ON OVERSIGHT AND GOVERNMENT REFORM

2157 RAYBURN HOUSE OFFICE BUILDING

WASHINGTON, DC 20515–6143

Majority (202) 225–5051
Minority (202) 225–5074

REVISED

To: Members, Committee on Oversight and Government Reform

From: Henry A. Waxman, Chairman

Re: Committee Hearing Schedule

Date: April 12, 2007

Date	Time	Room	Committee
Mon. Apr. 16th			Nothing Scheduled
Tues. Apr. 17th	10:00 a.m.	2154 RHOB	Subcommittee on National Security and Foreign Affairs hearing on "Is This Any Way to Treat Our Troops – Part II: Follow-up on Corrective Measures Taken at Walter Reed and Other Medical Facilities Caring for Wounded Soldiers"
	10:00 a.m.	2247 RHOB	Subcommittee on Federal Workforce, Postal Service, and the District of Columbia hearing on "The U.S. Postal Service: 101"
Wed. Apr. 18th	10:00 a.m.	2154 RHOB	**Full Committee hearing with invited witness Secretary of State Condoleezza Rice, on "Unanswered Questions Regarding the Administration's Claims that Iraq Sought Uranium from Niger, White House treatment of Classified Information, the Appointment of Ambassador Jones as 'Special Coordinator' for Iraq, and Other Subjects."**
	2:00 p.m.	2154 RHOB	Subcommittee on Information Policy, Census, and National Archives hearing on "Ensuring Fairness and Accuracy in Elections Involving Electronic Voting Systems"
Thurs. Apr. 19th	10:00 a.m.	2154 RHOB	Subcommittee on Government Management, Organization, and Procurement legislative hearing on H.R. __, the Contractor Tax Enforcement Act and H.R. ___, amends Title 31 of the United States Code by authorizing a pilot program for local governments to offset federal tax refunds to collect local tax debts
Fri. Apr. 20th			Nothing Scheduled

**If you are in need of special accommodations based on a disability, please contact the committee
at least 4 business days prior to the hearing (202) 225-5051
April 12, 2007

§ 8.42

Keeping Up with House and Senate Committee Hearings

See Chapters Eleven, Twelve, and Thirteen for descriptions of these and other sources.

Sources	Anticipating Hearings		During/After Hearings	
	Status	Substance	Status	Substance
Congressional Sources				
Congressional Record. See Daily Digest pages and advance Senate committee schedule. Also see announcements by committee chairs in House and Senate proceedings pages	x		x	
Committee web sites, available through the House <*www.house.gov*> and Senate <*www.senate.gov*> sites	x	x	x	x
Committee or committee members' press releases	x	x	x	x
For legislative hearings: the legislation itself (as introduced or committee draft); related documents such as draft administration legislation or a commission report		x		
For oversight hearings: relevant public law(s) and congressional documents from the law's legislative history		x		
For nomination hearings: press kits or other packets	x	x	x	x
Hearing transcripts, available from committee offices, some committee web sites, and eventually as printed congressional documents				x
Legislative Information System (Congress only)			x	x
THOMAS <*http://thomas.loc.gov*>	x		x	x
Non-Congressional Sources				
CongressDaily, from *National Journal* <*http://nationaljournal.com*>	x	x	x	x
CQ Today <*www.cq.com*>	x	x	x	x
CQ.com <*www.cq.com*>	x	x	x	x
C-SPAN (selectively) <*www.cspan.org*>				x
Prepared testimony, available from the witness's agency or organization				x
Trade press and daily newspapers	x	x	x	x
Relevant interest-group web sites	x	x	x	x
Other commercial database services	x	x	x	x
People *(Use these contacts after exhausting other resources.)*				
Committee professional staff (After hearings, what is the expected markup vehicle? When will markup begin?)		x	x	x
Documents clerks (What documents are available in advance or at the hearings? After hearings, are transcripts available?)		x		x
Committee and committee members' press assistants (What press releases or other press documents are available?)		x		x

88

cussion of the subject matter might endanger national security, compromise sensitive law-enforcement information, or violate a rule of the parent chamber. If testimony would defame, degrade, or incriminate a person, the testimony must be taken in closed session if a majority of committee members determines that the testimony might be problematic. Testimony taken in closed session can be released only by majority vote of the committee.

Quorums. Individual committees set their own quorum requirements to conduct a hearing. However, House rules require that not fewer than two members be present. Senate committees usually allow a single senator to be present to conduct a hearing. Individual House committee rules also set a quorum requirement for waiving a hearing notice, but House rules disallow the quorum from being less than one-third. Senate committees have no comparable rule. Finally, for House committees, a majority of members of a committee constitutes a quorum for authorizing a subpoena or closing a committee session.

Subpoena Power. Both House and Senate committees are authorized to issue subpoenas to witnesses and for documents. The rules of each committee delineate the procedures for issuing a subpoena. When a committee adopts its rules at the beginning of a Congress, it must decide how to issue subpoenas. A committee might determine that a subpoena can be issued under the signature of the chair or that the concurrence of the ranking minority member is required. Alternatively, it might choose to authorize a subpoena only by a majority vote of the committee.

Witnesses. Witnesses must be invited to appear before a committee or subcommittee. A formal letter of invitation is usually sent under the name of the chair or, sometimes, the chair and ranking minority member. Occasionally, a committee will ask for written witness testimony in lieu of an appearance before the committee. An organization or individual may also request an invitation to appear or to submit testimony for a hearing record. (*See § 10.75, Committee Investigations and Witness Protections.*)

House and Senate chamber rules, as well as individual committee rules, generally require a witness to file a specific number of copies of his or her prepared written statement in advance of an appearance. A nongovernmental witness appearing before a House committee is also required to comply with the so-called *truth in testimony* rule, which states that the witness should file a résumé and disclose the amount and source of any grant or contract money received from the federal government in the current or two preceding fiscal years. (*See § 8.43, Sample Truth in Testimony Form.*)

The minority party is entitled to one day of hearings to call its own witnesses if a majority of minority members so requests.

Conducting Hearings

Each committee determines if witnesses will appear individually or in a panel. In a panel format, committee members usually hold their questions until all panelists have made their presentations. A committee must also determine whether to swear in a witness.

§ 8.43

Sample Truth in Testimony Form

Committee on the Budget
Witness Disclosure Requirement – "Truth in Testimony"
Required by House Rule XI, Clause 2(g)

Your Name:		
1. Will you be representing a federal, State, or local government entity? (If the answer is yes please contact the committee).	Yes	No
2. Please list any federal grants or contracts (including subgrants or subcontracts) which <u>you</u> <u>have received </u>since October 1, 2002:		
3. Will you be representing an entity other than a government entity?	Yes	No
4. Other than yourself, please list what entity or entities you will be representing:		
5. Please list any offices or elected positions held and/or briefly describe your representational capacity with each of the entities you listed in response to question 4:		
6. Please list any federal grants or contracts (including subgrants or subcontracts) received by the entities you listed in response to question 4 since October 1, 2002, including the source and amount of each grant or contract:		
7. Are there parent organizations, subsidiaries, or partnerships to the entities you disclosed in response to question number 4 that you will not be representing? If so, please list:	Yes	No

Signature: _____ Date: _____

Please attach this sheet to your written testimony.

§ 8.44

Celebrity Witnesses

As a means of generating publicity and public support for public-policy issues, committees have turned increasingly in recent years to "celebrity witnesses." Celebrity witnesses who have testified at hearings before House and Senate committees in recent years, and the issues on which they testified, include the following:

Environmental and Agricultural Issues
- Ted Danson—American Oceans Campaign
- Jessica Lange—Farm bill

Health Issues
- Michael J. Fox—Parkinson's disease research
- Mary Tyler Moore—Diabetes disease research
- Ben Vereen—Deafness research
- Sally Field—Osteoporosis
- Jack Klugman—Cancer research
- Diane Keaton—Cancer research
- Olivia Newton John—Cancer research
- Christopher Reeve—Spinal-cord injuries research
- Jason Alexander—Scleroderma research
- Shawn Colvin—Drug addiction
- Robert Guillaume—Drug addiction
- Katie Couric—Colon cancer research
- David Hyde Pierce—Alzheimer's disease research
- Elton John—HIV/AIDS
- Julia Roberts—Rett syndrome

International Issues
- Richard Gere—Tibet
- Sam Waterston—Immigration

Labor Issues
- Charlton Heston—Unemployment benefits
- Muhammad Ali—Regulation of boxing

Treatment of Animals
- Alec Baldwin—End to animal testing
- Kim Basinger—End to animal testing

Other
- Denyce Graves—Arts funding
- Muhammad Ali—Boxing reform
- Pearl Jam—TicketMaster dispute
- Martin Short—Foster parents
- Jack Nicklaus—Education
- Elmo—Music education
- Stephen Sondheim, Arthur Miller, Wendy Wasserstein—Playwrights' Licensing Antitrust Initiative Act
- Bobby McFerrin—Arts funding
- Edward James Olmos—Volunteer service programs
- Doris Roberts—Ageism in media
- Jose Canseco, Mark McGwire, Sammy Sosa, Curt Schilling, and Frank Thomas—Steroids abuse in Major League Baseball

Protocol and tradition dictate that members of Congress wishing to testify at hearings do so before other witnesses testify. Executive-branch officials and former members are also afforded consideration in the order in which they appear. A "celebrity witness" is likely to be placed to generate maximum media coverage. A witness generally summarizes his or her written testimony before a committee. (See § 8.44, Celebrity Witnesses.)

As a general practice, each House member is entitled to five minutes of questioning of each witness. However, the chair and ranking member can designate specific members or staff

§ 8.45

Field Hearing Announcement

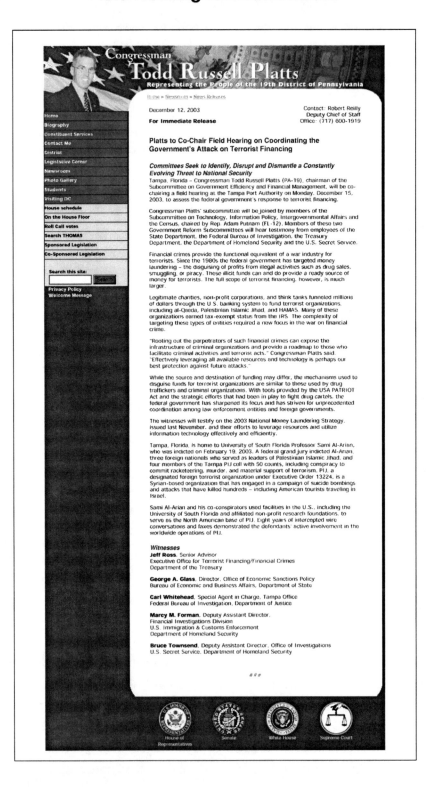

to pursue extended questioning of up to thirty minutes on behalf of their party's members. It is also possible for members to ask witnesses to respond to questions in writing after a hearing is concluded. Many Senate committees also have adopted committee rules limiting senators to five minutes for each witness.

An individual committee's rules spell out the order in which members are recognized to question witnesses. Many committees recognize members in order of their seniority on the committee. Several panels recognize members based on their "order of appearance" at a hearing, giving priority to those members who arrive early.

Most hearing rooms are equipped with small, color lights on the witness table. The green light is turned on when a member is recognized to speak or ask questions of a witness. The red light signifies a member's time has expired. An amber or orange light signifies that a member's time will soon expire. The committee chair or committee clerk controls the lights, but the lights are not always strictly monitored or even turned on. In many hearing rooms, digital clocks rather than lights have been installed on both the dais and the witness table.

Most committee hearings are held in Washington, DC. In recent years, however, committees have increased their use of *field hearings*. A field hearing is conducted the same way as a hearing in Washington, but is held in the home district or state of the member calling the hearing or in a locale relevant to the subject of the hearing. Field hearings allow local residents to attend or testify without coming to Washington *(see § 8.45, Field Hearing Announcement)*.

(For information on hearings transcripts and printed hearings, see § 12.10, Committee Documents.)

§ 8.50 Committee Markup

When hearings are completed, a committee may meet to *mark up* a measure. The connotation of a markup session is that the language of the original measure is analyzed line-by-line or section-by-section, and then *marked up*, that is, changed or amended. *(See § 8.51, Committee Markup and Reporting Glossary.)*

The rules of each chamber provide only general guidance to committees for conducting markups. The rules of the House and the Senate are the rules of their committees "so far as applicable." Each committee must also adopt written rules governing its procedures. House and Senate committee rules cannot be inconsistent with their chambers' rules. Committee markups follow committee rules made pursuant to these two guidelines. Subcommittees generally are covered by full committee rules. In recent years, several committees have conducted all markups at the full committee level after hearings were held at the subcommittee level. Both chambers require that markup sessions be open to the public unless a committee decides in open session by majority vote to close the markup.

Vehicle for Consideration and Amendment

A markup begins with the chair calling up a particular measure for consideration by the committee. The text the chair intends for the committee to consider is referred to as the *markup*

§ 8.51

Committee Markup and Reporting Glossary

Chairman's Mark/Staff Draft: Recommendation by chair of the measure to be considered in markup, usually drafted as a bill.

Clean Bill: New measure reported by a House committee, incorporating all changes made in markup. Measure, with new number, is introduced and referred to the committee, which then reports that measure.

Committee Report: Document accompanying measure reported from a committee, containing an explanation of the provisions of the measure, arguments for its approval, and certain other matters.

Cordon Rule: Senate rule that requires a committee report to show changes the reported measure would make in current law.

Mark: *See Vehicle.*

Minority, Supplemental, and Additional Views: Statements in a committee report, presenting individual or group opinions on the measure.

Ordered Reported: Committee's formal action of agreeing to report a measure to its chamber.

Original Bill: Bill drafted by a committee and introduced when the committee reports the measure to the chamber. Senate allows all committees to report original bills; House generally allows only the Appropriations Committee to do so.

Ramseyer Rule: House rule that requires a committee report to show changes the reported measure would make in current law.

Report/Reported: As a verb, formal submission of a measure to the chamber. As a noun, a committee document explaining the measure reported from committee. A report is designated *H. Rept.* in the House and *S. Rept.* in the Senate.

Vehicle/Legislative Vehicle: Term for legislative measure that is being considered.

A larger glossary is located at the back of the book.

vehicle, and the chair has several alternatives from which to choose. *(See § 8.52, Keeping Up with House and Senate Committee Markups.)*

Introduced Measure. Using an introduced measure as the vehicle is the easiest way to conduct a markup. The chair notifies committee members that the vehicle for the markup will be the introduced bill, identifying the bill number and, often, the original sponsor. At House markups, the measure is usually read for amendment by section. By unanimous consent, the measure can be open for amendment at any point or title by title. At Senate markups, measures are usually open to amendment at any point. In either case, each section

§ 8.52

Keeping Up with House and Senate Committee Markups[1]

See Chapters Eleven, Twelve, and Thirteen for descriptions of these and other sources.

Sources	Anticipating Markup		During/After Markup	
	Status	Substance	Status	Substance
Congressional Sources				
Congressional Record. See Daily Digest pages and advance Senate committee schedule. Also see announcements by committee chairs in House and Senate proceedings pages	x		x	
Committee and leadership web sites, available through the House <*www.house.gov*> and Senate <*www.senate.gov*> sites	x		x	
Committee or committee members' press releases	x	x	x	x
Committee markup vehicle		x		
Amendments printed or drafted by committee members (sometimes based on legislation previously referred to the committee)		x		x
Committee report and text of legislation as reported				x
Legislative Information System (Congress only)	x	x	x	x
THOMAS <*http://thomas.loc.gov*>	x	x	x	x
Non-Congressional Sources				
CQ Today <*www.cq.com*>	x	x	x	x
CQ.com <*www.cq.com*>	x	x	x	x
CQ Weekly (for major legislation) <*www.cq.com*>	x	x	x	x
CongressDaily, from *National Journal* <*http://nationaljournal.com*>	x	x	x	x
National Journal online service	x	x	x	x
National Journal (for major legislation) <*http://nationaljournal.com*>		x		x
Trade press and daily newspapers	x	x	x	x
Relevant interest-group web sites	x	x	x	x
Other commercial database services	x	x	x	x
People *(Use these contacts after exhausting other resources.)*				
Committee professional staff (What is expected to happen at markup? After markup, when is floor action expected?)		x	x	
Committee professional staff—*House only* (After markup, what type of rule will be sought? Is suspension of the rules an option?)			x	x
Committee clerks (When and where is markup scheduled? After markup, are amendment texts and recorded vote tallies available?)	x			x
Documents clerks (What documents are available?)		x		x
Committee and committee members' press assistants (What press releases or other press documents are available?)		x		x

1. Markups in a subcommittee do not usually result in formal documents. Information on substantive decisions must be gained from the media, subcommittee staff, and members who serve on the subcommittee or their personal staff.

can be amended in *two degrees. (See First-Degree Amendment and Second-Degree Amendment in § 8.121, Amendment Process Glossary.)*

Subcommittee Reported Version/Committee Print. Many measures considered by a full committee have already received subcommittee action. If a subcommittee reports its version of a text to the full committee, the product is often printed and referred to as a *committee print.* The committee print can then be used as the markup vehicle. An alternative is for a committee or subcommittee chair to offer the subcommittee reported version as an *amendment in the nature of a substitute* for the measure initially used as the markup vehicle. A third approach is for the subcommittee chair to introduce a new measure reflecting the subcommittee's changes to the earlier measure. This new measure could then be referred to the committee and used as the markup vehicle.

Staff Draft/Chairman's Mark. This option allows the committee to use as a vehicle a text that incorporates both changes made in subcommittee markup and additional changes negotiated afterward, yet before full committee markup. The product of these negotiations is incorporated into a *committee print*, often referred to as a *staff draft* or *chairman's mark.*

Amendment in the Nature of a Substitute. A chair sometimes prefers to offer an amendment in the nature of a substitute to the measure selected as the markup vehicle. This type of amendment, representing a full-text alternative, can be offered only at the outset of the amendment process, after the first section of the measure is read. (A full-text amendment can also be offered at the end of the markup process, but that practice is rare.)

Amendment Procedure

Committees do not actually amend measures during markup; instead, a committee votes on what amendments it wishes to recommend to its parent chamber. If a committee reports a measure with amendments, the parent chamber will ordinarily have to act on the amendments. How a panel conducts the amendment process in markup generally reflects procedures used in the chamber, possibly as modified by individual committee rules.

Reading the Measure. Bills must be *read* twice in committee. This second reading enables the amendment process to begin. Committees usually dispense with the first reading of a bill, either by unanimous consent or by a motion to dispense with the reading. A measure is not considered as read for a second time, for amendment, until a chair directs the clerk to read section one. A measure is usually read for amendment by section. By unanimous consent, a measure could be "considered as read and open for amendment at any point" or could be amended by title.

Recognition and Debate. In recognizing committee members to speak or offer amendments, the chair alternates between majority and minority members. The chair also gives preference to more senior members. When a member offers an amendment, the clerk reads the amendment and committee staff distribute copies of it. Reading of the amendment can be dispensed with by unanimous consent.

Before a sponsor speaks in support of an amendment, any committee member can either reserve or make a *point of order* against the amendment. A point of order must be reserved or made after the clerk reads but before the sponsor begins to speak. A point of order is a parliamentary device for questioning whether an amendment, measure, or motion is within the rules of a chamber or of a committee. If a point of order is sustained by a committee chair, the amendment cannot be offered. If the point of order is overruled, the amendment process can proceed. Although it is possible to appeal a chair's ruling—to question it—making a successful appeal is rare. (Although committee members and staff may seek advice from the parliamentarian before or during a markup, a parliamentarian is not present during a markup. Rather, a committee staff member is normally designated to be a committee's expert on chamber and committee rules.)

Amendments offered in House committee markups are considered under the five-minute rule; that is, any member may speak for up to five minutes. Additional time can be given by unanimous consent.

Amendments offered in Senate committee markups are generally not subject to debate limitations. Therefore, it is possible for opponents to filibuster an amendment. There is no Senate procedure for invoking cloture in a committee markup; however, several Senate committees have adopted committee rules to bring extended debate to an end.

An amendment may be agreed to or rejected by a voice, division, or roll-call vote. House committees may not use proxy voting; Senate committees may if a committee's rules authorize proxy voting. *(See § 8.131, House Voting Glossary.)*

Offering and Considering Amendments in House Markups. The most common method of conducting markups allows a member to offer an amendment to a section as it is read. When the last amendment to a section has been offered, the section is considered closed to further amendment, and the committee moves to the next section. By unanimous consent, amendments may be offered *en bloc*, that is, affecting more than one section of a measure.

Alternatively, the chair can open the bill to amendment at any point if unanimous consent is granted. This process enables members to offer amendments in an order convenient to the committee's members. Some committees use an amendment roster, a list agreed to in advance by all committee members, which provides the order in which amendments will be considered.

Another option is for the chair or another member, generally a senior majority member, to offer an amendment in the nature of a substitute. This is essentially a full-text alternative to the pending measure. This type of amendment can be offered only at the beginning or end of the markup process, and is itself open to amendment at any point (and may be made original text for the purpose of further amendment). An advantage of an amendment in the nature of a substitute is that a motion can be made after any debate on the amendment to cut off further debate and amendments. This motion is called the *previous question.*

An amendment must be read in full unless reading is dispensed with by unanimous consent. An amendment can be withdrawn if no action has occurred on it. Amendments are permitted only in *two degrees*, and they must be *germane*. *(See definitions in § 8.121, Amendment Process Glossary.)*

Ending the Amendment Process in House Markups. After the last section of the measure has been read, any committee member can move the previous question. A member can also move to *close debate* or *end debate* on amendments or to *limit debate* to a specified time. Unlike the previous question, closing or limiting debate does not preclude offering additional amendments, but it does mean that all subsequent amendments are decided without debate.

Offering and Considering Amendments in Senate Markups. A measure is usually open to amendment at any point in Senate committees. However, a committee can decide by unanimous consent to structure the amendment process. Otherwise, amendments are considered in whatever order senators offer them.

An amendment must be read in full unless reading is dispensed with by unanimous consent. An amendment can be withdrawn if no action has occurred on it. Germaneness of amendments is generally not required during markup; however, Senate rules prohibit the floor consideration of substantive committee amendments containing significant matter outside the jurisdiction of the reporting committee. Amendments are permitted in two degrees. *(See First-Degree Amendment, Second-Degree Amendment, and Germaneness at § 8.121, Amendment Process Glossary.)*

Reporting

At the end of the amendment process, a chair normally entertains a motion to report a measure favorably to its parent chamber. The motion is not a request for unanimous consent. In each chamber, a majority of the committee must be physically present in the committee when a measure is reported. Although Senate committees generally allow the use of proxies, proxy votes may not affect the outcome of the vote to report a measure from committee.

Once the motion to report is agreed to, a bill is *ordered reported*; it is not actually *reported* until the committee report is filed in the chamber. When a committee orders a measure reported, it is incumbent upon the chair to report it "promptly" and to take all steps necessary to secure its consideration by the House. Staff are usually granted authority to make "technical and conforming" changes to the measure reported.

Options for Reporting. A committee can report a measure without amendment. This means that the committee has made no changes to the text of the measure as introduced.

Second, a committee can report a measure "as amended" with an amendment or multiple amendments—so-called *cut and bite amendments*. Multiple amendments could be considered individually or adopted *en bloc* on the floor.

Third, a House committee can report a *clean bill*. That is a new bill incorporating the text of amendments adopted in markup. A committee member, often the chair, introduces the new measure in the House; it receives a new number and is referred to committee. By unanimous consent, a clean bill can be "deemed reported," thereby voiding the need for another committee meeting.

A Senate committee may report an *original bill* that embodies a text agreed to in markup. This new bill is given its own number when it is reported or called up or at another time after committee action has been completed. Reporting an original bill avoids separate floor votes on the changes adopted in markup.

Fourth, a committee can report an introduced measure with an amendment in the nature of a substitute. This is similar to reporting a clean bill, but it retains the original measure's number.

Which option a committee chooses may influence how the measure is considered on the floor of the respective chamber.

Options on How to Report. A committee can report a measure "favorably." This means that a majority of a committee is recommending that the full House or Senate consider and pass a measure. Alternatively, a committee can report "unfavorably" or "adversely." This often implies that the majority-party leadership believes that a majority of House members support a measure even though a majority of the committee does not. Third, a committee can report "without recommendation." This means that a committee believes a measure should receive floor consideration even though it could not find a majority to agree on what to report.

§ 8.60 Committee Reports

When a committee sends a measure to the floor by reporting it from the committee, the committee usually files a written report to accompany the measure. The report describes the purpose and intent of the legislation, and explains the committee's action on the measure, including votes taken in markup. The report indicates changes proposed to existing law, provides information on the measure's cost, and contains other information. Individual member statements can also be included in the report. A committee report provides a useful substantive and political explanation of a committee's intent.

Description and Requirements

The cover page of a committee report, usually formatted by the Office of Legislative Counsel, provides the title of the bill, the date the report was ordered printed, the name of the chair submitting the report, and a notation to the legislation it accompanies. There is a reference to the inclusion of a Congressional Budget Office (CBO) estimate and to any minority, supplemental, or additional views that were filed. The cover page also identifies committee action on the legislation and the number of the report itself. *(See § 8.61, Reading the Cover Page of a House Committee Report.)*

§ 8.61

Reading the Cover Page
of a House Committee Report

1 Committee reports, including those from conference committees, are numbered sequentially as the reports are filed by any committee with its parent chamber. "H. Rept." denotes a report from a House committee; "S. Rept." from a Senate committee. The numbers before the hyphen show the Congress; for example, "106" means 106th Congress. The numbers following the hyphen make up the unique, sequential number for the report.

2 If a measure is referred to more than one committee, each committee reporting the measure uses the same report number. But, each committee's report is printed separately and designated a "part" of the report. In this example, all reports were H. Rept. 106-74, but the Banking Committee reported "Part 1" and a supplement, "Part 2." The report from the Commerce Committee was then "Part 3." (Part designations may appear in Roman numerals.)

3 An identification of the measure, such as its "popular name" or "short title."

4 The reporting date and the calendar designation; in this case, the "Union Calendar."

5 The chair and committee reporting the measure.

6 The notation of minority, supplemental, or additional views, if one or more committee members requested their inclusion.

7 The measure that is being reported from the committee.

8 A brief description of the measure and the committee's recommendation to the parent chamber.

9 The report text begins, sometimes with a table of contents.

1

| 106TH CONGRESS
1st Session | HOUSE OF REPRESENTATIVES | REPT. 106–74
Part 3 |

2

3 FINANCIAL SERVICES ACT OF 1999

4 JUNE 15, 1999.—Committed to the Committee of the Whole House on the State of the Union and ordered to be printed

5 Mr. BLILEY, from the Committee on Commerce, submitted the following

R E P O R T

together with

6 ADDITIONAL VIEWS

7 [To accompany H.R. 10]

8 The Committee on Commerce, to whom was referred the bill (H.R. 10) to enhance competition in the financial services industry by providing a prudential framework for the affiliation of banks, securities firms, and other financial service providers, and for other purposes, having considered the same, report favorably thereon with an amendment and recommend that the bill as amended do pass.

CONTENTS

9

57–325

§ 8.62

House Committee Reports: Required Contents

Requirement	Applies to
Statement of committee action on all record votes	Record vote to report measure of public character and on any amendment offered in committee
Statement of committee oversight findings and recommendations	Measure approved; all committees except Committees on Appropriations and Budget
Statement on new budget authority and related items	Measure (except continuing appropriations measure) providing new budget authority, new spending authority, new credit authority, or increase or decrease in revenues or tax expenditures
Statement of Congressional Budget Office (CBO) cost estimate and comparison, if submitted in timely fashion	Measure of public character; all committees except Committee on Appropriations
Statement of general performance goals and objectives, including outcome-related goals and objectives	Measure approved
Statement of constitutional authority of Congress to enact	Measure of public character
Supplemental, minority, or additional views, if submitted in writing and signed, and filed within two calendar days	Measure approved; all committees except Committee on Rules
Recital on cover of report to show inclusion of certain material	Reports that include CBO cost estimate and comparison, oversight findings, and supplemental, minority, or additional views
Changes in existing law ("Ramseyer rule")	Measure that amends or repeals existing law
Statement of committee cost estimate	Measure of public character; Committees on Appropriations, House Administration, Rules, and Standards of Official Conduct are exempt; requirement does not apply if CBO cost estimate is in report
Determination regarding new advisory committee	Legislation establishing or authorizing establishment of advisory committee
Applicability to legislative branch, or statement explaining why not applicable	Measure relating to terms and conditions of employment or access to public services or accommodations
Statement of federal mandates	Measure of public character
Macroeconomic analysis	Ways and Means Committee; requirement does not apply if analysis is inserted in *Congressional Record*

§ 8.63

Senate Committee Reports: Required Contents

Committee reports must include:

- Record of roll-call votes
- Cost estimate prepared by Congressional Budget Office
- Regulatory impact statement
- Changes in existing law, a requirement called the "Cordon rule"
- Minority, supplemental, or additional views, if requested

Committee reports usually include:

- Text of committee's proposed amendments, if any
- Discussion of policy issue addressed
- Summary of committee's deliberations
- Discussion of committee's conclusions and recommendations
- Section-by-section analysis of measure's provisions and proposed amendments

A committee report's sections then begin, generally in the following sequence. The initial section provides a brief description of the purpose of the legislation, a brief summary of the bill itself (referred to as a "section-by-section"), and a legislative history of the legislation, including a detailed explanation of the actions taken by the committee in hearings and markup. A House report must contain details on all votes taken in committee on each amendment offered and on the motion to report, including how each member voted on each item. A hearing summary is often included as well. A committee report then addresses the need for the legislation and the intent of the measure; this portion of a report is often cited in court decisions and by future Congresses.

A House report must include oversight findings and recommendations, CBO estimates, information on unfunded mandates (if appropriate), and a statement of authority. (See § 8.62, House Committee Reports: Required Contents.)

A Senate report must include cost estimates, a paperwork impact statement, a regulatory impact statement, and information on unfunded mandates (if appropriate). If a roll-call vote was ordered to report a measure, the report must also include the vote results. Finally, if appropriate, a statement explaining the extent to which the measure preempts any state, local, or tribal law must be provided. (See § 8.63, Senate Committee Reports: Required Contents.)

Ramseyer/Cordon. A comparative section in contrasting typefaces must be included in a committee report. It shows the text of a statute, or a part thereof, that is proposed to be amended or repealed. This section is usually prepared by the respective chamber's Office of Legislative Counsel. In House reports, this comparative section is eponymously called a "Ramseyer," and in Senate reports, a "Cordon." (These sections are named, respectively, for Representative Christian W. Ramseyer, R-IA, 1915–1933, and Senator Guy Cordon, R-OR, 1944–1955.)

Minority, Additional, and Supplemental Views. Views of individual committee members or groups of committee members are required to be included if a member or members request permission to include them. Minority views may be filed by committee members who are not minority-party members.

§ 8.71

House Calendars

When a measure is reported from committee, it is placed on a calendar. These calendars are lists of pending measures. The calendars are not agendas, because measures are not assigned a day for consideration until the leadership determines when a measure will come up for consideration.

Union Calendar: All legislation dealing with raising, authorizing, or spending money.

House Calendar: Non-money measures, and measures dealing with internal House matters.

Private Calendar: Bills dealing with relief of a private individual or group of individuals.

Discharge Calendar (Calendar of Motions to Discharge Committees): All motions to take (discharge) a measure from a committee through the discharge procedure.

Individual Committee Requirements. Several House committees are required to include specific provisions in their committee reports. The Committee on Appropriations, for example, must provide a statement describing the effect of any provision of an appropriations bill that changes the application of a law, a list of appropriations for unauthorized expenditures, and a list of rescissions and transfers of unexpended balances.

In reports accompanying resolutions that change House rules, the Committee on Rules must include the text of the rule proposed to be changed and a comparative text showing the proposed change.

In reports on measures changing the Internal Revenue Code, the Committee on Ways and Means must include a tax complexity analysis prepared by the Joint Committee on Taxation. If the Ways and Means Committee reports legislation designated by the majority leader as major tax legislation, the report must include a *dynamic estimate* of the changes in federal revenues expected to result if the legislation is enacted.

(For additional information on committee documents, see § 12.10, Committee Documents.)

§ 8.70 House Floor: Scheduling and Privilege

Once a measure has been reported from committee, it goes on a calendar. The majority-party leadership is responsible for determining whether a measure should come off its respective calendar and when it should receive floor consideration. Working with the Rules Committee, the leadership also influences how a measure is considered. *(See § 8.71, House Calendars, and § 12.20, Floor Documents.)*

Decisions on how a measure comes to the floor are made within strictures in House rules that limit the kinds of measures that can go to the floor. The concept of *privilege* is used to categorize such procedures. *Privileged business* consists of those measures and matters that mem-

§ 8.72

Daily Starting Times
in the House

Starting times are usually announced early in each session by the majority-party leadership.

January 4, 2007, through May 13, 2007:

- 2:00 p.m. on Monday
  (12:30 p.m. for morning hour)
- 12:00 noon on Tuesday
  (10:30 a.m. for morning hour)
- 10:00 a.m. on all other days

May 14, 2007, until the end of the first session:

- 12:00 noon on Monday
  (11:00 a.m. for morning hour)
- 10:00 a.m. on Tuesday, Wednesday, and
  Thursday (9:00 a.m. for morning hour)
- 9:00 a.m. on Friday

bers can bring up for consideration on the House floor and that are *privileged* to interrupt the regular order of business.

In the House, measures on certain calendars, or to be brought up for consideration subject to certain procedures, are privileged on certain days. These calendars and procedures are the Discharge and Private Calendars; District Day; Calendar Wednesday; and suspension of the rules. Business privileged on any day the House meets includes general appropriations bills; privileged reports from committees that have the right to report at any time, including special rules from the Rules Committee; and reported resolutions of inquiry. Amendments in disagreement and Senate amendments that do not require consideration in the Committee of the Whole are also privileged.

When the House is in session, it tends to follow meeting times announced by the majority-party leadership at the beginning of each session. *(See § 8.72, Daily Starting Times in the House.)*

(For information on House floor documents, see § 12.20.)

§ 8.80 House Floor: Methods of Consideration

There are numerous ways to bring a measure to the House floor for debate, possible amendment, and a vote on passage. A measure might come to the floor because of the calendar on which it was placed or because it is a certain day of the week or the month. Another measure might find its fate in the hands of the majority leadership, especially the Speaker of the House. One measure might come to the floor because it is noncontroversial, and another might make it there only after complex negotiations.

Unanimous Consent

Noncontroversial measures, which have been cleared by the respective party leaders, can come to the floor by unanimous consent. Once cleared, a member can ask permission to bring up the particular measure. A single objection by another member will stop the process. A member can, alternately, "reserve the right to object" in order to ask about the request, traditionally to check if the measure has been cleared by the minority party. Once the member seeking to bring up the measure responds, the member reserving the right to object withdraws

104

the reservation, and the consent request is agreed to "without objection." This exchange, under the reservation, is all the discussion that occurs on a measure brought up by unanimous consent.

Suspension of the Rules

This procedure, for largely noncontroversial measures, accounts for more than half of all measures considered by the House. On Monday, Tuesday, and Wednesday of each week, and during the last six days of a session, the Speaker may recognize members to move to "suspend the rules and pass" a particular measure or conference report. Suspension measures can also be considered on other days by unanimous consent or pursuant to provisions of a special rule.

A measure traditionally will not be considered under the suspension procedure if it was controversial in committee. (The majority party's rules supplement House rules in guiding the leadership on legislative and other matters. However, party rules have no official status in House proceedings and cannot be a basis for a point of order.)

Debate on a motion to suspend the rules is limited to forty minutes, with twenty minutes controlled by a proponent and twenty minutes controlled by an opponent, regardless of party affiliation. In practice, a majority floor manager controls twenty minutes and a minority floor manager controls the other twenty minutes. Measures considered under this process are not subject to floor amendment, although the motion to suspend may incorporate an amendment. Because the motion would then be to "suspend the rules and pass the bill with an amendment," no separate vote is taken on the amendment. Points of order cannot be raised on a measure or conference report brought up under suspension of the rules.

To pass, a measure considered under the suspension procedure requires two-thirds of the members present and voting to vote for the motion. Unless a recorded vote is requested, however, a measure considered under this procedure can be passed by a voice vote.

Private Calendar

Bills on this calendar generally relate to individual immigration and claims matters and are placed there when reported by the Committee on the Judiciary or any committee considering a private bill. Measures on the Private Calendar can come to the floor on the first Tuesday of each month. At the discretion of the Speaker, private measures can also be considered on the third Tuesday of each month.

Each party usually appoints *official objectors* to review bills on the Private Calendar. If an official objector has a concern about a bill, there can be an objection to its consideration. More often, however, the bill is "passed over, without prejudice." It gives sponsors a chance to address concerns before the bill comes up under the next call of the Private Calendar.

Each bill is called up automatically in the order in which it was reported from committee and placed on the Private Calendar. A bill is considered under a special procedure, called "in the House as in the Committee of the Whole." Under this process, there is no general debate, but members may speak for five minutes. There is usually little debate and measures pass by voice vote.

Discharge Calendar

Any member may file a motion with the clerk of the House to discharge a committee from consideration of any measure that has been pending before the committee for thirty legislative days. A motion to discharge a special rule from the Committee on Rules can be filed if the special rule has been pending before that committee for seven legislative days. The Discharge Calendar is considered on the second and fourth Mondays of each month, although a measure eligible for discharge (by having 218 signatures on its discharge petition) must be on the Discharge Calendar for seven legislative days.

Discharge motions are considered in the House with twenty minutes of debate equally divided between a proponent and an opponent. The only intervening motion is a nondebatable motion to adjourn.

Special Rule

A measure not in order under the means discussed above generally comes to the floor under provisions of a *special rule*. A special rule sets the guidelines for a measure's consideration, including time for *general debate* and any limits on the *amendment process*. Most important and controversial legislation is considered under the terms of a special rule to enable the leadership to structure debate and amendments.

Rules are considered in the House under the *one-hour rule*, with time controlled by a majority floor manager. The majority floor manager customarily yields thirty minutes to the minority floor manager "for purposes of debate only." Accordingly, special rules can be amended only if the majority floor manager offers an amendment to the rule or yields time to another member to offer an amendment, or if the previous question on the rule is defeated. (The previous question is in the form of a motion ("I move the previous question"), which, if agreed to, cuts off further debate and the possibility of amendment.)

§ 8.90 Rules Committee and Special Rules

For most major legislation, it is the Rules Committee that determines if and how a measure will be considered on the floor. The Rules Committee is empowered to report *a special rule* in the form of a simple resolution (for example, H. Res. 123) to govern floor debate, the amendment process, and other procedures related to floor consideration of a measure. *(See § 8.91, Special Rules Glossary.)*

Requesting a Special Rule

When a committee reports a measure, the committee chair, usually by letter to the Rules Committee chair, requests that a Rules Committee hearing be scheduled on the measure. The

106

§ 8.91

Special Rules Glossary

Closed Rule: Permits general debate for a specified period of time but permits no floor amendments. Amendments reported by the reporting committee are allowed.

Modified Closed Rule: Permits general debate for a specified period of time, but limits amendments to those designated in the special rule or the Rules Committee report accompanying the special rule. May preclude amendments to particular portions of a bill.

Modified Open Rule: Permits general debate for a specified period of time, and allows any member to offer amendments consistent with House rules subject only to an overall time limit on the amendment process or a requirement that amendments be preprinted in the *Congressional Record*.

Open Rule: Permits general debate for a specified period of time and allows any member to offer an amendment that complies with the standing rules of the House.

Queen-of-the-Hill Rule: A special rule that permits votes on a series of amendments, usually complete substitutes for a measure, but directs that the amendment receiving the greatest number of votes is the winning amendment.

Rise and Report: Refers to the end of proceedings in the Committee of the Whole, which sends the measure it has been considering back to the House for final disposition.

Self-Executing Rule: If specified, the House's adoption of a special rule may also have the effect of amending or passing the underlying measure. Also called a "hereby" rule.

Structured Rule: Another term for a modified closed rule.

Waiver Rule: A special rule that waives points of order against a measure or an amendment.

A larger glossary is located at the back of the book.

letter often notes the type of rule requested, the amount of debate time needed, and whether any *waivers* of House rules are required. Individual members may also write to the Rules Committee requesting the opportunity to testify and make their cases for being allowed to offer amendments to the measure on the House floor. *(See § 8.92, Announcement on Amendments Prior to a Rules Committee Meeting.)*

Rules Committee Action

The Rules Committee hearing is typically scheduled after the majority leadership has decided to schedule floor time for a measure. The committee's hearing on this legislation resembles any other committee hearing, although only members of the House are witnesses. Following the hearing, the panel marks up a special rule, often drafted with the knowledge and input of the majority-party leadership.

§ 8.92

Announcement on Amendments Prior to a Rules Committee Meeting

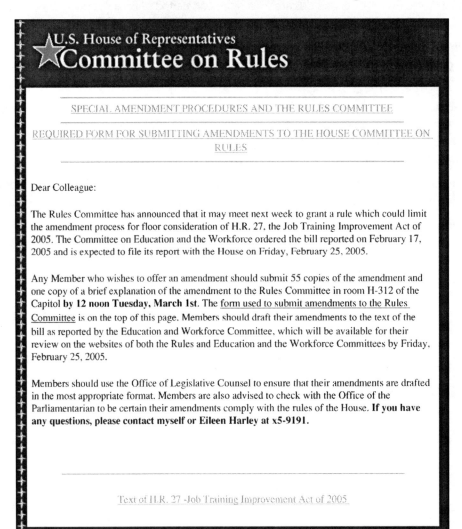

U.S. House of Representatives
Committee on Rules

SPECIAL AMENDMENT PROCEDURES AND THE RULES COMMITTEE

REQUIRED FORM FOR SUBMITTING AMENDMENTS TO THE HOUSE COMMITTEE ON RULES

Dear Colleague:

The Rules Committee has announced that it may meet next week to grant a rule which could limit the amendment process for floor consideration of H.R. 27, the Job Training Improvement Act of 2005. The Committee on Education and the Workforce ordered the bill reported on February 17, 2005 and is expected to file its report with the House on Friday, February 25, 2005.

Any Member who wishes to offer an amendment should submit 55 copies of the amendment and one copy of a brief explanation of the amendment to the Rules Committee in room H-312 of the Capitol **by 12 noon Tuesday, March 1st**. The form used to submit amendments to the Rules Committee is on the top of this page. Members should draft their amendments to the text of the bill as reported by the Education and Workforce Committee, which will be available for their review on the websites of both the Rules and Education and the Workforce Committees by Friday, February 25, 2005.

Members should use the Office of Legislative Counsel to ensure that their amendments are drafted in the most appropriate format. Members are also advised to check with the Office of the Parliamentarian to be certain their amendments comply with the rules of the House. **If you have any questions, please contact myself or Eileen Harley at x5-9191.**

Text of H.R. 27 -Job Training Improvement Act of 2005

Types of Special Rules

There are several types of rules the committee can craft. *(See § 8.93, Reading a Special Rule.)* Under each type, *general debate* is permitted for a specified period of time. Under an *open rule*, all *germane amendments* can be offered, provided they are offered in a timely manner, comply with all House rules, and fit on the *amendment tree*. Under a *closed rule*, no amendments can be offered to the bill. *(See § 8.120, Committee of the Whole: Amendment Process; and § 8.122, Basic House Amendment Tree.)*

Modified rules fall into several categories. A *modified open rule* generally requires that amendments be preprinted in the *Congressional Record*, and the special rule may place an overall time limit on the amendment process. A *modified closed rule*, often called a *structured rule*, permits only specified amendments, which are listed in the Rules Committee report. A *queen-of-the-hill rule* allows a specified number of full-text substitutes to a measure, with the amendment receiving the most votes being the only amendment deemed adopted. The *king-of-the-hill rule* has not been used in recent years. Under this procedure, the last amendment to receive a majority vote was the amendment adopted.

A *waiver rule* provides for consideration of amendments or measures that might otherwise be subject to points of order.

A *self-executing* or *hereby rule* stipulates that, upon adoption of the rule, the House is deemed to have passed a measure, adopted an amendment, or taken some other action. A self-executing rule precludes a separate vote on the measure, amendment, or action.

A special rule might include more than one of these features. For example, any of these types of rules might include waiver provisions.

Providing for Floor Consideration

A special rule designates which measure is to be considered on the floor; for example, a com-mittee-reported bill or a so-called leadership alternative. (Leadership alternatives appear reg-ularly.) After the House has voted to approve the rule, the rule then allows the Speaker to declare the House resolved into the *Committee of the Whole House on the State of the Union (Committee of the Whole)* for the consideration of the measure. (*See § 8.110, Committee of the Whole: Debate.*) The rule next generally waives the required *first reading* of a bill in full. Final-ly, the special rule states the amount of time available for discussion (called general debate), and further requires that debate be *germane*.

Structuring the Amendment Process

The special rule may address how the bill will be read for amendment; for example, by title, by section (which is the most common way), or open for amendment at any point. ("By section" is the default method for amending and would not typically be mentioned.) The rule also lays out the amendment process, although it does not state specifically that the rule is open, closed, or modified. The description of the amendment process in the rule enables one to clas-sify and refer to the rule as open, closed, or modified. The rule may also allow the chair of the Committee of the Whole to postpone or cluster votes on amendments and reduce to five min-utes the time for clustered votes after a fifteen-minute vote on the first amendment in a series.

Facilitating Final Passage

The special rule makes the motion for the Committee of the Whole to *rise and report* auto-matic upon completion of the amendment process, and further allows for a *separate vote* in the

§ 8.93

Reading a Special Rule

H. Res. 289

[Report No. 106–317]

Original Text of the Resolution

Providing for consideration of the bill (H.R. 1655) to authorize appropriations for fiscal years 2000 and 2001 for the civilian energy and scientific research, development, and demonstration and related commercial application of energy technology programs, projects, and activities of the Department of Energy, and for other purposes.

❶ Authorizes the Speaker to transform ("resolve") the House into the Committee of the Whole House to consider the measure after adoption of the special rule.

❶ *Resolved,* That at any time after the adoption of this resolution the Speaker may, pursuant to clause 2(b) of rule XVIII, declare the House resolved into the Committee of the Whole House on the state of the Union for consideration of the bill (H.R. 1655) to authorize appropriations for fiscal years 2000 and 2001 for the civilian energy and scientific research, development, and demonstration and related commercial application of energy technology programs, projects, and activities of the Department of Energy, and for other purposes.

❷ Dispenses with the first reading of the bill. (Bills must be read three times before being passed.) Sets the amount of general debate time—one hour—and specifies which members control that time—in this instance, the chair and ranking minority member of the Committee on Science. Specifies that debate should be relevant to the bill.

❷ The first reading of the bill shall be dispensed with. General debate shall be confined to the bill and shall not exceed one hour equally divided and controlled by the chairman and ranking minority member of the Committee on Science.

❸ Sets reading for amendment one section at a time (or one paragraph at a time for appropriations bills), and provides that each member can speak for five minutes on each amendment. Because this special rule sets no limitations on amendments that can be offered, it is an open rule. Nonetheless, amendments still must comply with the House's standing rules, such as that on germaneness.

❸ After general debate the bill shall be considered for amendment under the five-minute rule.

Continued on page 287

§ 8.93 *(continued)*

4 Identifies text to be open to amendment in the Committee of the Whole. A special rule can provide that a committee-reported substitute be considered as an original bill for the purpose of amendment. Allowing a full-text substitute to be considered as an original bill is usually done to permit second-degree amendments to be offered.

5 Determines recognition order for offering amendments. Open rules customarily grant the chair of the Committee of the Whole discretion to give priority recognition to members who submitted their amendments for preprinting in the *Congressional Record*. Absent this provision, the chair would follow the custom of giving preferential recognition to members, based on seniority, who serve on the reporting committee, alternating between the parties.

6 A special rule that allows amendments to be offered might allow the chair of the Committee of the Whole to postpone votes on amendments, as shown here. The chair may reduce to five minutes the time for electronic voting on a postponed question, provided that the voting time on the first in any series of questions is not less than fifteen minutes.

7 Provides for transformation ("to rise") back to the House from the Committee of the Whole. This provision eliminates the need for a separate vote on a motion to rise and report.

8 Enables separate votes to occur in the House on each amendment approved by the Committee of the Whole. House rules require the House to vote on each amendment approved by the Committee of the Whole.

9 Expedites final passage. By automatically imposing the "previous question," intervening debate and the offering of motions is precluded. The only motion allowed is a motion to recommit.

4 It shall be in order to consider as an original bill for purposes of amendment under the five-minute rule the amendment in the nature of a substitute recommended by the Committee on Science now printed in the bill. Each section of the committee amendment in the nature of a substitute shall be considered as read.

5 During consideration of the bill for amendment, the Chairman of the Committee of the Whole may accord priority in recognition on the basis of whether the Member offering an amendment has caused it to be printed in the portion of the Congressional Record designated for that purpose in clause 8 of rule XVIII. Amendments so printed shall be considered as read.

6 The Chairman of the Committee of the Whole may: (1) postpone until a time during further consideration in the Committee of the Whole a request for a recorded vote on any amendment; and (2) reduce to five minutes time for electronic voting on any postponed question that follows another electronic vote without intervening business, provided that the minimum time for electronic voting on the first in any series of questions shall be 15 minutes.

7 At the conclusion of consideration of the bill for amendment the Committee shall rise and report the bill to the House with such amendments as may have been adopted.

8 Any Members may demand a separate vote in the House on any amendment adopted in the Committee of the Whole to the bill or to the committee amendment in the nature of a substitute.

9 The previous question shall be considered as ordered on the bill and amendments thereto to final passage without intervening motion except one motion to recommit with or without instructions.

House on any amendment agreed to in the Committee of the Whole. Finally, the rule allows a *motion to recommit* to be offered before a vote on *final passage*, which may be a *voice, division,* or *recorded vote*.

§ 8.100 Consideration of a
Special Rule on the House Floor

When the House for parliamentary purposes is sitting as the House and has not resolved into the Committee of the Whole, House rules permit members, when recognized, to hold the floor for no more than one hour each. A special rule from the Rules Committee is privileged and is considered under this *hour rule*. *(See § 8.70, House Floor: Scheduling and Privilege.)* The *majority floor manager* for the Rules Committee, who calls up the simple resolution containing the special rule, customarily yields one half of this one hour to the control of a minority member of the committee, the *minority floor manager*, "for purposes of debate only."

When the House is meeting as the House, the Speaker or, more commonly, a Speaker pro tempore presides. The quorum in the House is a majority of the membership, or 218 representatives if there are no vacancies. *(See § 8.112, House versus Committee of the Whole.)*

Each floor manager then yields a portion of the time he or she controls to other members who wish to speak. The majority party has the right to close the debate—essentially to give the last speech. When all time has been consumed or yielded back, the majority floor manager "moves the previous question."

The *previous question* is a nondebatable motion that proposes to end debate on a measure, to preclude amendments, and to bring the House to a vote on a measure—in this case, the simple resolution containing the special rule. (A motion to adjourn, a motion to table, and a motion to recommit to committee are still in order.) The previous question requires a simple majority vote for adoption. After the previous question on a special rule is agreed to, there is a vote on adoption of the special rule.

There are three ways to offer amendments to a measure (such as a special rule) in the House sitting for parliamentary purposes as the House. First, a motion to recommit a measure can instruct a committee to report the measure back to the House with a specific amendment. The right to offer a motion to recommit is the prerogative of the minority party. Second, the majority floor manager can offer an amendment before the previous question is agreed to. In the case of a special rule, the majority party drafted the measure so that an amendment is rarely offered.

Third, an opponent of a measure can propose an amendment if he or she can gain control of the floor. To do this, the House would need to vote not to *order the previous question*, that is, to defeat it. Defeat of the previous question means that debate does not end, amendments are not precluded, and the resolution will not yet be voted on. If the previous question is defeated, a member, usually the minority floor manager, can proceed for one hour and offer an amendment to the special rule. At the end of the second hour, the minority floor manager would move the previous question on the measure and an amendment to it.

While neither the motion to recommit nor the defeat of the previous question routinely happen, the majority party occasionally mistakes majority sentiment. For example, when President Reagan's economic package was precluded from consideration in 1981 by the House by a special rule reported from the Rules Committee, the key vote was on ordering the previous question. A sufficient number of then-majority party Democrats joined Republicans to defeat the previous question and, subsequently, amend the special rule.

§ 8.110 Committee of the Whole: Debate

When the House is in session, it might be "sitting" in one of two ways for parliamentary purposes. For example, when the House considers and votes on a special rule, the House sits for parliamentary purposes as the House. The second way the House sits is as the *Committee of the Whole House on the State of the Union (Committee of the Whole)*, a parliamentary device created to expedite consideration of a measure.

The House "resolves" into the Committee of the Whole either by unanimous consent or by adoption of a special rule. The Committee of the Whole is a committee consisting of all members of the House. The Committee of the Whole meets in the House chamber, is presided over by a chair appointed by the Speaker of the House, and has a quorum requirement of 100 members. The mace, the symbol of the authority of the House, is removed from its pedestal when the Committee of the Whole is meeting. *(See § 8.111, The Mace.)* Measures from the Union Calendar are considered in the Committee of the Whole. *(See § 8.112, House versus Committee of the Whole.)*

General Debate

General debate is a period of time set aside for discussing a bill as a whole. During this period, no amendments or motions are in order.

The special rule specifies the amount of time available for general debate and how the time is allocated. (For those measures that are brought up by unanimous consent, but considered in the Committee of the Whole, the consent request specifies the time set aside for general debate.) The special rule typically provides one hour of general debate on a measure, with time usually divided equally between the control of the chair and ranking minority member of the committee of jurisdiction. These two members are referred to as the *floor managers* of the measure. (Once a special rule is adopted, the Rules Committee members' role as floor managers ends.)

The chair of the Committee of the Whole recognizes the majority floor manager to open the general debate. The majority floor manager reserves the balance of time after concluding

§ 8.111

The Mace

The mace is the symbol of authority of the House of Representatives. The following physical description of the mace appears with other information about the mace on the web site of the clerk of the House, at *<http://clerk.house.gov/art_history/art_artifacts/ virtual_tours/splendid_hall/artifacts.html>*:

> The mace is 46 inches high and consists of 13 thin ebony rods representing the original 13 states of the union. The rods are bound together by four crossing ribbons of silver, pinned together and held at the bottom and at the top by silver bands. The bands are decorated with floral borders and a repoussé design. The name "Wm. Adams/Manufacturer/New York/1841." is engraved in the cartouche, located in the front center of the bottom band. This shaft is topped by a silver globe 4-1/2 inches in diameter and engraved with the seven continents, the names of the oceans, lines of longitude, and the major lines of latitude. The Western Hemisphere faces the front. The globe is encircled with a silver rim marked with the degrees of latitude, on which is perched an engraved solid silver eagle with a wingspan of 15 inches. The total weight of the mace is 10 pounds.

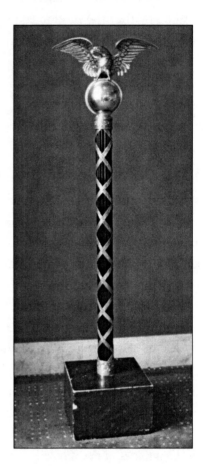

an opening statement. The minority floor manager then does the same. Thereafter, the two managers yield specific periods of time to individual members to speak on the measure.

Recognition by the chair of the Committee of the Whole usually alternates between the parties, although one party may yield to several members in a row to keep the remaining general debate time fairly equal between the parties. When a member who has been yielded time addresses issues that the manager does not want addressed, the manager reclaims the balance of time. Throughout the debate, it is common for the floor managers to inquire of the chair how much time remains. The floor managers are usually accompanied by committee staff, who can respond privately to questions from their party's members. *(See § 8.113, Who Is Allowed on the House Floor?)*

When all time for general debate has been consumed or yielded back, general debate ends, and the amendment process begins. *(See § 8.114, Committee of the Whole and the House: Stages of Action.)*

114

§ 8.112

House versus Committee of the Whole

House	Committee of the Whole
Established by Constitution	Established by House for consideration of a specific measure
Mace raised	Mace lowered
Speaker presides	Chair of Committee of the Whole presides, appointed by Speaker
One-hour rule	Five-minute rule for amendments; special rule from Rules Committee dictates procedure, after adoption of rule by House
Quorum of 218	Quorum of 100
One-fifth of members (44 with minimum quorum) to trigger a recorded vote	25 members to trigger a recorded vote
Motion for previous question in order	Motion for previous question not in order; motion to limit or end debate may be offered
Motion to recommit in order	Motion to recommit not in order
Motion to reconsider in order	Motion to reconsider not in order
Routine business of House in order	Routine business of House not in order

§ 8.113

Who Is Allowed on the House Floor?

In addition to the representatives and pages, a variety of staff have permanent or temporary privileges to be on the floor of the House.

Standing next to or near the presiding officer are the parliamentarian, sergeant at arms, clerk of the House, and Speaker's page. At the desk immediately in front of the Speaker are seated the journal clerk, tally clerk, and reading clerk. At the desk below the clerks are the bill clerk, enrolling clerk, and daily digest clerk. Reporters of debate sit at a table below the rostrum. Staff members of committees and individual representatives are allowed on the floor by unanimous consent.

(See § 14.11, House Floor Plan.)

§ 8.114

Committee of the Whole and the House: Stages of Action

- House resolves into Committee of the Whole
- General debate
- Measure read or considered for amendment
- Amendments debated under five-minute rule
- Committee of the Whole rises and reports
- House votes on Committee of the Whole-approved amendments
- Opportunity for motion to recommit
- House votes on final passage

§ 8.120 Committee of the Whole: Amendment Process

Unless a special rule provides otherwise, a bill is usually read for amendment "by section." Bills can alternatively be read for amendment by title or be "open for amendment at any point." Reading a bill for amendment is referred to as the *second reading.*

When the first section of a measure is read, or *designated,* amendments recommended by the committee reporting the bill, called *committee amendments,* are first considered without being offered from the floor. A special rule often provides that committee amendments become part of the text of the measure for further amendment. (The text for purposes of debate or amendment is sometimes referred to as the *base text.*)

After committee amendments become part of the base text, individual members are then recognized to offer individual amendments. Priority recognition is given to members of the committee of jurisdiction, by seniority on the committee, with recognition usually alternating between the parties.

Amendments are debated under the *five-minute rule,* with the proponent and an opponent speaking first for up to five minutes each. Members may then make a motion to "strike the last word" or "strike the requisite number of words," that is, offer a pro forma amendment to gain five minutes to speak on an amendment. At the end of five minutes, the pro forma amendment is considered withdrawn. Time under the five-minute rule cannot be reserved, and a member may not speak more than once on an amendment. (See § 8.121, *Amendment Process Glossary.*)

If the special rule does not provide a cap on time for debating amendments, debate can be limited or ended by unanimous consent or by a motion to end or limit debate. (The previous question is not in order in the Committee of the Whole.) Such a motion may limit debate on a specific amendment, a section, or the entire measure. The motion can specify a specific time or a specific duration of minutes or hours for the consideration of amendments to continue. The motion may also designate how the remaining time is to be divided.

Amendment Tree

An amendment to the base text is called a *first-degree amendment.* Such an amendment can be further amended by either a *substitute amendment* (which is also a first-degree amendment) or a *perfecting amendment*—a *second-degree amendment.* The substitute is also subject to a perfecting amendment. These four amendments constitute what is referred to as the *amendment tree.* Once an amendment to a measure is pending, either a perfecting amendment or a substitute amendment can be offered first. (See § 8.122, *Basic House Amendment Tree.*)

If all four of these amendments are pending, the order of voting is as follows:

1. the perfecting amendment to the amendment to the bill (a second-degree amendment)
2. the perfecting amendment to the substitute (a second-degree amendment)
3. the substitute (considered a first-degree amendment)
4. the base amendment to the text

§ 8.121

Amendment Process Glossary

Amendment: Proposal of a member of Congress to alter the text of a measure.

Amendment in the Nature of a Substitute: Amendment that seeks to replace the entire text of the underlying measure. The adoption of such an amendment usually precludes any further amendment to that measure.

Amendment Tree: Diagram showing the number and types of amendments to a measure permitted by the chamber. It also shows the relationship among the amendments, their degree or type, the order in which they may be offered, and the order in which they are voted on.

"Bigger Bite" Amendment: Amendment that, although it amends previously amended language (not allowed under the rules), can be offered because it changes more of the measure than the original amendment.

Degrees of Amendment: Designation that indicates the relationship of an amendment to the text of a measure and of one amendment to another. Amendments are permitted only in two degrees.

En Bloc Amendment: Several amendments offered as a group, after obtaining unanimous consent.

First-Degree Amendment: Amendment offered to the text of a measure or a substitute offered to a first-degree amendment.

Five-Minute Rule: House rule that limits debate on an amendment offered in the Committee of the Whole to five minutes for its sponsor and five minutes for an opponent. In practice, the Committee of the Whole permits the offering of pro forma amendments, each debatable for five minutes.

Germaneness: Rule in the House requiring that debate and amendments pertain to the same subject as the bill or amendment under consideration. In the Senate, germaneness is not generally required.

Insert: Amendment to add new language to a measure or another amendment.

Perfecting Amendment: Amendment that alters—but does not substitute or replace—language in another amendment.

Point of Order: Objection to the current proceeding, measure, or amendment because the proposed action violates a rule of the chamber, written precedent, or rule-making statute.

Pro Forma Amendment: Motion whereby a House member secures five minutes to speak on an amendment under debate, without offering a substantive amendment. The member moves to "strike the last word" or "strike the requisite number of words." The motion requires no vote and is deemed automatically withdrawn at the expiration of the five minutes.

Second-Degree Amendment: Amendment to an amendment. It is also called a perfecting amendment.

Continued on page 294

§ 8.121 *(continued)*

Strike: Amendment to delete a portion of a measure or an amendment.

Strike and Insert: Amendment that replaces the text of a measure or an amendment.

Strike the Last Word/Strike the Requisite Number of Words: Also called a pro forma amendment. Means of obtaining time to speak on an amendment without offering a substantive change.

Substitute Amendment: Amendment that replaces the entire text of a pending amendment.

Unprinted Amendment: Senate amendment not printed in the *Congressional Record* before its offering. Unprinted amendments are numbered sequentially in the order of their submission during a Congress.

A larger glossary is located at the back of the book.

When an amendment has been disposed of, a branch of the amendment tree is open. An additional amendment may then be offered, provided that the new amendment does not propose to change what has already been amended. *(See § 8.123, Keeping Up with the House Floor: Scheduling and Proceedings.)*

Restrictions on Amendments

In general, an amendment must be in writing at the time it is offered. The amendment must be a first- or second-degree amendment. It is not in order to reoffer an identical amendment to an amendment that has already been acted upon.

An amendment may not amend text that has already been amended. In some circumstances, however, a bigger bite can be taken from the measure or amendment. A *bigger-bite amendment* substantively changes the unamended parts of the provision in which the previously amended language appears and is in order.

An amendment must be offered in a timely fashion—only at the time the Committee of the Whole is considering the section or title the amendment seeks to change. An amendment may not affect different parts of a bill unless unanimous consent is granted to offer the amendment *en bloc*.

Germaneness. In addition to the restrictions previously described, an amendment must be germane, or relevant, to the text it would amend. House Rule XVI, clause 7 is one of the most discussed rules of the House. Three tests of germaneness are noted in the rule. First, the amendment must relate to the subject matter under consideration. Second, the fundamental purpose of the amendment must be germane to the fundamental purpose of the bill or amendment. Third, the amendment should be within the jurisdiction of the committee reporting the

§ 8.122

Basic House Amendment Tree

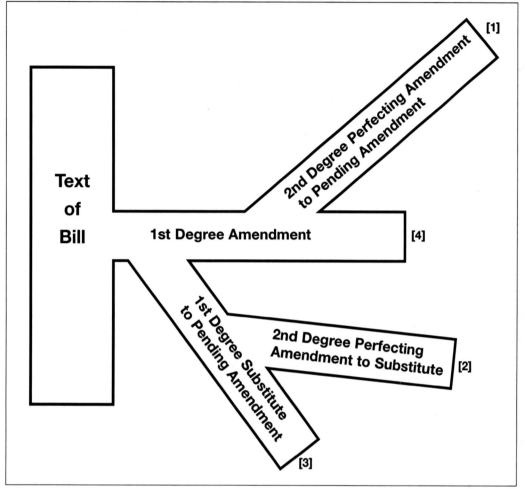

[Note: Bracketed numbers indicate voting order.]

bill. Hence, subject matter, fundamental purpose, and committee jurisdiction represent key tests of germaneness.

Beyond these tests, several principles also relate to germaneness. First, an individual proposition cannot be amended by another individual proposition. Second, a specific subject may not be amended by a general subject. Third, a general subject may be amended by a specific subject. These principles are difficult to interpret, and the Speaker or chair of the Committee of the Whole seeks the advice of the House parliamentarian if a ruling is required. If a point of order is raised that an amendment is not germane, and the point of order is sustained, the amendment cannot be considered. On the other hand, if the question of germaneness is

§ 8.123

Keeping Up with the House Floor: Scheduling and Proceedings

See Chapters Eleven, Twelve, and Thirteen for descriptions of these and other sources.

Sources	Anticipating Scheduling		During/After Proceedings	
	Status	Substance	Status	Substance
Congressional Sources				
Congressional Record (for leadership announcement of legislative program; printed amendments; special rules; and House proceedings)	x	x	x	x
Reporting committee's, Rules Committee's and leadership web sites available through the House site, *<www.house.gov>*	x	x	x	x
Rules Committee announcement of deadline for providing it with proposed floor amendments, before reporting a special rule	x			
Rules Committee "special rule," for major legislation (Text different from that reported by committee *may* be made in order by special rule.)		x		
Amendments printed in Rules Committee's report on special rule or, if made in order by special rule, printed in *Congressional Record* or announced by members		x		
"Whip notices" from party leadership	x		x	
Committee report and text of legislation as reported		x		x
Text of legislation as passed ("engrossed measure")				x
Legislative Information System (Congress only)	x	x	x	x
THOMAS *<http://thomas.loc.gov>*	x	x	x	x
Non-Congressional Sources				
C-SPAN *<www.cspan.org>*			x	x
CQ Today *<www.cq.com>*	x	x	x	x
CQ.com *<www.cq.com>*	x	x	x	x
CQ Weekly (for major legislation) *<www.cq.com>*	x	x	x	x
CongressDaily, from *National Journal* *<http://nationaljournal.com>*	x	x	x	x
National Journal (for major legislation) *<http://nationaljournal.com>*		x		x
Trade press and daily newspapers	x	x	x	x
Relevant interest-group web sites	x	x	x	x
Other commercial database services	x	x	x	x
People *(Use these contacts after exhausting other resources.)*				
Reporting committee professional staff and leadership staff (When is floor action anticipated? What amendments, if any, are expected? What debate is anticipated? After the measure's passage, what is anticipated in dealing with the Senate?)	x	x	x	x
Chamber leaders, committee members, and interested members (What amendments or debate is anticipated? What happens next?)		x		x
Committee and interested members' press assistants (What press releases and other press documents are available?)		x		x

not raised, or if a special rule waives the point of order, it is possible for a nongermane but popular amendment to be agreed upon.

Over 2,000 pages of precedents in *Hinds and Cannon, Deschler's Precedents,* and the parliamentarian's annotations in the House *Rules Manual* address germaneness.

Ending the Amendment Process

In the Committee of the Whole, a member can move to *close debate* (end debate) on a pending amendment or to *limit debate* at a specified time. (After the last section of the bill has been read in the House sitting as the House, a member can move the previous question. This motion is not in order in the Committee of the Whole.) Unlike the previous question, closing or limiting debate does not preclude offering additional amendments. It means that all subsequent amendments are decided without debate.

At the conclusion of the amendment process, a member moves that the *committee rise and report.* The motion to rise and report in effect takes a measure from the Committee of the Whole back to the House for final disposition. A *motion to rise,* on the other hand, reports a measure back to the House temporarily. The adoption of a motion to rise indicates that the Committee of the Whole may reconvene at a later time to continue work on a measure.

Separate Vote on Amendments

Once the Committee of the Whole has risen and the House is again sitting as the House, any member may demand a separate vote on any amendment to the text of the measure under consideration agreed to in the Committee of the Whole.

§ 8.130 House Floor: Voting
Voting in the House

There are four types of votes: voice, division, yea and nay, and record votes. *Voice vote* means that members call out "yea" or "nay" when a question is put in the House. The Speaker determines the outcome of the vote by the volume of each response. On occasion, the Speaker can say "without objection," a variation on a voice vote meaning the question is adopted.

A *division vote* can be demanded by any member after a voice vote is taken. First the members in favor stand and are counted; then, those opposed stand and are counted. A division vote shows only vote totals and does not provide a record of how individual members voted. In recent times, there have been only a few division votes on the floor each year.

Under an automatic *yea and nay vote,* a member may "object on the ground that a quorum is not present and make a point of order that a quorum is not present." The actual vote then determines both the presence of a quorum and the outcome of the pending question.

A *record vote* is taken if one-fifth of a quorum, forty-four members, stand and support the request. Like a yea and nay vote, a record vote is taken by the electronic voting system. *(See § 8.131, House Voting Glossary.)*

§ 8.131

House Voting Glossary

Agreed To: Usual parliamentary term for approval of motions, amendments, and simple and concurrent resolutions.

Cluster Voting: Allowance for sequential recorded votes on a series of measures or amendments that the House finished debating at an earlier time or on a previous date. The Speaker can reduce the minimum time for the second and subsequent votes in the series to five minutes each.

Division Vote: A vote in which a committee chair or the House presiding officer counts those in favor and those in opposition, with no record made of how each member votes. The chair or presiding officer can either ask for a show of hands or ask members to stand.

Electronic Vote: A vote in the House using the electronic voting machine. Members insert voting cards into one of the boxes located throughout the House chamber.

Proxy Vote: The committee practice of permitting a member to cast the vote of an absent colleague. Proxy voting is not permitted in House committees.

Quorum Call: A procedure for determining whether a quorum is present—218 in the House and 100 in the Committee of the Whole House on the State of the Union.

Roll-call (Record) Vote: A vote in which members are recorded by name for or against a measure.

Second: The number of members required to indicate support for an action, such as calling for a vote.

Teller Vote: A House procedure in which members cast votes by passing through the center aisle of the chamber to be counted; now used only when the electronic voting system breaks down.

Voice Vote: A method of voting where members who support a question call out "aye" in unison, after which those opposed answer "no" in unison. The chair decides which position prevails.

Yea and Nay: A vote in which members respond "aye" or "no" on a question when their names are called in alphabetical order.

A larger glossary is located at the back of the book.

Voting in the Committee of the Whole

Both voice votes and division votes are taken in the Committee of the Whole. To obtain a record vote, twenty-five members must support a member's request for a record vote. If fewer than one hundred members are present, which is the minimum number required for a quorum in the Committee of the Whole, a member may demand a record vote, and pending that make a point of order that a quorum is not present. The record vote would then be automatic.

122

Time for Voting

The minimum time for a record vote or quorum call is fifteen minutes in both the House and the Committee of the Whole. The Speaker has the authority to postpone and cluster certain votes and to reduce to five minutes votes after an initial fifteen-minute vote. The chair of the Committee of the Whole is usually granted the same authority in a special rule.

§ 8.140 House Floor: Motion to Recommit and Final Passage

After the third reading of a bill, but before the vote on final passage, a *motion to recommit* is in order. (The third reading is the required reading to a chamber of a measure by title only before the vote on passage.) The motion is traditionally the prerogative of a minority member to offer, providing the minority with one last opportunity to kill or amend a measure.

A member stands and says, "Mr. Speaker, I have a motion to recommit at the desk." The Speaker then asks if the member is opposed to the measure. That member signifies that he or she is opposed to the measure "in its current form."

There are two types of motions to recommit. Adoption of a motion to recommit *without instructions* kills a measure. If such a motion is offered, it is not debatable.

A motion to recommit *with instructions* attempts to amend a measure. The motion normally instructs that the measure be referred to the reporting committee and that the committee "report the bill back to the House forthwith with the following amendment. . . ." A motion to recommit with instructions is debatable for ten minutes, equally divided between the proponent and an opponent. The time is not controlled, meaning members may not yield or reserve time. At the request of the majority floor manager, the ten minutes can be extended to one hour, equally divided and controlled. If a motion to recommit with instructions is agreed to, the measure is immediately reported back to the House with the amendment, the amendment is voted on, and the House then votes on final passage of the bill.

The vote on final passage is then taken. (See § 11.40, *Versions of Legislation.*) When the results of the vote on final passage are announced, a pro forma *motion to reconsider* is made and *laid on the table,* that is, postponed indefinitely. There is rarely a vote on these motions. To table the motion to reconsider prevents a measure from being reconsidered at a later date. (See § 8.141, *Approval Terminology.*)

§ 8.141
Approval Terminology

Term	Used For
Adopted	Conference Reports
Agreed To	Amendments Simple Resolutions Concurrent Resolutions
Concur	Amendment of Other Chamber
Ordered	Engrossment Previous Question Third Reading Yeas and Nays
Passed	Bills Joint Resolutions
Sustained	Points of Order Rulings of Chair

§ 8.151

Comparison of Selected House and Senate Procedures

House	Senate
Four calendars (Union, House, Private, and Discharge)	Two calendars (Legislative and Executive)
Scheduling by Speaker and majority-party leadership, with limited consultation among members	Scheduling by majority-party leadership, with broad consultation among all senators
Role of Rules Committee and special rules to govern floor consideration	Unanimous consent and complex unanimous consent time agreements to govern floor consideration
Presiding officer has considerable discretion in recognition; rulings rarely challenged	Presiding officer has little discretion in recognition; rulings frequently challenged
Debate always restricted	Debate rarely restricted
Debate-ending motions by majority vote (218 representatives)	Cloture invoked by three-fifths vote (60 senators)
Germaneness of amendments generally required	Germaneness of amendments rarely required
Quorum calls permitted in connection with record votes	Quorum calls permitted almost any time and used for constructive delay
Adjourns at end of day	Recesses at end of many days

§ 8.150 House and Senate Compared

The Senate has an extensive framework of parliamentary procedure to guide its actions. Nevertheless, in practice, its procedures are more flexible than those of the House. While the House emphasizes its procedures, the Senate functions in a more ad hoc manner, adapting its procedures to accommodate individual senators. For example, scheduling and consideration of legislation can be accomplished in almost any manner the party leaders and individual senators can devise. (*See § 8.151, Comparison of Selected House and Senate Procedures.*)

§ 8.160 Senate Scheduling

The Senate sets its floor agenda to accommodate individual senators and to prepare for almost any contingency. Because of the privileges accorded individual senators, the Senate can rarely rely on its rules or customs to set the order of business. Because the rules have different influences at certain times, no Senate session day is truly typical. Scheduling the consideration of a measure can be accomplished in almost any manner the party leaders can arrange. Because the majority leader has priority recognition on the floor, it is that person's job to arrange the schedule.

Some measures can be raised for consideration, or even passage without debate, by *unan-*

§ 8.161

Keeping Up with the Senate Floor: Scheduling and Proceedings

See Chapters Eleven, Twelve, and Thirteen for descriptions of these and other sources.

Sources	Anticipating Scheduling		During/After Proceedings	
	Status	Substance	Status	Substance
Congressional Sources				
Congressional Record (for leadership announcement of legislative program; printed amendments; time agreements; and Senate proceedings)	x	x	x	x
Reporting committee's and leadership web sites available through the Senate site, *<www.senate.gov>*	x	x	x	x
Amendments printed in the *Congressional Record,* announced by members or made in order by unanimous consent agreement(s)		x		
Time agreements (A text different from that reported by a committee *may* be made in order by the time agreement.)		x		
"Whip notices" from party leadership	x		x	
Text of legislation as originated in committee or reported by committee; possibly a House measure reported from a Senate committee or placed directly on the Senate Calendar		x		x
Committee report, if there is one		x		x
Text of legislation as passed ("engrossed measure")				x
Legislative Information System (Congress only)	x	x	x	x
THOMAS *<http://thomas.loc.gov>*	x	x	x	x
Non-Congressional Sources				
C-SPAN *<www.cspan.org>*			x	x
CQ Today <www.cq.com>	x	x	x	x
CQ.com *<www.cq.com>*	x	x	x	x
CQ Weekly (for major legislation) *<www.cq.com>*	x	x	x	x
CongressDaily, from *National Journal <http://nationaljournal.com>*	x	x	x	x
National Journal (for major legislation) *<http://nationaljournal.com>*		x		x
Trade press and daily newspapers	x	x	x	x
Relevant interest-group web sites	x	x	x	x
Other commercial database services	x	x	x	x
People *(Use these contacts after exhausting other resources.)*				
Senators' and reporting committee professional staff, and leadership staff (When is floor action anticipated? What amendments, if any, are expected? What is the status of holds or requests for consultation? After passage, what is anticipated in dealing with the House?)	x	x	x	x
Chamber and committee leaders, and interested members (What debate is anticipated? What happens next?)		x		x
Committee and interested members' press assistants (What press releases and other press documents are available?)		x		x

imous consent. However, a single objection can derail a unanimous consent request. Accordingly, the majority leader checks with all interested senators before bringing legislation to the floor by unanimous consent. Other measures are scheduled for consideration pursuant to a *unanimous consent time agreement.* A time agreement is negotiated among interested parties to avoid an objection to the unanimous consent request. Still other measures are brought up by a *motion to proceed to consider.* However, a motion to proceed in most instances is debatable. *(See § 8.161, Keeping Up with the Senate Floor: Scheduling and Proceedings.)*

§ 8.170 Legislative and Calendar Days; Morning Hour and Morning Business

How the Senate begins its session depends on how it ended its business the previous day.

Legislative and Calendar Days

A calendar day is recognized as each twenty-four-hour period. A *legislative day* begins when the Senate next meets after adjourning, rather than recessing, the previous daily session. Indeed, a legislative day can stretch over several calendar days or even weeks.

This practice enables the Senate to maintain flexibility. Because procedures are so strictly determined when a new legislative day is created, the Senate often recesses rather than adjourns at the end of the previous day's session. Recessing does not create a new legislative day. A legislative day continues until the Senate adjourns at the end of a daily session.

At the beginning of each day, whether a calendar day or legislative day, a period of *leader time* is set aside. During this time, the majority and minority leaders can be recognized by the presiding officer for ten minutes each to speak on whatever subjects they choose. They often discuss the legislative schedule for the day and the next several days.

Morning Hour and Morning Business

If it is a new legislative day, the Senate proceeds to *morning hour,* which constitutes the first two hours of a legislative day. Based on traditional Senate schedules, morning hour usually extends from 12:00 noon to 2:00 p.m. Within the morning hour, the Senate entertains *morning business.* The first hour is reserved for individual senators to deliver *morning hour speeches* on any subject. Each speech is usually limited to five minutes. By unanimous consent, morning business can be conducted throughout the day, and usually is.

After the completion of morning business, or at the end of the first hour, the other morning hour business occurs. It consists of messages from the president, messages from the House of Representatives, the presentation of petitions and memorials, reports of committees, and the introduction of bills and resolutions.

Because the Senate may remain in the same legislative day for several days, a morning business period is held almost every calendar day.

§ 8.180 Senate Calendars and Legislative and Executive Business before the Senate

The Senate has two calendars. The *Calendar of Business* contains all legislation, both bills and resolutions. The *Executive Calendar* is reserved for executive business, that is, business requiring the Senate to advise and consent on treaties and nominations. Both calendars are published every day the Senate is in session.

Calendar of Business

The *Calendar of Business* contains a list called "General Orders, under Rule VIII," which details all measures that committees have reported and any bills or joint resolutions that have been placed directly on the calendar without first being referred to committee. The order number reflects the chronological order in which a measure was placed on the calendar. Noted on the general order list are the following items:

- the measure's number
- the measure's sponsor
- the measure's title
- date the measure was placed on the calendar
- whether the measure was placed directly on the calendar without being referred to committee
- whether the measure is an original bill
- whether the measure was reported with or without amendment
- whether there is an accompanying report
- whether the report contains minority or additional views

Also included in the Calendar of Business are the following:

- a calendar that shows the days on which the Senate was in session and the anticipated recesses and nonlegislative periods
- a list of senators and the year in which each senator's term expires
- membership lists of Senate committees and Senate membership on joint committees
- a list of bills sent to conference, the names of House and Senate conferees on each bill, and the date either chamber acted on a conference report

The Calendar of Business also contains the text of unanimous consent time agreements and a list of "resolutions and motions over, under the rule." This is a list of simple and concurrent resolutions that have been placed directly on the calendar without first being referred to committee.

The back cover of the calendar shows the history of legislative action on appropriations bills during the current session of Congress.

Executive Calendar

The Executive Calendar has five sections:

- texts of any unanimous consent agreements, which have not been fully implemented, concerning executive business
- Senate executive resolutions that concern executive business (it is rare for there to be any resolutions listed)
- treaties that have been reported from committee, including each treaty's calendar number, document number, and subject, as well as information on how it was reported from the Foreign Relations Committee
- nominations that have been reported from committee, including each nomination's calendar number, the number of the presidential message transmitting the nomination, the name of the nominee and the office for which he or she has been nominated, and information on how the nomination was reported (a nomination listed for the first time appears under a heading of "new reports")
- routine nominations, such as those in the armed services and the Public Health Service

(For additional information on the calendars, see § 12.20, Floor Documents.)

§ 8.190 Holds, Clearance, and Unanimous Consent

By custom, the majority leader of the Senate, or that person's designee, has the right to set the agenda on the floor. The majority leader decides the order in which bills on the calendar should come to the floor for action, and negotiates with other senators to agree to take up measures the majority leader wishes to consider.

Custom, however, also allows a senator to place a *hold* on the consideration of any legislative or executive business. A hold is a notice that a senator intends to object to any unanimous consent request made on the floor to bring up a matter for consideration by the Senate. Current policy regarding holds, which has not been consistently followed, dictates that a senator placing a hold should notify the sponsor of the legislation (if legislation is the object of the hold) and the committee of jurisdiction that he or she is concerned about the measure. A written notice should also be provided to the senator's respective party leader and placed in the *Congressional Record*. Before the 106th Congress, holds could be placed anonymously.

In addition, to learn whether there may be objection to bringing up a measure or executive matter if no hold has been placed, or to identify controversy associated with a measure, the party leadership attempts to obtain *clearance* to have a measure considered. To obtain clearance, the party leaders ask individual senators to file *requests to be consulted* with the party leaders. A request signifies that a senator wants to participate in any negotiations regarding when and how a measure or executive matter might be considered on the Senate floor. Further, quorum calls conducted throughout the day—a form of constructive delay—

allow the leadership time to conduct negotiations. A hotline telephone, provided to all Senate offices, is often used to obtain clearance. Once all requests have been considered and addressed, the majority leader may choose to call up a measure or executive matter on the floor.

Through these negotiations, the majority leader can determine how best to bring a measure or executive matter to the floor. For most noncontroversial items, the majority leader, or that person's designee, asks "unanimous consent to proceed to the consideration" of a measure or executive matter. By bringing a measure or executive matter to the floor by *unanimous consent*, debate and amendment options are usually unlimited, although a further unanimous consent request could be made to set debate and amendment limitations. A *complex unanimous consent agreement*, also called a *time agreement*, generally limits debate and amendments.

Finally, there is also a class of routine unanimous consent requests that allows senators to obtain floor privileges for selected staff and to "proceed as if in morning business" throughout the day. *(See § 8.191, Who Is Allowed on the Senate Floor?)* Unanimous consent is also obtained to allow the Senate to go into *executive session* to consider business on the Executive Calendar.

---

§ 8.191

Who Is Allowed on the Senate Floor?

In addition to senators, a variety of staff have permanent or temporary privileges to be on the floor of the Senate.

At the desk immediately in front of the presiding officer are seated the parliamentarian, legislative clerk, journal clerk, and, often, the executive clerk and bill clerk. Reporters of debates sit at a table below the rostrum. Seats near the rostrum are reserved for the secretary and assistant secretary of the Senate and the sergeant at arms. Majority- and minority-party secretaries and other staff members who have floor privileges may be seen on the floor. Pages sit on either side of the presiding officer's desk. Staff members of individual senators are allowed on the floor by unanimous consent.

(See § 14.21, Senate Floor Plan.)

---

§ 8.200 Time Agreements and Motions to Proceed on the Senate Floor

There are three typical ways to bring a measure to the Senate floor for consideration. *Unanimous consent*, often referred to as a *simple unanimous consent agreement*, implies agreement among all senators, as a single objection can stop its implementation. A *complex unanimous consent agreement*, referred to as a time agreement, and a *motion to proceed to consideration*, called a motion to proceed, are the other options available to the majority leader to bring up a measure for consideration.

Time Agreements

The Senate conducts much of its work by agreeing to unanimous consent requests. *Simple unanimous consent requests* cover noncontroversial and routine matters. Complex unanimous

§ 8.201

Example of a Senate Unanimous Consent Time Agreement

S. 343 (ORDER NO. 118)

2. – *Ordered,* That prior to the Senate recessing for Independence Day, debate only be in order on S. 343, with the exception of the withdrawal of the committee amendments, and the offering of a substitute amendment by the Majority Leader.

Ordered further, That at 1:00 p.m. on Monday, July 10, 1995, the Senate resume consideration of S. 343, the Regulatory Reform bill, and that the Senator from Michigan (Mr. Abraham) be recognized to offer an amendment to the Dole substitute relative to small business; that no second degree amendments be in order; and that a vote occur on, or in relation to, the Abraham amendment at 5:00 p.m., Monday, July 10, 1995.

Ordered further, That at 3:00 p.m. on Monday, July 10, 1995, the Abraham amendment be laid aside, and the Senator from Georgia (Mr. Nunn) be recognized to offer a Nunn/Coverdell amendment, relative to the Regulatory Flexibility Act; that no second degree amendments be in order; and that a vote occur on, or in relation to, the Nunn/Coverdell amendment immediately following the vote on the Abraham amendment. (June 28, 1995.) (June 29, 1995.)

S. 343 (ORDER NO. 118)

2. – *Ordered,* That during the pendency of S. 343, a bill to reform the regulatory process, and for other purposes, no amendments regarding the USDA's HACCP rule, proposed on February 3, 1995, be in order. (July 12, 1995.)

Ordered further, That during the pendency of S. 343, no amendments regarding mammography be in order. (July 13, 1995.)

consent requests, often called *time agreements*, establish another procedure under which measures are considered on the floor. Without a time agreement, a measure could be debated for as long as senators spoke on the floor, and amendments, whether germane or not, could be offered without restriction. Time agreements are intended to expedite consideration and establish predictability by imposing restrictions on the time available and limiting the amendments that could be offered. *(See § 8.201, Example of a Senate Unanimous Consent Time Agreement.)*

After consultation and negotiation with other senators, which can take days or weeks or months on highly contentious matters, the majority leader obtains a time agreement that satisfies all concerned senators and that meets the policy objectives of the majority party. The majority leader then asks on the Senate floor that a measure be considered "under the following time agreement."

A time agreement can cover consideration of an entire measure or consideration for just

§ 8.202

Comparing a House Special Rule and a Senate Time Agreement

House Special Rule	Senate Time Agreement
Called up as a simple resolution	Called up by unanimous consent
Requires majority vote for passage	Agreed to by unanimous consent
Specifies time for general debate	Specifies time for debating amendments
Permits or prohibits amendments	Generally restricts only the offering of nongermane amendments
Does not specify date for vote on passage of measure	Generally sets date for vote on final passage
Effect is often to waive House rules	Effect is often to waive Senate rules

one day. It can cover time allocation for all amendments or debate on a particular amendment. It can limit debate on the measure itself or on part of the measure. A time agreement can limit senators to offering only germane amendments, or it can contain a negotiated list of nongermane amendments. It can also restrict the offering of amendments to pending amendments. (*See § 8.202, Comparing a House Special Rule and a Senate Time Agreement.*)

The Senate often begins consideration of a measure by unanimous consent without a time agreement but then adopts piecemeal agreements. A time agreement can be changed by agreeing to a subsequent unanimous consent agreement.

Time agreements are printed in the *Congressional Record* and the daily Calendar of Business.

Motions to Proceed

Because of the difficulty of negotiating a time agreement, which can be stopped by a single objection, any senator as an alternative can attempt to call up a measure by making a "motion to proceed to consideration," usually referred to as a *motion to proceed.* Although any senator may offer a motion to proceed, by custom the Senate reserves the right to the majority leader or that person's designee. A motion to proceed is generally debatable, and there is no limit on the duration of the debate under Senate rules. Debate on the motion to proceed can be ended by unanimous consent or by invoking cloture. (*See § 8.230, Cloture in Senate Floor Proceedings.*) A motion to proceed, however, needs only a majority vote for passage. (The motion to proceed is not debatable under certain circumstances, such as during a new legislative day.)

§ 8.211

Longest Senate Filibusters

- Strom Thurmond, 1957
  24 hours, 18 minutes on civil rights bill

- Wayne Morse, 1953
  22 hours, 26 minutes on Tidelands oil bill

- William Proxmire, 1961
  19 hours, 6 minutes (held floor for 25 hours, 36 minutes, but yielded for 6 hours and 30 minutes to other senators to debate foreign aid bills) on confirmation of Lawrence O'Connor for post at Federal Power Commission

- Robert LaFollette, Sr., 1908
  18 hours, 23 minutes on Aldrich-Vreeland currency bill

- William Proxmire, 1981
  16 hours, 12 minutes on bill raising public debt limit

- Huey Long, 1935
  15 hours, 30 minutes on extension of National Industrial Recovery Act

- Alfonse D'Amato, 1992
  15 hours, 14 minutes on tax bill

- Robert C. Byrd, 1964
  14 hours, 13 minutes on civil rights bill

§ 8.210 Consideration and Debate on the Senate Floor
Presiding Officer and Recognition to Speak

The presiding officer of the Senate is the vice president of the United States. However, the vice president rarely presides over daily sessions of the Senate. He presides only when a close vote is anticipated and when his vote may be needed to break a tie vote, the only occasion under the Constitution when he is allowed to cast a vote in the Senate.

The president pro tempore, the most senior majority-party senator, generally opens a day's session. Yet, the president pro tempore does not preside throughout the day. The president pro tempore designates other majority-party senators to preside, usually in one-hour or two-hour blocks of time. Junior majority-party senators preside often early in their careers, providing them opportunities to learn Senate procedures. In fact, a *golden gavel award* is granted to the first senator in each Congress to preside for one hundred hours.

The main authority of the presiding officer is to recognize members to speak. Priority recognition is almost always granted to the majority and minority leaders if they are seeking recognition, and then to the floor managers of pending legislation. In the absence of any of these senators, the presiding officer must recognize the first senator on his or her feet seeking recognition. The presiding officer is addressed as "Mr. (Madam) President."

Filibusters

When a senator is recognized to speak on a pending measure, few limitations are placed on him or her. Debate is generally unlimited on all pending measures. A senator may yield to another senator for a question, but the senator still controls the floor. One of the most visible of Senate characteristics is the right of an individual senator to maintain the floor, that is, to speak for an extended period of time. Continuing, extended debate is referred to as a *filibuster*. The image of James Stewart in the film, *Mr. Smith Goes to Washington*, presents an exaggerated picture of one senator tying up the work of the Senate. *(See § 8.211, Longest Senate Filibusters.)*

A contemporary approach to filibusters is the so-called "tag-team filibuster." A senator speaks for a period and then yields to another senator. When several senators participate in extended debate, it takes some time for the Senate to realize a filibuster is being conducted. Therefore, even the threat of a filibuster carries weight as the Senate attempts to schedule and consider legislation.

Debate is limited only when the Senate:

1. invokes cloture (*see § 8.230, Cloture in Senate Floor Proceedings*),
2. limits debate by unanimous consent or operates under a unanimous consent time agreement,
3. considers a motion to table, or
4. considers a measure governed by a rule-making statute. (Examples of rule-making statutes with built-in debate limitations include the Congressional Budget Act of 1974, and the 1974 Trade Act, which allows so-called *fast-track* procedures.)

Senate rules prohibit a senator from speaking more than twice on the same subject on the same legislative day. Because each amendment is considered a different subject, the so-called two-speech rule is not a practical limit on debate.

§ 8.220 Senate Amendment Procedure

Amendments to a measure in the Senate can be offered at practically any time during consideration of the measure, can be debated for an unlimited amount of time, and, in most situations, can deal with any subject, even if it is unrelated to the measure being amended.

When a measure is being considered on the floor of the Senate, committee amendments are considered first. The Senate often agrees by unanimous consent to committee amendments as a package, called *en bloc amendments*. By unanimous consent, the Senate might then provide that the measure, as amended by the committee amendments, be "considered as an original bill for the purpose of further amendment." This facilitates further amending on the floor by not taking up a branch on the *amendment tree*. (*See one amendment tree in § 8.122, Basic House Amendment Tree.*)

Amendments can be either printed or unprinted. *Printed amendments* are provided in advance of floor consideration of a measure and are printed in the *Congressional Record*. Although a sponsor usually calls up his or her own amendment, any senator can call up a printed amendment. *Unprinted amendments* are not available in advance and may be drafted on the floor while a measure is being considered.

Senate amendments do not usually need to be *germane*, that is, relevant to the measure. Nongermane amendments are often referred to as *riders*. Measures that contain numerous nongermane amendments have been called *Christmas-tree bills*. Germaneness, however, is necessary for general appropriations bills, bills on which cloture has been invoked, concurrent budget resolutions, and measures regulated by unanimous consent time agreements.

An amendment can also be classified as either *first degree* or *second degree*. A first-degree amendment would change the text of the measure under consideration; a second-degree amendment proposes to change the text of the first-degree amendment.

Both *perfecting amendments* and *substitute amendments* can be offered. Perfecting amendments change or modify language. Substitute amendments add new language as an alternative to the existing text. Perfecting amendments are considered second-degree amendments, and are always voted on before substitute amendments.

Separate *amendment trees* are possible based on the effect of the initial amendment offered. One tree is designed for *motions to strike and insert*, another for *insert*, and a third to *strike*. This complexity is rare in the Senate. Unanimous consent is more likely to be reached so that one amendment can be temporarily set aside to consider a different amendment.

A *motion to table* is frequently offered to avoid voting directly on an amendment. To "table" means to kill a provision. Any senator can make a nondebatable motion to table. Often, a senator announces that he or she intends to offer a motion to table an amendment but does not do so until debate has occurred on the amendment. By agreeing to a motion to table, the Senate does not vote directly on an amendment, and thereby avoids having to vote against it.

§ 8.230 Cloture in Senate Floor Proceedings

A filibuster can be ended by negotiation among senators or by *invoking cloture*. Cloture is the only procedure by which the Senate can vote to set an end to debate without also rejecting the measure under consideration.

Invoking Cloture

Senate Rule XXII describes several stages to invoke cloture. To begin the process, at least sixteen senators sign a *cloture motion*, often referred to as a *cloture petition*. The motion is presented on the Senate floor, where the clerk reads it. The motion needs to "mature" or "ripen" before it can be considered. To do this, it lies over until the second calendar day on which the Senate is in session. For example, if a petition is filed on Monday, it ripens on Wednesday.

On the day the motion is ready for consideration, Senate rules require a vote on cloture one hour after the Senate convenes and after a quorum call establishes the presence of a quorum. However, the Senate can waive the quorum call or change the time by unanimous consent, and often does so. When the vote occurs, it generally requires three-fifths of the senators chosen and sworn; that is, sixty votes if there are no vacancies. (However, to invoke cloture on a motion to amend Senate rules, a two-thirds vote, or sixty-seven senators, is required.)

There are no limits to the number of cloture petitions that can be filed on any measure or amendment. Often, senators file petitions every day so that a vote occurs almost daily with the expectation that cloture will eventually be invoked. *(See § 8.231, Steps to Invoke Cloture.)*

134

§ 8.231

Steps to
Invoke Cloture

- Must be filed on a pending question
- At least sixteen senators must sign a cloture motion (also called "cloture petition")
- Amendments must be filed before the vote
- Vote on a motion occurs two days of session later
- Live quorum call precedes the vote and occurs one hour after the Senate convenes
- Vote immediately follows the quorum call
- Roll-call vote is automatic
- Affirmative vote by three-fifths of the senators chosen and sworn is required, except on a rules change, which requires two-thirds of the senators present

§ 8.232

Senate Procedures
under Cloture

- Thirty-hour cap on post-cloture consideration
- One hour maximum for debate for each senator
- Amendments must have been submitted before the vote on the cloture motion
- Presiding officer may count for a quorum rather than conduct a quorum call
- No nongermane amendments
- No dilatory motions
- Points of order and appeals not debatable

Limitations Following Cloture

If cloture is invoked, certain limitations on how the Senate considers a measure are put into place. Generally, this period, often referred to as *post-cloture consideration*, operates under procedures different from normal Senate process. *(See § 8.232, Senate Procedures under Cloture.)*

Time Cap. The most important effect of invoking cloture is the cap of thirty hours of time for the Senate to continue consideration of a measure. The filibuster—one senator's or a group of senators' unfettered control of the floor—is over. Time for recorded votes, quorum calls, and points of order count in the cap, as does all debate time. Within the cap, each senator is guaranteed at least ten minutes to speak. No senator can speak for more than one hour, although time can be yielded to other senators.

Amendments. Once cloture is invoked, all amendments to be considered must have been submitted in writing during the time the Senate was in session before invoking cloture. First-degree amendments must be filed by 1:00 p.m. on the day the cloture motion is filed, and second-degree amendments must be filed at least one hour before a cloture vote begins. In addition, unlike normal amendment procedures, no amendment is in order unless it is germane to the matter on which cloture was invoked.

Presiding Officer. The presiding officer has the authority to count to determine the presence of a quorum. The presiding officer may also make rulings without a point of order being raised. Finally, the presiding officer may rule out of order certain motions or quorum calls if he or she deems them dilatory. In contrast to regular procedures, no senator can suggest the absence of a quorum once cloture is invoked.

§ 8.240 Senate Floor:
Motion to Reconsider and Final Passage

After passage of an amendment, measure, or motion, a senator *moves to reconsider the vote.* Approving this motion to reconsider allows the Senate an opportunity to review its decision and, essentially, revote. Therefore, once a proposition has been agreed to, a senator immediately moves to reconsider the vote, and another senator immediately moves to table the motion to reconsider. The motion to table effectively kills the motion to reconsider and makes the original vote final. Approval of the motion to table also blocks any future attempts to reverse the vote.

Only a senator who voted on the prevailing side or who did not vote at all on a proposition can offer a motion to reconsider. The motion is usually offered by the majority floor manager. The motion to table is made immediately after the motion to reconsider and is generally made by the minority floor manager. Usually, the motion to table is then routinely disposed of: "Without objection, the motion to table is agreed to."

The motion to reconsider can be made on the same day or within the next two days in which the Senate is in session.

When action is completed, a measure is ready for *engrossment and third reading.* Third reading is usually by title only. The measure is then ready for a vote on final passage.

§ 8.250 Voting in the Senate

Voting in the Senate is by *voice, division,* or *roll call.* On a voice vote, the presiding officer normally announces which side seems to have won based on how loudly they voted. More typically, the presiding officer states that "without objection the item is agreed to." This is a variation of a voice vote.

Division votes, often called standing votes, are rarely employed. If used, any senator may demand a division vote. Those senators in favor stand and the chair counts. Those opposed then stand and are counted. A division vote does not provide a record of how each senator voted.

Roll-call votes are known as *yea and nay votes* in the Senate. There is not an electronic voting device as there is in the House. Any senator can seek the yeas and nays. The presiding officer asks if there is a sufficient second. A sufficient second is one-fifth of a quorum—a minimum of eleven senators—which is an easy threshold to reach. Often, a senator receives support for the yeas and nays well in advance of the time the vote actually occurs. Thus, it is possible for debate on a proposition to be held and a request made for a vote. Yet, the vote does

§ 8.261

Reconciling Differences Glossary

Amendments between the Houses: Basic method for reconciling differences between two chambers' versions of a measure by passing the measure back and forth between them until both have agreed to identical language.

Amendments in Disagreement: Provisions in dispute between the two chambers.

Amendments in Technical Disagreement: Amendments agreed to in a conference but not included in the conference report because they may violate the rules of one of the houses and would open the conference report to a point of order.

Concur: Agree to amendment of the other house, either as is or with an amendment.

Conference Committee: Temporary joint committee of representatives and senators created to resolve differences between the chambers on a measure.

Conference Report: Document containing the conference committee's agreements and signed by a majority of conferees from each chamber.

Conferees: The representatives and senators from each chamber who serve on a conference committee; also referred to as managers.

Custody of the Papers: Custody of the engrossed measure and other documents that the two houses produce as they try to reconcile differences in their versions of a measure. *(See Papers.)*

Disagree: To reject an amendment of the other chamber.

Insist: Motion by one house to reiterate its previous position during amendments between the houses.

Instruct Conferees: Formal action by one chamber urging its conferees to uphold a particular position in conference.

Joint Explanatory Statement of Managers: Portion of the conference report providing the history, explanation, and intent of the conferees.

Managers: Representatives and senators serving on a conference committee; also called conferees.

Papers: Documents—including the engrossed measure, the amendments, the messages transmitting them, and the conference report—that are passed back and forth between the chambers.

Recede: Motion by one chamber to withdraw from its previous position during amendments between the houses.

Recede and Concur: Motion to withdraw from a position and agree with the other chamber's position.

Recede and Concur with an Amendment: Motion to withdraw from a position and agree, but with a further amendment.

Scope of Differences: Limits within which a conference committee is permitted to resolve the chambers' disagreement.

Stage of Disagreement: Stage when one house formally disagrees with an amendment proposed by the other house, and insists on its amendment. A measure generally cannot go to conference until this stage is reached.

A larger glossary is located at the back of the book.

§ 8.262

Keeping Up with Reconciling House-Senate Differences

See Chapters Eleven, Twelve, and Thirteen for descriptions of these and other sources.

Sources	Anticipating Conference Procedures		During/After Conference Procedures	
	Status	Substance	Status	Substance
Congressional Sources				
Congressional Record (for the appointment of full and partial conferees)	x			
Congressional Record (for leadership announcement of legislative program; text of conference report and joint explanatory statement; and House and Senate proceedings, including motions to instruct conferees)	x		x	x
Congressional Record Daily Digest (for scheduling of full conference meetings, appointment of additional full or partial conferees, or replacement of a conferee)	x		x	
Reporting committee's and leadership web sites available through the House <*www.house.gov*> and Senate <*www.senate.gov*> web sites	x	x	x	x
Announcements from the conference committee chair and from other House or Senate committee chairs serving on the conference	x	x	x	x
House and Senate engrossed measures		x		
For conference, possibly side-by-side analysis		x		
Depending on procedure used: measure passed in identical form by both chambers, amendments between the houses, or conference report and joint explanatory statement				x
Special rule from Rules Committee (House only)				x
Completion of House and Senate action on the same measure, text of the enrolled measure				x
"Whip notices" from party leadership (conference report on floor)			x	
Legislative Information System (Congress only)	x	x	x	x
THOMAS <*http://thomas.loc.gov*>	x	x	x	x
Non-Congressional Sources				
C-SPAN (floor proceedings) <*www.cspan.org*>		x		x
CQ Today <*www.cq.com*>	x	x	x	x
CQ.com <*www.cq.com*>	x	x	x	x
CQ Weekly (for major legislation) <*www.cq.com*>	x	x	x	x
CongressDaily, from *National Journal* <*http://nationaljournal.com*>	x	x	x	x
National Journal (for major legislation) <*http://nationaljournal.com*>		x		x
Trade press and daily newspapers	x	x	x	x
Other commercial database services	x	x	x	x

Continued on page 315

People (Use these contacts after exhausting other resources.)				
Professional staff of reporting committees, leadership staff, and interested members:				
• Will differences between the houses be reconciled with amendments between the houses or a conference?	x			
• Under what circumstances might a conference be necessary, even if a process of amendments between the houses is tried?	x			
• How might conference proceed? Which issues will be delegated to staff and which will the conferees handle? In what order might conference proceed?	x	x		
• For floor action between the houses or on a conference report, when will action occur?			x	
• During floor proceedings, what debate is anticipated?			x	x
• For floor action between the houses or on a conference report, what outcome is anticipated?			x	x
• What is anticipated on presidential action?				x
Chamber and committee leaders, and interested members (What are your expectations for a conference? After conference, how might specific sections be interpreted?)		x		x
Leadership, committee, and interested members' press assistants (What press releases and other press documents are available?)		x		x

not occur until after debate has concluded, which may be minutes or hours after the request for the vote was made. A fifteen-minute period is the time allocated for yea and nay votes, although votes are often kept open beyond this time to accommodate senators trying to reach the floor. (See § 11.40, Versions of Legislation.)

§ 8.260 Reconciling Differences between House-Passed and Senate-Passed Legislation

Legislation must pass both chambers in identical form before it can be sent to the president for signature or veto. Differences between the two versions can be worked out either by *amendments between the houses* or by convening a *conference committee*. (See § 8.261, Reconciling Differences Glossary.)

After a measure has been passed by one house, an *engrossed version* is transmitted to the other chamber. When a measure is received in the second chamber, it is either ordered "held at the desk" or referred to the appropriate committee.

When the second chamber considers and passes the measure in identical form to that passed by the first chamber, the measure can be sent to the president without further consideration in either chamber.

If the second chamber, the recipient chamber, considers and passes the measure with changes, it returns it to the chamber of origin. The originating chamber has several options. It can accept the second chamber's amendment, it can accept the second chamber's amendment with a further amendment, or it can disagree to the other chamber's amendment and request a conference.

The second chamber can also request a conference immediately rather than returning the measure to the first chamber with an amendment. A chamber must possess the *papers* to request a conference. The papers are the *engrossed measure* (measure as passed by the first chamber), *engrossed amendments* (measure as passed by the second chamber), and *messages of transmittal* between the chambers. *(See § 8.262, Keeping Up with Reconciling House-Senate Differences.)*

§ 8.270 Amendments between the Houses

The House and Senate must approve identical versions of a measure before it can be sent to the president. This process begins with one house notifying the second house that it has passed a measure and transmitting to the second chamber the measure as passed (the *engrossed measure*). If the second house passes the measure with changes, the two houses can opt to either offer *amendments between the houses* or convene a conference committee to resolve differences.

When one chamber sends a measure, it is *messaged* to the other chamber. At this stage, several actions are possible. The second chamber can ultimately approve, or *concur*, in the first chamber's version. If that happens, the measure is cleared and sent to the president.

Or, the second chamber can ultimately pass the measure with one or more amendments, that is, *to concur with a further amendment*. If that happens, the measure is returned to the originating chamber with "an amendment to the measure."

The first chamber may accept the amendment. If that occurs, the amended measure is cleared and sent to the president. Alternatively, the first chamber may propose a further amendment.

This first option of resolving differences between the two houses—the process of amendments between the houses—allows two degrees of amendments. The amendment of the second chamber is considered text that is subject to amendment. Each chamber has one opportunity to propose an amendment to the amendment of the other chamber. The process is often conducted by informal negotiations between the members and staff of the committees of jurisdiction in the two houses. An extended exchange of amendments is rare.

At any point in the process, either house may choose not to act on the version sent by the other house. It may insist on its own position, and formally disagree with the version sent by the other house. If a chamber insists on its own position, it reaches a *stage of disagreement*. This

140

allows the houses to proceed to the second option of resolving differences by convening a conference committee. *(See § 8.280, Conference Committees.)*

Amendments between the houses is an attempt to reconcile differences in lieu of a conference committee, or even after a conference if items are reported in *true disagreement* or *technical disagreement*. The process of amendments between the houses is most often used when a measure is not controversial, there are few differences between the two chambers' versions of a measure, or it is late in a session and there is insufficient time or will to convene a conference.

House Consideration of Senate Amendments

Assume a fictitious bill, H.R. 1111, is messaged to the Senate and then returned from the Senate with an amendment. Several scenarios are then possible. The House floor manager could ask unanimous consent to "concur" in the Senate amendment. If that option is selected, the house bill as amended by the Senate amendment is the version sent to the president. Alternatively, the House floor manager could ask unanimous consent to concur in the Senate amendment with a further amendment. If unanimous consent is granted, the House bill with the "House amendment to the Senate amendment to the House bill" is returned to the Senate. If objection is heard to either scenario, or is even anticipated, the House manager could seek to bring up the Senate amendment under suspension of the rules or under the terms of a special rule.

Senate Consideration of House Amendments

Assume a fictitious bill, S. 2222, is messaged to the House, which returns it to the Senate with a "House amendment to the Senate bill." The Senate can accept the House amendment by unanimous consent, that is, concur in the House amendment. The measure is then sent to the president. Alternatively, the Senate can concur in the House amendment with a further amendment.

Senate rules provide that a motion to proceed to consider a House amendment to a Senate measure is not debatable. However, if the Senate agrees to concur in the House amendment or to concur with a further Senate amendment to the House amendment, then the amendment itself is debatable. Therefore, the Senate normally disposes of House amendments by unanimous consent or agrees to proceed to conference.

§ 8.280 Conference Committees

Either chamber can request a conference once both houses have passed versions of a measure treating the same subject and using the same bill or resolution number but containing substantive differences. Generally, the chamber that first approved the legislation disagrees to the amendments made by the other chamber and requests that a conference be convened. Sometimes, however, the second chamber requests a conference immediately after it passes legisla-

§ 8.281

Size of Conference Committees

The conference committee delegation on the 1981 Budget Reconciliation Act had 280 conferees—208 representatives and 72 senators. This is believed to be the largest conference committee ever assembled.

The smallest conference committee would have 6 members, 3 from the House and 3 from the Senate. That was the practice in early Congresses.

tion, making the assumption that the other chamber will not accept its version.

A conference cannot be held until both chambers formally agree to convene one. The House generally requests a conference by unanimous consent, by motion, or by adoption of a special rule. The Senate usually agrees to a conference by unanimous consent or by motion.

Selection of Conferees

Although House rules grant the Speaker the right to appoint conferees, the Speaker usually does so after consultation with the chair(s) of the committee(s) of jurisdiction. The Senate presiding officer appoints Senate conferees, although the presiding officer, too, draws selections from recommendations of the chair of the committee of jurisdiction and party leaders. Conferees are also referred to as *managers*.

Although seniority on a committee of jurisdiction plays a role in selecting conferees, junior committee members are also appointed to conference committees. A member not on the committee of jurisdiction may be appointed if he or she had an important amendment included in the chamber's version of the measure or in the other chamber's version. In some instances, especially when a measure was considered by multiple committees, representatives or senators can be appointed as *limited-purpose conferees*. Precedents in both chambers indicate that conferees are supposed to support their chamber's legislation in conference.

The number of conferees can range from three to every member of a chamber. Generally, the size of a chamber delegation reflects the complexity of a measure. Moreover, the size of one chamber's delegation does not necessarily affect the size of the other chamber's delegation. Decisions are made by majority vote of *each delegation*, never by a majority vote of all the conferees. Each chamber appoints a majority of conferees to its delegation from the majority party. *(See § 8.281, Size of Conference Committees.)*

Instructing Conferees

Because a conference committee is a negotiating forum, there are few rules imposed on conferees. However, there are two circumstances under which House conferees may be given direction: first, before conferees are named, and second, when conferees have been appointed for twenty calendar days and ten legislative days and have not yet filed a report.

By custom, recognition to offer a *motion to instruct conferees*—a motion before the conferees are named—is a prerogative of the minority party. The motion is debatable for one hour. Only one motion to instruct conferees before their being named is in order.

For a motion to instruct conferees who have been appointed but not yet reported, any

§ 8.282

Authority of Conferees

Provision in First Chamber's Measure	Provision in Second Chamber's Measure	Contents Permitted in Conference Report
No provision	No provision	No provision
Provision A	Provision A	Provision A
Provision A	No provision	Provision A or current law or a compromise position between Provision A and current law
Provision A	Provision B	Between Provision A and Provision B

member, regardless of party, can be recognized to make a motion to instruct, and numerous motions to instruct can be offered.

Motions to instruct House conferees are not binding but express the sentiment of the House on a particular issue in either the House or Senate version of a measure sent to conference.

Motions to instruct in the Senate are rarely made. If made, a motion to instruct is both debatable and amendable, and, as in the House, must be offered before conferees are named. Unlike the House, however, a motion to instruct is not available after conferees have been appointed but the conference committee has not yet reported.

Authority of Conferees

Conferees are expected to meet to reconcile differences between the competing versions of a bill. As such, they are generally limited to matters in disagreement between the versions. They cannot delete provisions that exist in both measures or add provisions not in either measure. However, when the second chamber has adopted a full-text substitute, the latitude in such matters has proven to be quite wide. In appropriations measures, it is often easier to determine the *scope* of differences between House and Senate versions because specific dollar amounts can often be used to determine scope. *(See § 8.282, Authority of Conferees.)*

Conference Committee Deliberations

Conference committees are bargaining sessions. As such, they are characterized by inter-chamber negotiations and trade-offs as each chamber's conferees try to fashion a compromise that will pass their chamber while upholding the basic position their chamber brought into conference.

There are no formal rules in conference. Staff negotiations are customary, often leaving only the most contentious issues to the members themselves. Decisions on how managers work through these issues are determined by the conferees themselves. All conferees may meet together to consider the two chambers' full alternatives. Conferees might agree to consider a measure in conference title by title and to close a title after it has been considered and reconciled. Conferees sometimes create subgroups or subconferences to consider specific issues in the measure in conference.

There is one restriction placed on House managers. The House in the 110th Congress agreed to new chamber rules that House conferees should "endeavor to ensure" that conference meetings occur only if notice is provided and House managers are given the opportunity to attend.

Conference chairs are determined informally; however, when committees conference regularly, the chair normally rotates between the chambers.

When agreement is reached, a majority of each chamber's conference delegation must agree to the *conference report*. No vote is taken seeking a majority of all conferees. The agreement is formally indicated by signing the report. *(See § 8.283, Conference Signature Sheet.)*

Conference Report and Joint Explanatory Statement

The conference report and joint explanatory statement are two distinct documents. The conference report contains a formal statement of the procedural actions the conferees took and the formal legislative language the conferees propose. The joint explanatory statement is a more readable document. It identifies the major matters in disagreement, and then summarizes each chamber's position and the conferees' recommendations. The joint explanatory statement also often contains an explanation of the conferees' intent. Two copies of each document must be signed by a majority of the House conferees and a majority of the Senate conferees.

The documents are printed in the House portion of the *Congressional Record,* and are also printed together as a single House committee report. Although Senate rules require printing as a Senate document as well, the Senate usually waives this requirement.

Consideration of Conference Report

The chamber that agrees to a request for a conference is normally the chamber that considers the conference report first. That chamber can agree to, or disagree with, a conference report, or it can agree to a motion to recommit a conference report to conference. However, after one chamber has acted on a conference report, its conferees are discharged, and the second chamber may only accept or reject the conference report.

Consideration on House Floor. House rules provide that a conference report cannot be called up for consideration until the third calendar day (excluding Saturday, Sunday, or holidays, unless the House is in session) after the conference documents have been filed. Furthermore, copies of the conference report and joint explanatory statement must be available at least two hours before the chamber begins consideration. Both requirements can be waived

§ 8.283

Conference Signature Sheet

S. 2845	
Managers on the part of the HOUSE	Managers on the part of the SENATE
Mr. HOEKSTRA	
Mr. DREIER	
Mr. HYDE	
Mr. HUNTER	
Mr. SENSENBRENNER	

Managers on the part of the House	Managers on the part of the Senate
	Susan M. Collins
Peter Hoekstra, Chair	
Jane Harman	Joseph I. Lieberman
David Dreier	Trent Lott
Robert Menendez	Carl Levin
Henry J. Hyde	Richard J. Durbin
Ike Skelton	Mike DeWine
Duncan Hunter	Pat Roberts
James F. Sensenbrenner, Jr.	John D. Rockefeller, IV
	George V. Voinovich
	John E. Sununu
	Bob Graham
	Frank Lautenberg
	Norm Coleman

S. 2845—Continued	
Managers on the part of the HOUSE	Managers on the part of the SENATE
Ms. HARMAN	
Mr. MENENDEZ	
Mr. SKELTON	

by unanimous consent or by adoption of a special rule from the Rules Committee containing a waiver of the requirements.

Conference reports are privileged and can be brought up when available. They are considered under the one-hour rule. Occasionally, conference reports are brought to the floor by a special rule or under suspension of the rules.

Consideration on Senate Floor. When available, a conference report can be called up. A conference report is debatable under normal Senate rules and procedures. A motion to proceed to consider a conference report, however, is not debatable. A conference report can also be considered under the provisions of a time agreement.

145

§ 8.290 Presidential Action on Enacted Measures

When a measure has been approved by both chambers, the original papers are provided to the *enrolling clerk* of the chamber that originated the legislation. The enrolling clerk prepares an *enrolled version* of the measure—essentially, the measure printed on parchment. (In infrequent circumstances, Congress may submit to the president a *hand-enrolled measure*, one in draft form and not printed on parchment.) This enrolled measure is then certified by the clerk of the House or the secretary of the Senate, depending on the house in which the measure originated, and signed—first by the Speaker of the House and then by the president pro tempore of the Senate.

The enrolled measure is subsequently sent to the White House, although transmittal can occur any time from a few hours to several weeks after an enrolling clerk has been provided with the original papers. At the White House, the Office of the Executive Clerk logs the receipt of the enrolled measure. *(Information on the status of presidential receipt and action on measures is available from the Executive Clerk's Office, 202-456-2226.)*

Within ten days, not counting Sundays, the president must act on the legislation. Counting begins at midnight of the day he receives the enrolled measure. If the president wishes to approve the measure, he signs it, dates it, and writes "Approved" on it, although the Constitution requires only his signature.

Signing ceremonies for major pieces of legislation are often held on the White House lawn, in the Rose Garden, or in a place related to or signified by the legislation. Presidential pens are given to selected people at the ceremony, with the president using several pens to sign and date the document—essentially one pen for each letter or number, to accommodate all those wanting a pen used to sign the measure.

Contemporary presidents have often issued *signing statements* when they signed a measure into law. These statements are often congratulatory toward Congress and the president for having enacted a new law that the president believes will benefit the American people. However, they have in the last three decades become an additional source of information on the president's attitude toward a new law, perhaps expanding on views expressed in statements of administration policy issued during floor and conference consideration of legislation. *(See § 10.20, Congress and the Executive: Legislation.)* Although a president will not have vetoed a measure passed by Congress, he might nonetheless have reservations about provisions in the measure. He may then use a signing statement to explain his reservations and indicate how he will deal with them. A president might indicate that he will seek new legislation from Congress to overcome perceived problems, that implementation of certain provisions will occur pursuant to a certain interpretation of those provisions, or that certain provisions will be carried out consistent with the president's perceived constitutional prerogatives.

A signing statement does not amend or nullify a provision of a law—only Congress and the president together may do that. It may show how the president will use his constitutional duty to execute a law. If the president's interpretation offends Congress, Congress through

§ 8.291

Vetoes and Veto Overrides: Presidential Clout
(as of May 1, 2007)

Of the 1,448 vetoes exercised by President Washington through President Bush, only 104 were overridden by Congress. Of the 36 vetoes exercised by President Clinton, only 2 were overridden. In addition, presidents, including President Clinton, pocket vetoed another 1,066 measures enacted by Congress, for which Congress had no recourse.
The record for contemporary presidents follows:

President	Regular Vetoes	Regular Vetoes Overridden	Pocket Vetoes
Carter (1977–1981)	13	2	18
Reagan (1981–1989)	39	9	39
Bush, G.H.W. (1989–1993)	29	1	15
Clinton (1993–2001)	36	2	1
Bush, G.W. (2001–)	2	0	0

Through the end of his term, President Clinton vetoed 36 measures and returned the vetoed measures to Congress. No override attempt was made on 23 of his vetoes. On seven occasions, the House voted first and sustained his veto. On three occasions, the House overrode a veto only to have the Senate sustain the veto twice and not attempt an override the third time. On one occasion, the Senate voted first and sustained President Clinton's veto. On the two remaining occasions, the House voted to override the president's veto, and the Senate followed suit. The House failed to override either of President Bush's vetoes.

oversight, appropriations, or new legislation may seek to redirect the president. If the president's interpretation is challenged in court, courts have generally looked to the law and its textual development in Congress in their decision making. *(See § 10.73, Legislative History.)*

If the president does not want to approve the legislation, he may *veto* it. He does this by returning the measure without his signature, but including his objections in writing, called a *veto message*. If Congress, or one chamber of Congress, takes no action on a veto, the measure dies. Neither chamber must take action.

Alternately, Congress can attempt to override a veto and enact the bill "the objections of the president to the contrary notwithstanding." A two-thirds vote of those present and voting is required in each chamber to override a veto. The vote must be by roll call. Once the first chamber successfully overrides a veto, the measure is sent to the second house. The second house does not have to attempt a veto override. However, if a veto override in the second house is attempted and is successful, the measure becomes law. Procedures in each chamber allow debate and motions to table, postpone action, or refer a veto message to committee.

Under the Constitution, a measure may become law without the president's signature if the president does not sign it within ten days, not counting Sundays, provided Congress is in session. Why might a president choose this course of action? President George H. W. Bush allowed two measures to become law without his signature. In both cases he cited his agreement with the legislation's goals, but he also in both cases expressed his belief that the laws would be found to be unconstitutional violations of First Amendment rights in any court challenges. The two measures that became law were the Children's Television Act of 1990 (P.L. 101-385) and the Flag Protection Act of 1989 (P.L. 101-131).

If Congress is not in session, a measure not signed does not become law. Such measures are considered to be *pocket vetoed*. Current understanding of the pocket veto allows the practice after Congress has adjourned *sine die*. Pocket vetoes at other times have been challenged in both Congress and the courts. *(See § 8.291, Vetoes and Veto Overrides: Presidential Clout.)*

§ 8.300 Publication of Public Laws

Once the president has signed a measure into law, the president has not signed it within the constitutional ten days, or Congress has passed it over his veto, the measure is transmitted to the National Archives and Records Administration (NARA) and within NARA to the Office of the Federal Register (OFR). At OFR, the measure is assigned a sequential public-law number, such as P.L. 107-8, which would indicate that the law was enacted in the 107th Congress and that it was the eighth public law of that Congress. *(Public-law numbers are announced in the Congressional Record, Federal Register, and other print and electronic resources, including the NARA web site at <www.archives.gov/federal-register/laws/current.html>; they are also available by phone at 202-741-6043.)*

The law is first published in *slip form*, essentially a pamphlet form similar to that of other congressional documents, and is referred to as a *slip law*. *(Slip laws are available from the House Legislative Resource Center, the Senate Document Room, the Government Printing Office, and other print and electronic resources.)*

OFR also assigns each new public law a *Statutes at Large* page citation. Each new public law is added sequentially to the Statutes at Large. Once a slip law is out-of-print, it is easy to find provisions of a specific public law by using its statutory cite.

Finally, the House's Office of Law Revision Counsel organizes the parts of a new public law in the *U.S. Code*. Unlike the organization scheme of the Statutes at Large—sequential—the U.S. Code organizes all laws by subject matter, and the user can readily understand what is current law. Other print and electronic resources also provide U.S. Code reporting. *(Additional information and samples of the Statutes at Large and U.S. Code are found in § 11.50, Laws and Their Implementation by the Executive.)*

148

Introducing a House Bill or Resolution

Betsy Palmer
Analyst on the Congress and Legislative Process

November 25, 2008

Congressional Research Service

7-5700

www.crs.gov

98-458

CRS Report for Congress——————————
Prepared for Members and Committees of Congress

Developing Ideas for Legislation

Ideas and recommendations for legislation come from a wide variety of sources, such as individual Representatives, committees and other House working groups, party and chamber leaders, executive branch agencies and the White House, states and localities, and citizens or interest groups. Any or all of these individuals or entities may participate in drafting legislation, although only a Member may formally introduce legislation. For more information on legislative process, see http://www.crs.gov/products/guides/guidehome.shtml.

Some of the most common considerations that might be taken into account when drafting a bill are

- To what committee or committees is the measure likely to be referred?

- Will the bill attract cosponsors?

- Does the measure have bipartisan appeal?

- Is the measure best introduced at the beginning or toward the end of a Congress?

- What are the budgetary or appropriations implications?

- Should there be a companion measure introduced in the Senate?

Drafting Legislation

Although there is no requirement that bills and other measures introduced in the House be prepared by the House Office of Legislative Counsel, the office plays an important role in drafting legislation. Its staff attorneys are both subject-matter specialists and experts in legislative drafting. Legislative counsel staff are often assigned to serve a specific committee or committees and focus almost exclusively on related policy areas in which they are expert. They act as nonpartisan, shared staff, working closely with committee members and staff. Numerous drafts of a bill or resolution may be required before a measure is formally introduced.

Staff drafting legislation may seek assistance from legislative counsel at any stage. All communications with the office are considered confidential. The office is located at 136 Cannon House Office Building (5-6060).

After introduction, a bill will normally be referred to the committee (or committees) having jurisdiction, under House Rule X, over the subject the bill addresses. (For detail, see CRS Report 98-175, *House Committee Jurisdiction and Referral: Rules and Practice*, by Judy Schneider.) The referral will be made by the Office of the Parliamentarian, acting as agent of the Speaker (Rule XII, clause 2). Members and staff drafting legislation may consult the Office of the Parliamentarian on the referral that a draft bill would be likely to receive, and on the possibility of securing a different referral by making adjustments in its text before introduction.

Introducing a Bill

The formal procedures that govern the practical activity of introducing legislation are few and are found in House Rule XII. Former House Parliamentarian Wm. Holmes Brown in *House Practice: A Guide to the Rules, Precedents and Procedures of the House* (Washington: GPO, 2003) has stated: "The system for introducing measures in the House is a relatively free and open one." House rules do not limit the number of bills a Representative may introduce.

When a Representative who is the primary sponsor has determined that a bill or resolution is ready for introduction, the measure is printed in a form that leaves room for the parliamentarian's office to note the committee or committees of referral and for a clerk to insert a number. The Member must sign the measure and attach the names of any cosponsors on the form provided by the Clerk's office; cosponsors do not affix their signatures to the bill. The Member then deposits the measure in the box, or "hopper," at the bill clerk's desk in the House chamber when the House is in session. A Member need not seek recognition in order to introduce a measure.

If a Member has second thoughts after introducing a measure, he or she may reclaim it from the clerk so long as the measure has not been assigned a number and referred to committee (a process that normally takes one day). Once a measure has been numbered and referred, it becomes the property of the House and cannot be reclaimed. The House has the authority to consider an introduced bill or resolution even if the primary sponsor resigns from the House or dies.

In the first days of a new Congress, hundreds of bills and resolutions are introduced. Measures are numbered sequentially and Representatives may seek to reserve numbers, as these are sometimes seen as providing a shorthand meaning to the legislation, or having some other symbolic meaning. In recent years, the House has ordered that bill numbers one through 10 be reserved for majority party leaders.

Author Contact Information

Betsy Palmer
Analyst on the Congress and Legislative Process
bpalmer@crs.loc.gov, 7-0381

Acknowledgments

This report was originally prepared by former CRS Specialist Richard C. Sachs. Please direct any inquiries to the listed author.

The Legislative Process on the House Floor: An Introduction

Christopher M. Davis
Analyst on the Congress and Legislative Process

February 2, 2009

Congressional Research Service

7-5700

www.crs.gov

95-563

CRS Report for Congress ————————————————————
Prepared for Members and Committees of Congress

Summary

With very few exceptions, the House determines and enforces its own procedures for considering legislation on the floor. Its standing rules include several alternative sets of procedures for acting on individual bills and resolutions. The choices made among these procedures usually depend on how important and controversial each measure is. In general, though, all these procedures permit a majority of Members to work their will without excessive delay.

The House passes many bills by motions to suspend the rules, with limited debate and no floor amendments, with the support of at least two-thirds of the Members voting. Most major bills first are considered in Committee of the Whole before being passed by a simple majority vote of the House. The Committee of the Whole is governed by more flexible procedures than the basic rules of the House, under which a majority can vote to pass a bill after only one hour of debate and with no floor amendments. The Rules Committee is instrumental in recommending procedures for considering major bills, and may propose restrictions on the floor amendments that Members can offer.

The daily order of business on the House floor is governed by standing rules that make certain matters and actions privileged for consideration, and by House decisions to grant other individual bills privileged access to the floor, usually upon recommendation of the Rules Committee. Although a quorum is supposed to be present on the floor when the House is conducting business, the House assumes a quorum is present unless a quorum call or electronically recorded vote demonstrates that it is not. However, the standing rules preclude quorum calls at most times other than when the House is voting. Questions are first decided by voice vote, though any Member then may demand a division vote. Before the final result of a voice or division vote is announced, Members can secure an electronically-recorded vote instead, if enough Members desire it or if a quorum is not present in the House.

Congressional Research Service

The Legislative Process on the House Floor: An Introduction

Contents

Contacts

Introduction

A complicated body of rules, precedents, and practices governs the legislative process on the floor of the House of Representatives. The official manual of House rules is more than a thousand pages long and is supplemented by more than 25 volumes of precedents, with more volumes to be published in coming years. Yet there are two reasons why gaining a fundamental understanding of the House's legislative procedures is not as difficult as the sheer number and size of these documents might suggest.[1]

First, the ways in which the House applies its rules are largely predictable, at least in comparison with the Senate. Some rules certainly are more complex and more difficult to interpret than others, but the House does tend to follow similar procedures under similar circumstances. Even the ways in which the House frequently waives, supplants, or supplements its regular rules with special, temporary procedures generally fall into a limited number of recognizable patterns.

Second, underlying most of the rules that Representatives may invoke and the procedures the House may follow is a fundamentally important premise—that a majority of Members ultimately should be able to work their will on the floor. While House rules generally do recognize the importance of permitting any minority, partisan or bipartisan, to present its views and sometimes to propose its alternatives, the rules do not enable that minority to filibuster or use other devices to prevent the majority from prevailing without undue delay.[2] This principle provides an underlying coherence to the various specific procedures that are discussed briefly in this report.

The Nature of the Rules

Article I of the Constitution imposes a few restrictions on House (and Senate) procedures—for example, requirements affecting quorums and roll call votes—but otherwise the Constitution authorizes each house of Congress to determine for itself the "Rules of its Proceedings" (Article 1, Section 5).

This grant of authority has several important implications. First, the House can amend its rules unilaterally; it need not consult with either the Senate or the President. Second, the House is free to suspend, waive, or ignore its rules whenever it chooses to do so. By and large, the Speaker or whatever Representative is presiding usually does not enforce the rules at his or her own initiative. Instead, Members must protect their own rights and interests by making points of order whenever they believe that the rules are about to be violated. In addition, House rules include several formal procedures for waiving or suspending certain other rules, and almost any rule can be waived by unanimous consent. Thus, the requirements and restrictions discussed in this report generally apply only if the House chooses to enforce them.

---

[1] This report was written by Stanley Bach, a former Senior Specialist in the Legislative Process at CRS. The listed author updated the report and can respond to inquiries on the subject.

[2] This premise is not characteristic of Senate rules and procedures, and this difference most clearly distinguishes between the general approaches that the two chambers traditionally have taken to the legislative process.

The House and the Committee of the Whole

Actually, much of the legislative process on the floor occurs not "in the House," but in a committee of the House known as the Committee of the Whole (formally, the Committee of the Whole House on the State of the Union). Every Representative is a member of the Committee of the Whole, and it is in this Committee, meeting in the House chamber, that most major bills usually are debated and amended before being passed or defeated by the House itself. Most bills first are referred to, considered in, and reported by a standing committee of the House before coming to the floor. In much the same way, once bills do reach the floor, many of them then are referred to a second committee, the Committee of the Whole, for further debate and for the consideration of amendments.

The Speaker presides over meetings of the House but not over meetings of the Committee of the Whole. Instead, she appoints another member of the majority party to serve as the chair of the Committee of the Whole during the time the Committee is considering a particular bill or resolution. In addition, the rules that apply in Committee of the Whole are somewhat different from those that govern meetings of the House itself. The major differences are discussed in the following sections of this report. In general, the combined effect of these differences is to make the procedures in Committee of the Whole—especially the procedures for offering and debating amendments—considerably more flexible than those of the House.

Limitations on Debate

If for no other reason than the size of its membership, the House has found it necessary to limit the opportunities for each Representative to participate in floor deliberations. Whenever a Member is recognized to speak on the floor, there always is a time limit on his or her right to debate. The rules of the House never permit a Representative to hold the floor for more than one hour. Under some parliamentary circumstances, there are more stringent limits, with Members being allowed to speak for no more than 5, 20, or 30 minutes.

Furthermore, House rules sometimes impose a limit on how long the entire membership of the House may debate a motion or measure. Many bills and resolutions, for instance, are considered under a set of procedures called "suspension of the rules" (discussed later in this report), that limits all debate on a measure to a maximum of 40 minutes. Under other conditions, when there is no such time limit imposed by the rules, the House (and to some extent, the Committee of the Whole as well) can impose one by simple majority vote. These debate limitations and debate-limiting devices generally prevent a minority of the House from using opportunities for delay to thwart the will of the majority.

House rules also limit debate in other important respects. First, all debate on the floor must be germane to whatever legislative business the House is conducting. Representatives may speak on other subjects only in "one-minute" speeches made at the beginning of each day's session, "special order" speeches occurring after the House has completed its legislative business for the day, and during "morning hour" debates that are scheduled on certain days of the week. Second, all debate on the floor must be consistent with certain rules of courtesy and decorum. For example, a Member should not question or criticize the motives of a colleague.

Four Modes of Consideration

There is no one single set of procedures that the House always follows when it considers a public bill or resolution on the floor. Instead, there are four main modes of consideration, or different sets of procedural rules, that the House uses. In some cases, House rules require that certain kinds of bills be considered in certain ways. By various means, however, the House chooses to use whichever mode of consideration is most appropriate for a given bill. Which of these modes the House uses depends on such factors as the importance and potential cost of the bill and the amount of controversy over it among Members. The differences among these sets of procedures rest largely on the balance that each strikes between the opportunities for Members to debate and propose amendments, on the one hand, and the ability of the House to act promptly, on the other.

Under Suspension of the Rules

The House frequently resorts to a set of procedures that enables it to act quickly on bills that enjoy overwhelming but not unanimous support. Although this set is called "suspension of the rules," clause 1 of Rule XV provides for these procedures as an alternative to the other modes of consideration. The essential components of suspension of the rules are (1) a 40-minute limit on debate, (2) a prohibition against floor amendments, and (3) a two-thirds vote of those present and voting for passage.

On every Monday, Tuesday, and Wednesday, and often during the closing days of a session, the Speaker may, if she chooses, recognize Members to move to suspend the rules and pass a particular bill (or take some other action, such as agreeing to the Senate's amendments to a House bill). Once such a motion is made, the motion and the bill itself together are debatable for a maximum of 40 minutes. Half of the time is controlled by the Representative making the motion, often the chair of the committee with jurisdiction over the bill; the other half usually is controlled by the ranking minority member of the committee (or sometimes the subcommittee) of jurisdiction, especially when he or she opposes the motion. The motion may propose to pass the bill with certain amendments, but no Member may propose an amendment from the floor.

During the debate, the two Members who control the time yield parts of it to other Members who wish to speak. Once the 40 minutes is either used or yielded back, a single vote occurs on suspending the rules and simultaneously passing the bill. If two-thirds of the Members present vote "Aye" the motion is agreed to and the bill is passed. If the motion fails, the House may debate the bill again at another time, perhaps under another mode of consideration that permits floor amendments and more debate and that requires only a simple majority vote for passage.

The House frequently considers several suspension motions on the same day, which could result in a series of electronically recorded votes taking place at 40-minute intervals if such votes are requested. For the convenience of the House, therefore, clause 8 of Rule XX permits the Speaker to postpone electronic votes that Members have demanded on motions to suspend the rules until a later time on the same day or the following day. When the votes do take place, they are "clustered," occurring one after the other without intervening debate.

In the House under the Hour Rule

One of the ironies of the legislative process on the House floor is that the House does relatively little business under the basic rules of the House. Instead, most of the debate and votes on amendments to major bills occur in Committee of the Whole. This is largely because of the rule that generally governs debate in the House itself.

The rule controlling debate during meetings of the House (as opposed to meetings of the Committee of the Whole) is clause 2 of Rule XVII, which states in part that "[a] Member, Delegate, or Resident Commissioner may not occupy more than one hour in debate on a question in the House.... " In theory, this rule permits each Representative to speak for as much as an hour on each bill, on each amendment to each bill, and on each of the countless debatable motions that Members could offer. Thus, there could be more than four hundred hours of debate on each such question, a situation that would make it virtually impossible for the House to function effectively.

In practice, however, this "hour rule" usually means that each measure considered "in the House" is debated by all Members for no more than a total of only one hour before the House votes on passing it. The reason for this dramatic difference between the rule in theory and the rule in practice lies in the consequences of a motion to order what is called the "previous question."

When a bill or resolution is called up for consideration in the House—and, therefore, under the hour rule—the Speaker recognizes the majority floor manager to control the first hour of debate. The majority floor manager usually is the chair of the committee or subcommittee with jurisdiction over the measure, and most often supports its passage without amendment. This Member will yield part of his or her time to other Members, and may allocate control of half of the hour to the minority floor manager (usually the ranking minority member of the committee or subcommittee). However, the majority floor manager almost always yields to other Representatives "for purposes of debate only." Thus, no other Member may propose an amendment or make any motion during that hour.

During the first hour of debate, or at its conclusion, the majority floor manager invariably "moves the previous question." This non-debatable motion asks the House if it is ready to vote on passing the bill. If a majority votes for the motion, no more debate on the bill is in order, nor can any amendments to it be offered; after disposing of the motion, the House usually votes immediately on whether to pass the bill. Only if the House votes not to order the previous question can debate on the bill continue into a second hour, during which the bill may be amended. Thus, Members who want to amend the measure first must convince the House to vote against ordering the previous question. If they are successful, then the Member controlling the second hour of debate may propose an amendment. However, it is very unusual for the House not to vote for the previous question; so the House disposes of most measures considered in the House, under the hour rule, after no more than one hour of debate, and with no opportunity for amendment from the floor.

These are not very flexible and accommodating procedural ground rules for the House to follow in considering most legislation. Debate on a bill usually is limited to one hour, and only one or two Members control this time. Before an amendment to the bill can even be considered, the House first must vote against a motion to order the previous question. For these reasons, most major bills are not considered in the House under the hour rule. Instead, they are considered under a third and more complicated mode of consideration, a set of procedures involving the Committee of the Whole.

In Committee of the Whole and the House

Clause 3 of Rule XVIII requires that most bills affecting federal taxes and spending be considered in Committee of the Whole before the House votes on passing them. Most other major bills also are considered in this way. Most commonly, the House adopts a resolution, reported by the Rules Committee, that authorizes the Speaker to declare the House "resolved" into Committee of the Whole to consider a particular bill.

General Debate

There are two distinct stages to consideration in Committee of the Whole. First, there is a period for general debate, which routinely is limited to an hour.[3] Each of the floor managers usually controls half the time, yielding parts of it to other Members who want to participate in the debate. During general debate, the two floor managers and other Members discuss the bill, the conditions prompting the committee to recommend it, and the merits of its provisions. Members may describe and explain the reasons for the amendments that they intend to offer, but no amendments can actually be proposed at this time. During or after general debate, the majority floor manager may move that the Committee "rise"—in other words, that the Committee transform itself back into the House. When the House agrees to this motion, it may resolve into Committee of the Whole again at another time to resume consideration of the bill. Alternatively, the Committee of the Whole may proceed immediately from general debate to the next stage of consideration, the amending process.

Amending Process

The Committee of the Whole usually considers a bill for amendment section by section or, in the case of appropriations measures, paragraph by paragraph. Amendments to each section or of the bill are in order after the part they would amend has been read or designated, and before the next section is read or designated. Alternatively, the bill may be open to amendment at any point, usually by unanimous consent. The first amendments considered to each part of the bill are those (if any) recommended by the committee that reported it. Thereafter, members of the committee usually are recognized before other Representatives to offer their own amendments. All amendments must be germane to the text they would amend. Germaneness is a subject matter standard more stringent than one of relevancy and reflects a complex set of criteria that have developed by precedent over the years.

The Committee of the Whole only votes on amendments; it does not vote directly on the bill as a whole. And like the standing committees of the House, the Committee of the Whole does not actually amend the bill; it only votes to recommend amendments to the House. The motion to order the previous question may not be made in Committee of the Whole, so Members usually may offer whatever germane amendments they wish, unless prevented from doing so by the terms of a special rule. After voting on the last amendment to the last portion of the bill, the Committee rises and reports the bill back to the House with whatever amendments it has agreed to.

---

[3] The length of general debate on a bill is determined either by unanimous consent or by adoption of a procedural resolution reported by the Committee on Rules, that typically affects various aspects of the procedures for considering that bill. These resolutions are discussed in the section of this report on "The Rules Committee and Special Rules".

An amendment to a bill is a first-degree amendment. After such an amendment is offered, but before the Committee votes on it, another Member usually may offer a perfecting amendment to make some change in the first degree amendment. A perfecting amendment to a first-degree amendment is a second-degree amendment. After debate, the Committee first votes on the second-degree perfecting amendment and then on the first-degree amendment as it may have been amended. Clause 6 of Rule XVI also provides that a Member may offer a substitute for the first-degree amendment, before or after a perfecting amendment is offered, and this substitute may also be amended. Although a full discussion of these possibilities is beyond the scope of this report, it is important to note that the amending process can become complicated, with Members proposing several competing policy choices before the Committee of the Whole votes on any of them.

Debate on amendments in Committee of the Whole is governed by the five-minute rule, not the hour rule that governs debate in the House. The Member offering each amendment (or the majority floor manager, in the case of a committee amendment) first is recognized to speak for five minutes. Then a Member opposed to the amendment may claim five minutes for debate. Other Members also may speak for five minutes each by offering a motion "to strike the last word." Technically, this motion is an amendment that proposes to strike out the last word of the amendment being debated. But it is a "pro forma amendment" that is offered merely to secure time for debate, and so is not voted on when the five minutes expire. In this way, each Representative may speak for five minutes on each amendment. However, a majority of the Members can vote (or agree by unanimous consent) to end the debate on an amendment immediately or at some specified time.

Final Passage

When the Committee finally rises and reports the bill back to the House, the House proceeds to vote on the amendments the Committee has adopted. It usually approves all these amendments by one voice vote, though Members can demand separate votes on any or all of them as a matter of right. After a formal and routine stage called third reading and engrossment (when only the title of the bill is read), there is then an opportunity for a Member, virtually always from the minority party, to offer a motion to recommit the bill to committee. If the House agrees to a "simple" or "straight" motion to recommit, which only proposes to return the bill to committee, the bill is taken from the floor and returned to committee. While the committee technically has the power to re-report the bill, in practice, the adoption of a straight motion to recommit is often characterized as effectively "killing" the measure.

Alternately, motions to recommit frequently include instructions that the committee report the bill back to the House "forthwith" with an amendment that is stated in the motion. If the House agrees to such a motion, it then immediately votes on the amendment itself, so a motion to recommit with instructions is really a final opportunity to amend the bill before the House votes on whether to pass it.

Thus, this complicated mode of consideration, which the House uses to consider most major bills, begins in the House with a decision to resolve into Committee of the Whole to consider a particular bill. General debate and the amending process take place in Committee of the Whole, but ultimately it is the House that formally amends and then passes or rejects the bill.

In the House as in Committee of the Whole

A fourth mode of consideration, which the House does not use very often, is a hybrid form that combines features of the procedures that apply in the House under the hour rule and those that apply in the Committee of the Whole. This set of procedures, known as the House meeting "as in Committee of the Whole," has evolved by precedent, and no House rules explicitly define its elements. It may be used to consider private bills, and it was used routinely, although only by unanimous consent, to consider bills reported by the Committee on the District of Columbia before the House abolished that committee in 1995.

A measure considered in this way is debated under the five-minute rule; the hour rule does not apply, nor is there a period for general debate. The majority floor manager secures time to make his opening statement on the bill by moving to strike the last word that is, the last word of the bill. All other Members who want their own time to speak use the same device. The bill is open to amendment at any point; it is not read for amendment, as are bills being amended under the five-minute rule in Committee of the Whole. But like procedures in the House under the hour rule, the majority floor manager may move the previous question on an individual amendment or on the bill and all amendments to it. Votes on amendments are final because they occur in the House itself. After acting on the last amendment and ordering the bill engrossed and read the third time (by title only), the House votes on final passage.

The Calendars and the Order of Business

When a House committee reports a public bill or resolution that had been referred to it, the measure is placed on the House Calendar or the Union Calendar. In general, tax, authorization, and appropriations bills are placed on the Union Calendar; all others go to the House Calendar. In effect, the calendars are catalogues of measures that have been approved, with or without proposed amendments, by one or more House committees, and now are available for consideration on the floor.[4] Because it would be impractical or undesirable for the House to take up measures in the chronological order in which they are reported and placed on one of the calendars, there must be some procedures for deciding the order in which measures are to be brought from the calendars to the House floor—in other words, procedures for determining the order of business.

Clause 1 of Rule XIV lists the daily order of business on the floor, beginning with the opening prayer, the approval of the Journal, which is the official record of House proceedings required by the Constitution, and the Pledge of Allegiance. Apart from these routine matters, however, the House never follows the order of business laid out in this rule. Instead, certain measures and actions are privileged, meaning that they may interrupt the regular order of business. In practice, all the legislative business that the House conducts comes to the floor by interrupting the order of business under Rule XIV, either by unanimous consent or under the provisions of another House rule. Every bill and resolution that cannot be considered by unanimous consent must become privileged business if it is going to reach the floor at all.

---

[4] Committees also may report measures unfavorably or without recommendation, but they rarely do so. Instead, committees usually do not report the bills and resolutions they do not approve.

Measures considered under some of the modes of consideration discussed above are privileged on certain days. For example, on any Monday, Tuesday, or Wednesday, the Speaker can recognize Members to move to suspend the rules and pass bills. As has been noted, suspension motions are privileged on those days and so the bills they involve may be considered. Private bills are privileged for consideration on the first and third Tuesdays of each month (under clause 5 of Rule XV). Clause 4 of the same rule makes bills relating to the District of Columbia, if reported by the Committee on Oversight and Government Reform, in order on the second and fourth Mondays.

In addition, clause 5(a) of Rule XIII grants certain committees the right to report certain kinds of measures at any time, meaning that those measures may be called up on the floor as privileged business whenever another matter is not already pending. These privileged measures include general appropriations bills (from the Appropriations Committee), budget resolutions and reconciliation bills (from the Budget Committee), resolutions to fund House committees (from the Committee on House Administration), and measures changing House rules (from the Rules Committee). However, most major bills do not fall into one of these categories, nor do they usually enjoy enough support to pass under suspension of the rules. Another approach is necessary for them to become privileged for floor action. This approach is based on the Rules Committee's jurisdiction over measures affecting the order of business on the floor.

The Rules Committee and Special Rules

Clause 1(m) of Rule X authorizes the Rules Committee to report resolutions affecting the order of business. Such a resolution—which is called a "rule" or "special rule"—usually proposes to make a bill in order for floor consideration so that it can be debated, amended, and passed or defeated by a simple majority vote. In effect, each special rule recommends to the House that it take from the Union or House Calendar a measure that is not otherwise privileged business and bring it to the floor out of its order on that calendar. Typically, such a resolution begins by providing that, at any time after its adoption, the Speaker may declare the House resolved into the Committee of the Whole for the consideration of that bill. Because the special rule itself is privileged, under clause 5(a) of Rule XIII, the House can debate and vote on it promptly. If the House accepts the Rules Committee's recommendation, it proceeds to consider the bill itself.

One fundamental purpose of most special rules, therefore, is to make another measure privileged so that it may interrupt the regular order of business. Their other fundamental purpose is to set special procedural ground rules for considering that measure; these ground rules may either supplement or supplant the standing rules of the House. For example, the special rule typically sets the length of time for general debate in Committee of the Whole and specifies which Members are to control that time. In addition, the special rule normally includes provisions that expedite final House action on the bill after the amending process in Committee of the Whole has been completed. Special rules also may waive points of order that Members otherwise could make against consideration of the bill, against one of its provisions, or against an amendment to be offered to it.

The most controversial provisions of special rules affect the amendments that Members can offer to the bill that the resolution makes in order. An "open rule" permits Representatives to propose any amendment that meets the normal requirements of House rules and precedents—for example, the requirement that each amendment must be germane. At the other extreme, a "closed rule" prohibits all amendments, except perhaps for committee amendments and pro forma amendments (to strike the last word) offered only for purposes of debate. The Rules Committee also has proposed a variety of restrictive special rules, most often called "structured" or "modified open" rules, that either permit only certain amendments or require Members to pre-print their amendments in the *Congressional Record* before they can be considered on the floor. These provisions are very important because they can prevent Representatives from offering amendments as alternatives to provisions of the bill, thereby limiting the policy choices that the House can make.

However, like other committees, the Rules Committee only makes recommendations to the House. Members debate each of its procedural resolutions in the House under the hour rule and then vote to adopt or reject it. If the House votes against ordering the previous question on a special rule, a Member may offer an amendment to it, proposing to change the conditions under which the bill itself is to be considered. Because the adoption of a special rule is often viewed as a "party loyalty" vote, however, such a development is exceedingly rare. All the same, it is important to remember that while the Rules Committee is instrumental in helping the House formulate its order of business and in setting appropriate ground rules for considering each bill, the House retains ultimate control over what it does, when, and how.

Senate Amendments and Conference Reports

Before any bill can become law, both the House and the Senate must pass it, and the two houses must agree on each and every one of its provisions. This basic constitutional requirement means that the House must have procedures to respond when the House and Senate pass different versions of the same bill. For example, the House may pass a Senate bill with House amendments, or the Senate may pass a House bill with Senate amendments and then send its amendments to the House. In either case, the two houses must resolve their differences over these amendments before the legislative process is completed.

There are essentially two ways to approach this stage of the process: either (1) by dealing with the amendments individually, through a process of exchanging amendments between the chambers, with the bill being sent back and forth between the House and Senate, or (2) by dealing with the amendments collectively, through a conference committee of Representatives and Senators who negotiate a series of compromises and concessions that are compiled in a conference report that the two houses can vote to accept. Because the process of resolving differences between the houses can be quite complicated, only some of its basic elements are summarized here.

The House normally considers Senate amendments to a House bill by unanimous consent or by suspension of the rules; the House may accept the amendments (concur in them) or amend them (concur in them with House amendments). Alternatively, the committee with jurisdiction over the bill may authorize its chair to move that the House disagree to the Senate's amendments and send them to a conference committee. When the House amends and passes a Senate bill, it may request a conference with the Senate immediately, or it may simply send its amendments to the Senate in the hope that the Senate will accept them. If the Senate refuses to do so, it may request a conference with the House instead. On the other hand, if the House and Senate can reach agreement by proposing amendments to each other's positions, the bill can be sent to the President for his signature or veto without the need to create a conference committee.

If the House and Senate agree to send their versions of the bill to a conference committee, the Speaker appoints the House conferees. These conferees usually are drawn from the standing committee (or committees) with jurisdiction over the bill, although the Speaker may appoint some other Representatives as well. When the House and Senate conferees meet, they are to deal only with provisions of the bill on which the two houses disagree. They should not insert new provisions or change provisions that both houses already have approved. Furthermore, as the conferees resolve each provision or amendment in disagreement, they should accept the House position, the Senate position, or a compromise between them. Like almost all other House rules, the rules limiting the authority of conferees are enforced only if Members make points of order at the appropriate time. The House also may adopt a special rule, reported by the Rules Committee, waiving points of order against a conference report.

To complete their work successfully, a majority of the House conferees and a majority of the Senate conferees must sign a report that recommends all the agreements they have reached.[5] The conferees also sign a "joint explanatory statement" that describes the original House and Senate positions and the conferees' recommendations, and which is the functional equivalent of a committee report.

After Representatives have had three days to examine a conference report, it is privileged for floor consideration; it may be called up at any time that the House is not already considering something else. The report may be debated in the House, under the hour rule, so the vote almost always occurs after no more than one hour of debate. No amendments to the report are in order. In practice, however, the House almost always considers conference reports under the terms of a special rule which waives points of order against the report and its consideration.

The conference report is a proposed package settlement of a number of disagreements, so the House and Senate may accept it or reject it but they may not change it.[6] If the two houses agree to the report, by simple majority vote, all their differences have been resolved and the bill is then "enrolled," or reprinted, for formal presentation to the President.

In rare instances, conferees cannot reach agreement on one or more of the amendments in conference, or they may reach an agreement that they cannot include in their conference report because their proposal exceeds the scope of the differences between the House and Senate positions (and thus violates the rules governing the content of conference reports). In either case, the conferees may report back to the two houses with an amendment (or amendments) in disagreement. After acting on the conference report, dealing collectively with all the other amendments that were sent to conference, the House acts on each of the amendments in disagreement by considering motions such as a motion to accept the Senate's amendment or a motion to amend it with a new House amendment. The Senate takes similar action until the disagreements on these amendments are resolved, or until the two houses agree to create a new conference committee only to address the remaining amendments that are still in disagreement.

---

[5] There are other procedures for the conferees to follow if they cannot reach full agreement or if they want to propose something that is not within the scope of the differences between the original House and Senate positions.

[6] However, the first house to consider a conference report also has the option of recommitting it to the conference committee in the hope that the conferees can reach a different and more acceptable agreement. House rules also include provisions for voting separately on conference report provisions, originating in the Senate, that would not have been germane if offered as House floor amendments to the bill. But these are often dealt with instead by a waiver in a special rule. Finally, the Senate has adopted special procedures whereby, under certain circumstances, "new matter" or new directed spending in a conference report might be stricken if a point of order is raised against it. For information, see CRS Report RS22733, *Senate Rules Changes in the 110th Congress Affecting Restrictions on the Content of Conference Reports*, by Elizabeth Rybicki.

The bill cannot become law until the two houses resolve all the differences between their positions.

Voting and Quorum Procedures

Whenever Representatives vote on the floor, there first is a "voice vote," in which the Members in favor of the bill, amendment, or motion vote "Aye" in unison, followed by those voting "No." Before the Speaker (or the chair of the Committee of the Whole) announces the result, any Representative can demand a "division vote," in which the Members in favor stand up to be counted, again followed by those opposed. But before the result of either a voice vote or a division vote is announced, a Member may try to require another vote in which everyone's position is recorded publicly.

This vote is taken by using the House's electronic voting system. In Committee of the Whole, an electronic vote is ordered when 25 Members request it. In the House, such a vote occurs when demanded by at least one-fifth of the Members present. Alternatively, any Member can demand an electronically recorded vote in the House if a quorum of the membership is not present on the floor when the voice or division vote takes place.

The Constitution requires that a quorum must be present on the floor when the House is conducting business. In the House, a quorum is a majority of the Representatives; in Committee of the Whole, it is only 100 Members. However, the House traditionally has assumed that a quorum is always present unless a Member makes a point of order that it is not. The rules restrict when Members can make such points of order, and they occur most often when the House or the Committee of the Whole is voting. In the House, for example, a Representative can object to a voice or division vote on the grounds that a quorum is not present, and make that point of order. If a quorum is not present, the Speaker automatically orders an electronically recorded vote during which Members record their presence on the floor by casting their votes. The issue is decided and a quorum is established at the same time. A voice or division vote is valid even if less than a quorum participates in the vote, so long as no one makes a point of order that a quorum is not present. For this reason, Members can continue to meet in their committees or fulfill their other responsibilities off the floor when the House is doing business that does not involve publicly recorded votes.

The Daily Order of Business

After the opening prayer on each day, the Speaker announces his approval of the Journal of the previous day's proceedings. A Member may require a recorded vote on agreeing to the Speaker's approval of the Journal—not because of any question about the accuracy of the Journal, but to determine which Representatives may not be in the Capitol or the House office buildings that day. Following the Pledge of Allegiance, some Members then ask unanimous consent to address the House for one minute each on whatever subjects they wish, including subjects unrelated to the scheduled legislative business of the day.

Generally speaking, to the extent possible, the majority party leaders and the committee chairmen arrange the legislative schedule for each week in advance. During the last floor session of the week, the Majority Leader normally announces the expected schedule for the coming week in a "wrap-up" colloquy with a minority party leader. Changes in the schedule may be announced as they are made. To be considered, a bill or resolution must enjoy the privilege to interrupt the regular order of business. Various kinds of legislative business are privileged, however. So the Speaker enjoys considerable discretion in deciding the order in which privileged matters should be considered, and, therefore, the order in which she recognizes Members to call them up on the floor. On the other hand, the Speaker's discretion is limited by rules such as the ones that set aside specific days for considering certain kinds of business, such as bills concerning the District of Columbia.

As each item of business is completed, the Speaker anticipates which Member should be seeking recognition to call up the next bill or resolution. If another Representative requests to be recognized instead, the Speaker may ask, "For what purpose does the gentleman rise?," and she may decline to recognize that Member if he wants the House to consider another privileged bill, motion, or conference report. If a bill is to be considered in Committee of the Whole, the majority party leaders and the committee chair may decide in advance whether the Committee should only complete general debate on that day or whether to proceed with the amending process as well. The ability to set the House's floor schedule is one of the primary powers and responsibilities of the majority party leaders, though they often consult with the minority party leaders. On rare occasion, however, a majority of the Members have voted against a special rule—and, therefore, against considering a bill—even when the Speaker and his leadership colleagues wish the House to debate and pass it.

At the end of legislative business on most days, some Members address the House for as much as an hour each on subjects of their choice. These "special order" speeches are arranged in advance by unanimous consent and organized by the parties. In this way, Representatives can comment at length on current national and international issues, and discuss bills that have not yet reached the House floor. The House often adjourns by late afternoon, although it may remain in session throughout the evening when an emergency arises or when the end of the annual session or some other deadline approaches.

Sources of Additional Information

The House rules for each Congress are published in a volume often called the House manual, but officially entitled *Constitution, Jefferson's Manual and Rules of the House of Representatives*. A new edition of this collection is published each Congress. The precedents of the House established through 1935 have been compiled in the 11-volume set of *Hinds' and Cannon's Precedents of the House of Representatives*. More recent precedents are in the process of being published as *Deschler's* or *Deschler-Brown Precedents of the U.S. House of Representatives*; 16 volumes of this set now are available. The House's procedures are explained in *House Practice: A Guide to the Rules, Precedents and Procedures of the House*, by Wm. Holmes Brown, Parliamentarian Emeritus of the House, and Charles W. Johnson, Parliamentarian of the House. The latest version of *House Practice* was published in 2003. The Parliamentarian and his assistants welcome inquiries about House procedures and offer expert assistance compatible with their other responsibilities.

CRS Reports

CRS Report 98-995, *The Amending Process in the House of Representatives*, by Christopher M. Davis.

CRS Report RS20147, *Committee of the Whole: An Introduction*, by Judy Schneider.

CRS Report RL32200, *Debate, Motions, and Other Actions in the Committee of the Whole*, by Bill Heniff Jr. and Elizabeth Rybicki.

CRS Report 96-708, *Conference Committee and Related Procedures: An Introduction*, by Elizabeth Rybicki.

CRS Report 97-552, *The Discharge Rule in the House: Principal Features and Uses*, by Richard S. Beth.

CRS Report RL30787, *Parliamentary Reference Sources: House of Representatives*, by Richard S. Beth and Megan Suzanne Lynch.

CRS Report 98-696, *Resolving Legislative Differences in Congress: Conference Committees and Amendments Between the Houses*, by Elizabeth Rybicki.

CRS Report 97-780, *The Speaker of the House: House Officer, Party Leader, and Representative*, by James V. Saturno.

CRS Report 98-314, *Suspension of the Rules in the House: Principal Features*, by Elizabeth Rybicki.

CRS Report 98-870, *Quorum Requirements in the House: Committee and Chamber*, by Christopher M. Davis.

Author Contact Information

Christopher M. Davis
Analyst on the Congress and Legislative Process
cmdavis@crs.loc.gov, 7-0656

Congressional Research Service

Introducing a Senate Bill or Resolution

Betsy Palmer
Analyst on the Congress and Legislative Process

November 25, 2008

Congressional Research Service

7-5700

www.crs.gov

98-459

CRS Report for Congress

Prepared for Members and Committees of Congress

Developing Ideas for Legislation

Ideas and recommendations for legislation come from a wide variety of sources, from individual Senators, committees and other Senate work groups, and party and chamber leaders; executive branch agencies and the White House; states and localities; and ordinary citizens or interest groups. Any or all of these entities may also participate in drafting measures.

Some of the most common considerations that may be taken into account when preparing the initial draft of a bill are

- To which committee is the measure likely to be referred?

- How can the measure attract cosponsors?

- Does the measure have bipartisan appeal?

- Is the measure best introduced early or late in a session of Congress?

- What are the budgetary or appropriations implications?

For more information on legislative process, see http://www.crs.gov/products/guides/guidehome.shtml.

Senate Office of Legislative Counsel

The Senate Office of Legislative Counsel usually plays a critical role in drafting legislation, although there is no requirement that they draft bills or resolutions. Its staff attorneys are both subject-matter specialists and experts in legislative drafting. The office is at 668 Dirksen Senate Office Building (4-6461). Legislative counsel staff are often assigned to a committee or committees, and focus almost exclusively on related policy areas in which they are expert. They act as nonpartisan, shared staff, working closely with committee members and staff. Personal office staff assigned responsibility for drafting legislation may seek assistance from legislative counsel at any stage. Numerous drafts of a bill or resolution may be required before the measure is formally introduced.

The Senate Committee on Rules and Administration has set the drafting priorities of the Office of the Legislative Counsel as follows: (1) measures in conference; (2) measures pending on the floor; (3) measures pending before a committee; and (4) measures to be prepared for individual Senators. Within each of these categories, priority is given to requests in the order they are received.

Guidelines for expediting requests for assistance from the Office of the Legislative Counsel are to be found on the Senate Webster website. Only Senate offices have access to Webster. See http://webster.senate.gov/other/solc/Requests/requests.htm.

Seeking Cosponsors

When a Senator introduces a measure, he or she commonly attaches a form bearing the names of cosponsors. Before the bill is introduced, Senators may become cosponsors by contacting the office of the chief sponsor and requesting that their names be added to the bill or resolution. Initial cosponsors can be added until the measure is presented to the clerk in the Senate chamber. There is no limit on the number of cosponsors.

One of the most common techniques for informing Senators of the pending introduction of a bill or resolution, and for soliciting support, is the "Dear Colleague" letter, sent to most or all Senators. Typically, these letters briefly state the issue the measure addresses, the measure's significant features and an appeal to become a cosponsor. Almost always, they carry the name and phone number of a staff aide to contact about cosponsoring the bill. (See CRS Report 98-279, *Sponsorship and Co-sponsorship of Senate Bills*, by Betsy Palmer and CRS Report RL34636, *"Dear Colleague" Letters: Current Practices*, by Jacob R. Straus.)

Introducing a Bill or Resolution

Senate Rule VII requires measures to be introduced from the floor as part of "morning business." In practice, however, morning business seldom occurs as provided in Rule VII. Instead, on most days, the Senate provides by unanimous consent that a period for transacting routine morning business occur at some point. Senators may introduce measures from the floor during this period. Also, at the beginning of each new Congress, the Senate adopts a standing order allowing Senators to introduce measures at any time the chamber is in session by presenting them to a clerk at the desk. Most measures are introduced in this fashion. However, no bill may be introduced on a day in which there has been no period for morning business.

To be introduced for Senate consideration, a measure must be signed by the sponsoring Senator. If Senators wish to accompany the measure with a statement, they may either deliver the statement during morning business, or at any other time, or they may ask unanimous consent to insert the statement in the *Congressional Record*. By unanimous consent, the text of the measure also is typically included.

Referral

Senate Rule XIV requires that all bills and resolutions be read twice before they are referred to committees. Committee jurisdictions are set forth in Rule XXV. Referral decisions are made by the Senate parliamentarian's office acting on behalf of the presiding officer. Under the provisions of Rule XVII, a measure is referred to the committee with "jurisdiction over the subject matter which predominates." Multiple referrals occur only occasionally. A procedure in Rule XIV allows an introduced measure to be placed directly on the calendar of business without being first referred to a standing committee (see CRS Report RS22309, *Senate Rule XIV Procedures for Placing Measures Directly on the Senate Calendar*, by Michael L. Koempel).

Author Contact Information

Betsy Palmer
Analyst on the Congress and Legislative Process
bpalmer@crs.loc.gov, 7-0381

Congressional Research Service

The Legislative Process on the Senate Floor: An Introduction

Valerie Heitshusen
Analyst on the Congress and Legislative Process

November 26, 2008

Congressional Research Service

7-5700

www.crs.gov

96-548

CRS Report for Congress
Prepared for Members and Committees of Congress

Summary

The standing rules of the Senate promote deliberation by permitting Senators to debate at length and by precluding a simple majority from ending debate when they are prepared to vote to approve a bill or other matter. This right of extended debate permits filibusters that can be brought to an end if the Senate invokes cloture, usually by a vote of three-fifths of all Senators. Even then, consideration can continue under cloture for an additional thirty hours. The possibility of filibusters encourages the Senate to seek consensus whenever possible and to conduct business under the terms of unanimous consent agreements that limit the time available for debate and amending.

Except when the Senate is considering appropriations, budget, and certain other measures, Senators also may propose floor amendments that are not germane to the subject or purpose of the bill being debated. This permits individual Senators to raise issues and have the Senate vote on them, even if they have not been studied and evaluated by the appropriate standing committees. Similarly, Senators can bypass the committee system by introducing measures and having them placed directly on the Calendar of Business without having been referred to committee at all.

These characteristics of Senate rules make the Senate's daily floor schedule potentially unpredictable unless all Senators agree by unanimous consent to accept limits on their right to debate and offer non-germane amendments to a bill. Also to promote predictability and order, Senators traditionally have agreed to give certain procedural privileges to the Majority Leader. The Majority Leader enjoys priority in being recognized to speak, and the Majority Leader (or a Senator acting at his behest) alone proposes what bills and resolutions the Senate should consider.

Thus, the legislative process on the Senate floor reflects a balance between the rights guaranteed to Senators under the standing rules and the willingness of Senators to forego exercising some of these rights in order to expedite the conduct of business.

Congressional Research Service

174

Contents

Contacts

Introduction

The legislative process on the Senate floor is governed by a set of standing rules, a body of precedents created by rulings of Presiding Officers or by votes of the Senate, a variety of established and customary practices, and ad hoc arrangements the Senate makes to meet specific parliamentary and political circumstances. A knowledge of the Senate's formal rules is not sufficient to understand Senate procedures, and Senate practices cannot be understood without knowing the rules to which the practices relate.

The essential characteristic of the Senate's rules, and the characteristic that most clearly distinguishes its procedures from those of the House of Representatives, is their emphasis on the rights and prerogatives of individual Senators. Like any legislative institution, the Senate is both a deliberative and a decision-making body; its procedures must embody some balance between the opportunity to deliberate or debate and the need to decide. Characteristically, the Senate's rules give greater weight to the value of full and free deliberation than they give to the value of expeditious decisions. Put differently, legislative rules also must strike a balance between minority rights and majority prerogatives. The Senate's standing rules place greater emphasis on the rights of individual Senators—and, therefore, of minorities within the Senate—than on the powers of the majority. The Senate's legislative agenda and its policy decisions are influenced not merely by the preferences of its members but also by the intensity of their preferences.

Precisely because of the nature of its standing rules, the Senate cannot rely on them exclusively. If all Senators took full advantage of their rights under the rules whenever it might be in their immediate interests, the Senate would have great difficulty reaching timely decisions. Therefore, the Senate has developed a variety of practices by which Senators set aside some of their prerogatives under the rules to expedite the conduct of its business or to accommodate the needs and interests of its members. Some of these practices have become well-established by precedent; others are arranged to suit the particular circumstances the Senate confronts from day to day and from issue to issue. In most cases, these alternative arrangements require the unanimous consent of the Senate—the explicit or implicit concurrence of each of the one hundred Senators. The Senate relies on unanimous consent agreements every day for many purposes—purposes great and small, important and routine. However, Senators can protect their rights under Senate rules simply by objecting to a unanimous consent request to waive one or more of the rules.

Generally, the Senate can act more efficiently and expeditiously when its members agree by unanimous consent to operate outside of its standing rules. Generally also, Senators insist that the rules be enforced strictly only when the questions before it are divisive and controversial. Compromise and accommodation normally prevail. Senators exercise great self-restraint by not taking full advantage of their rights and opportunities under the standing rules, and often by agreeing to unanimous consent requests for arrangements that may not promote their individual legislative interests. The standing rules remain available, however, for Senators to invoke when, in their judgment, the costs of compromise and accommodation become too great.

Thus, the legislative procedures on the Senate floor reflect a balance—and sometimes an uneasy balance—between the operation of its rules and the principles they embody, on the one hand, and pragmatic arrangements to expedite the conduct of business, on the other. The interplay between the principles of the Senate's standing rules and the pragmatism of its daily practices will be a theme running throughout the following sections of this report.

The Right to Debate

The standing rule that is probably most pivotal for shaping what does and does not occur on the Senate floor is paragraph 1(a) of Rule XIX, which governs debate:

> When a Senator desires to speak, he shall rise and address the Presiding Officer, and shall not proceed until he is recognized, and *the Presiding Officer shall recognize the Senator who shall first address him*. No Senator shall interrupt another Senator in debate without his consent, and to obtain such consent he shall first address the Presiding Officer, and no Senator shall speak more than twice upon any one question in debate on the same legislative day without leave of the Senate, which shall be determined without debate. (Emphasis added.)

The Presiding Officer of the Senate (unlike the Speaker of the House) may not use the power to recognize only certain Senators in order to control the flow of business. If no Senator holds the floor, any Senator seeking recognition has a right to be recognized. Moreover, once a Senator has been recognized, he or she may make any motion that Senate rules permit, including motions affecting what bills the Senate will consider (though a Senator loses the floor when he or she makes a motion, offers an amendment, or takes one of many other actions). In practice, however, the Senate has modified the effect of this rule by precedent and custom. By precedent, the Majority and Minority Leaders are recognized first if either leader and another Senator are seeking recognition at the same time. In addition, by custom, only the Majority Leader (or another Senator acting at his behest) makes motions or requests affecting when the Senate will meet and what legislation it will consider.

In these respects, Senators relinquish their equal right to recognition and their right to make certain motions, and they do so in order to lend some order and predictability to the Senate's proceedings. Otherwise, it would be nearly impossible for any Senator to predict with assurance when the Senate will be in session and what legislation it will consider. For example, during debate on one bill, any Senator could move that the Senate turn to another bill instead. This would make it very difficult for the Senate to conduct its business in an orderly fashion, and it would be equally difficult for Senators to plan their own schedules with any confidence. Thus, Senate precedents and practices modify the operation of this rule, as it affects recognition, in the interests of the Senate as an institution and in the interests of its members individually.

Even more important is what paragraph 1(a) of Rule XIX says and does not say about the length of debate. The rule imposes a limit of two speeches per Senator per question per day, but it imposes no limit at all on the number of Senators who may make those two speeches, nor on the length of the speeches. In fact, there are few Senate rules that limit the right to debate, and no rules that permit a simple majority of the Senate to end a debate whenever it is ready to vote for a bill, amendment, or other question that is being considered. When Senators are recognized by the Presiding Officer, the rules normally permit them to speak for as long as they wish, and questions generally cannot be put to a vote so long as there are Senators who still wish to make the speeches they are permitted to make under Rule XIX.

The House of Representatives may bring a question to a vote if a simple majority agrees to a motion to order the previous question. When meeting in Committee of the Whole, a majority of Representatives also can move to close debate on a pending amendment or sometimes on a bill and all amendments to it. No such motions are possible in the Senate. As a result, a majority of

Senators does not have nearly the same control over the pace and timing of their deliberations as does a majority of the House.

There is one partial exception to this generalization. The Senate often disposes of an amendment by agreeing to a motion to lay the amendment on the table. When a Senator who has been recognized makes this motion, it cannot be debated (except by unanimous consent, of course). If the Senate agrees to this motion to table, the amendment is rejected; to table is to kill. On the other hand, if the Senate defeats the motion, debate on the amendment may resume; the Senate only has determined that it is not prepared at that time to reject the amendment. Thus, a tabling motion can be used to stop debate even if there still are Senators wishing to speak, but only by defeating the amendment at issue. Although the effect of the motion is essentially negative, it frequently is a test vote on Senate support for an amendment. If the motion fails, the Senate may agree to the amendment shortly thereafter. But this is a reflection of political reality, not a requirement of Senate rules or precedents.

Filibusters and Cloture

The dearth of debate limitations in Senate rules creates the possibility of filibusters. Individual Senators or minority groups of Senators who adamantly oppose a bill or amendment may speak against it at great length, in the hope of changing their colleagues' minds, winning support for amendments that address their objections, or convincing the Senate to withdraw the bill or amendment from further consideration on the floor. Opposing Senators also can delay final floor action by offering numerous amendments and motions, insisting that amendments be read in full, demanding roll call votes on amendments and motions, and by using a variety of other devices.

The only formal procedure that Senate rules provide for breaking filibusters is to invoke cloture under the provisions of paragraph 2 of Rule XXII. Under the rules however, cloture cannot be voted until two days after it is proposed, and a simple majority of the Senate is insufficient to invoke cloture.

Cloture requires the support of three-fifths of the Senators duly chosen and sworn, or a minimum of 60 votes if there are no vacancies (unless the matter being considered changes the standing rules, in which case cloture requires a vote of two-thirds of the Senators present and voting). For this reason alone, cloture can be difficult to invoke and almost always requires some bipartisan support. In addition, some Senators are reluctant to vote for cloture, even if they support the legislation being jeopardized by the filibuster, precisely because the right of extended debate is such an integral element of Senate history and procedure.

Even if the Senate does invoke cloture on a bill (or anything else), the result is not an immediate vote on passing the bill. The cloture rule permits a maximum of thirty additional hours for considering the bill, during which each Senator may speak for one hour. The time consumed by rollcall votes and quorum calls is deducted from the thirty hour total; as a result, each Senator does not have an opportunity to speak for a full hour, although he or she is guaranteed at least ten minutes for debate. Thus, cloture does not stop debate immediately; it only ensures that debate cannot continue indefinitely. Even the thirty hours allowed under cloture is quite a long time for the Senate to devote to any one bill, especially since Senators may not be willing to invoke cloture until the bill already has been debated at considerable length.

Restraint and Delay

Any Senator can filibuster almost any legislative proposal the Senate is considering. The only bills that cannot be filibustered are the relatively few which are considered under provisions of law that limit the time available for debating them. For example, Section 305(b)(1) of the Budget Act of 1974 restricts debate on a budget resolution, "and all amendments thereto and debatable motions and appeals in connection therewith," to not more than fifty hours. If no such provision applies, Senators can prolong the debate indefinitely on any bill or amendment, as well as on many motions, subject only to tabling motions or cloture.

Although there may be many bills to which some Senators may be adamantly opposed, filibusters are not daily events. One reason is that conducting a filibuster is physically demanding, but there are more compelling reasons for self-restraint. If Senators filibustered every bill they opposed, the Senate as an institution would suffer. It could not meet its constitutional responsibilities in a timely fashion and it could not respond effectively to pressing national needs. Public support for the Senate as an institution, and for its members as individuals, would be undermined. Furthermore, all Senators have legislation they want to promote. They appreciate that if they used the filibuster regularly against bills they oppose, other Senators would be likely to do the same, and every Senator's legislative objectives would be jeopardized. In short, Senators resort to filibusters only on matters of the greatest importance to them because this practice serves the long-term interests of the Senate and all Senators alike.

Nonetheless, the right to debate at length remains, and the possibility of filibusters affects much of what happens on the Senate floor. Many of the ways in which the Senate agrees to set aside its standing rules are designed in response to the possibility of filibusters. Simply threatening to filibuster can give Senators great influence over whether the Senate considers a bill, when it considers it, and how it may be amended.

If a majority of Senators support a bill that is being filibustered, they may be able to pass it eventually if they are committed and patient enough—and especially if they are able to invoke cloture. Even if cloture is not invoked, devices such as late-night sessions can strain the endurance and determination of the filibustering Senators. The potency of filibusters does not depend, however, solely on Senators' ability to prolong the debate indefinitely. From the right to debate flows the ability to delay, and the prospect of delay alone can often be sufficient to influence the Senate's agenda and decisions.

The legislative process is laborious and time-consuming, and the time available for Senate floor action each year is limited. Every day devoted to one bill is a day denied for consideration of other legislation, and there are not enough days to act on all the bills that Senators and Senate committees wish to see enacted. Naturally, the time pressures become even greater with the approach of deadlines such as the date for adjournment and the end of the fiscal year. So, for all but the most important bills, even the threat of a filibuster can be a potent weapon. Before a bill reaches the floor or while it is being debated, its supporters often seek ways to accommodate the concerns of opponents, preferring an amended bill that can be passed without protracted debate to the time, effort, and risks involved in confronting a filibuster.

Scheduling Legislative Business

Routine Agenda Setting

One way in which the possibility of extended debate affects the Senate's procedures is in how the Senate determines its legislative agenda—the order in which it decides to consider bills and other business on the floor. When one or more of the Senate's standing committees reports a bill back to the Senate for floor debate and passage, the bill is placed on the Senate's Calendar of Business (under the heading of "General Orders").

The Senate gives its Majority Leader the primary responsibility for deciding the order in which bills on the Calendar should come to the floor for action. The Majority Leader's right to preferential recognition already has been mentioned, as has Senators' willingness to relinquish to him the right to make the motion (provided for in the standing rules) for deciding the order of legislative business—namely, the motion that the Senate proceed to the consideration of a particular bill.

Whenever possible, however, bills reach the Senate floor not by motion but by unanimous consent. The motion to proceed to a bill usually is debatable and, therefore, subject to a filibuster. Even before the bill can reach the floor (and perhaps face a filibuster), there may be extended debate on the question of whether or not the Senate should even consider the bill at all.

It is to avoid this possibility that the Majority Leader attempts to get all Senators to agree by unanimous consent to take up the bill he wishes to have debated. If Senators withhold their consent, they are implicitly threatening extended debate on the question of considering the bill. Senators may do so because they oppose that bill or because they wish to delay consideration of one measure in the hope of influencing the fate of some other, possibly unrelated, measure. Senators can even place a "hold" on a bill, by which they ask their party's floor leader to object on their behalf to any unanimous consent request to consider the bill, at least until they have been consulted. The practice of holds is not recognized in Senate rules or precedents (though a recent change in public law has established guidelines for their use); more often than not, however, the Majority Leader will not even make such a unanimous consent request if there is a hold on a bill.

In attempting to devise a schedule for the Senate floor, the Majority Leader seeks to promote the legislative program of his party (and perhaps the President) as he also tries to ensure that the Senate considers necessary legislation in a timely fashion.

When the Majority Leader is confronted with two bills, one of which can be brought up by unanimous consent and the other of which cannot, he is naturally inclined to ask the Senate to take up the bill that can be considered without objection. Time is limited, and the Majority Leader is concerned to use that time with reasonable efficiency. Some bills, of course, are too important to be delayed only because some Senators object to considering them. Most are not, however, especially if the objections can be met through negotiation and compromise. Thus, the possibility of extended debate affects decisions for scheduling legislation in two ways: by discouraging the Majority Leader and the Senate from attempting to take up bills to which some Senators object, and by encouraging negotiations over substantive changes in the bills in order to meet these objections.

The right of Senators to debate at length is not the only way in which they can influence the Senate's legislative agenda. The standing rules of the Senate give its members at least two other opportunities to influence the matters that reach the Senate floor for debate and decision. One opportunity affects the prerogatives of Senate committees; the other affects the amendments that Senators may propose on the floor.

Committee Referral and Rule XIV

The Senate's standing committees play an essential part in the legislative process, as they select the small percentage of the bills introduced each Congress which, in their judgment, deserve the attention of the Senate as a whole, and as they recommend amendments to these bills based on their expert knowledge and experience. Most bills are routinely referred to the committee with appropriate jurisdiction as soon as they are introduced. However, if a Senator plans to introduce a bill and believes that the committee to which it would be referred will be unsympathetic, Rule XIV, paragraph 4, permits the Senator to bypass the standing committee system altogether and have the bill placed directly on the Calendar of Business, with exactly the same formal status the bill would have if it had been the subject of extensive hearings and exhaustive mark-up meetings in committee.

By the same token, if a committee fails to act on a bill that was referred to it, while this may mean the bill will die for lack of action, the proposal it embodies may not. The Senator sponsoring the bill may introduce a new bill with exactly the same provisions as the first, and have the second bill placed directly on the Calendar. In either event, the committee that has been circumvented may oppose bringing the bill from the Calendar to the floor by unanimous consent or by motion, but now the fate of the bill can be decided by the Senate as a whole, not only by one of its committees. Senators generally view this use of Rule XIV as a last resort, both because it undermines the committee system as a whole and because they do not wish to encourage a practice that can be used against their own committees. In recent practice, the Majority Leader sometimes also uses this method to put a measure directly on the Calendar—often to expedite consideration of a complicated or high-profile bill that has been drafted outside of the committee process.

Non-Germane Amendments

An even more important opportunity for individual Senators is a result of the absence in the standing rules of any general requirement that the amendments offered by Senators on the floor must be germane or relevant to the bill being considered. The rules impose a germaneness requirement only on amendments to general appropriations and budget measures and to matters being considered under cloture, and various statutes impose such a requirement on a limited number of other bills. (The Senate generally interprets germaneness strictly, to preclude amendments that expand the scope of a bill or introduce a specific additional topic.) In all other cases, Senators are free to propose whatever amendments they choose on whatever subjects to whatever bill the Senate happens to be considering.

The right to offer non-germane amendments is extraordinarily important because it permits Senators to present issues to the Senate for debate and decision, without regard to the judgments of the Senate's committees or the scheduling decisions and preferences of its Majority Leader. Again consider the position of a Senator whose bill is not being acted on by the committee to which it was referred. Instead of introducing an identical bill and having it placed directly on the

Calendar, he or she has a second and usually more attractive option: to offer the text of the bill as a floor amendment to another bill that has reached the floor and that can serve as a useful legislative "vehicle."

The existence of this opportunity can make it extremely difficult to anticipate what will happen to a bill when it reaches the floor and how much of the Senate's time it will consume. The party leaders and the floor managers of the bill may know what amendments on the subject of the bill will be offered, but they cannot be certain that there will be no other, perhaps far more controversial, non-germane amendments. In fact, it is not unusual for one or more non-germane amendments to occupy far more of the Senate's attention than the subject the bill itself addresses.

Time Agreements

The Nature of Time Agreements

Just as the right of extended debate encourages Senate committee and party leaders to bring up bills for consideration by unanimous consent, the right to debate combined with the right to offer non-germane amendments encourages the same leaders to seek unanimous consent agreements limiting or foreclosing the exercise of these rights while a bill is being considered. Without such an agreement, the bill could be debated for as long as Senators wish—as could each amendment, whether germane or not—unless the Senate votes to table it. These are the essential conditions under which the Senate considers a bill if it adheres to its standing rules.

It is precisely to avoid these conditions that the Senate often debates, amends, and passes bills under very different sets of parliamentary ground rules—ground rules that are far more restrictive but that require unanimous consent to be imposed. One of the frequent purposes of these unanimous consent agreements is to limit the time available for debate, and thereby ensure that there will be no filibuster. Complex unanimous consent agreements of this special kind are frequently called "time agreements."

In addition, before taking up a bill, or after the Senate has begun debating it, Senators often reach unanimous consent agreements to govern consideration of individual amendments that have been or will be offered. Less often today, the Senate reaches an encompassing agreement, limiting debate on a bill and all amendments to it, before or at the time the bill is called up for floor action.

The following example illustrates such a comprehensive time agreement "in the usual form":

> *Ordered*, That when the Senate proceeds to the consideration of S. 1651 (Order No. 636), the Veterans' Dioxin and Radiation Exposure Compensation Standards Act, debate on any amendment in the first degree shall be limited to 1 hour, to be equally divided and controlled by the mover of such and the manager of the bill, and debate on any amendment in the second degree, debatable motion, appeal, or point of order which is submitted or on which the Chair entertains debate shall be limited to 30 minutes, to be equally divided and controlled by the mover of such and the manager of the bill: *Provided*, That in the event the manager of the bill is in favor of any such amendment or motion, the time in opposition thereto shall be controlled by the Minority Leader or his designee; *Provided Further*, That no amendment that is not germane to the provisions of the said bill shall be received.

Ordered Further, That on the question of final passage of the said bill, debate shall be limited to 4 hours, to be equally divided and controlled by the Majority Leader and the Minority Leader, or their designees: *Provided*, That the said Senators, or either of them, may, from the time under their control on the passage of the said bill, allot additional time to any Senator during the consideration of any amendment, debatable motion, appeal, or point of order.

Before discussing the effect of this agreement, some of its terms require definition. A first degree amendment is an amendment that proposes to change or add to the text of the bill, while a second degree amendment proposes to change or replace the text of a first degree amendment that has been proposed but not yet voted on. The manager of the bill usually is the chair of the standing committee that had considered and reported it (although it may be the chair of one of the committee's subcommittees instead). Finally, debate on the question of final passage is debate on the bill as a whole, not on any amendment or motion affecting the bill; this debate may occur throughout the time the Senate considers the bill.

The two essential features of this and comparable time agreements are (1) a prohibition against non-germane amendments, and (2) strict limitations on the time available for debating the bill and every question that may arise during its consideration. Under the terms of this agreement, for example, the Senate as a whole may debate each first degree amendment for no more than one hour. Moreover, only a very few Senators have a right to speak during that hour; other Senators may speak only if one of their colleagues agrees to yield them part of the time that he or she controls. Senators still may offer as many amendments as they wish, but they have lost their valued right of unlimited debate. There are also even more stringent time limits for debate on second degree amendments and other questions, as well as a limit on time for debating the bill itself.

The differences between considering a bill under the terms of the Senate's standing rules and considering it under this kind of time agreement are so great and so fundamental that they bear repeating. Under the standing rules, Senators may offer whatever non-germane amendments they want; under the time agreement, no non-germane amendments at all are permitted. Under the standing rules, Senators may debate the bill, each amendment, and a variety of other questions for as long as they want; under the time agreement, on each question, only two Senators may speak as a matter of right, and all time for debate is severely limited. The differences could hardly be more dramatic. It must be emphasized, however, that time agreements are unanimous consent agreements. They cannot be imposed on the Senate by any vote of the Senate; they require the concurrence or acquiescence of each and every Senator.

Negotiating Time Agreements

Negotiating these complex unanimous consent agreements can be a difficult and time-consuming process, the responsibility for which falls primarily on the Majority and Minority Leaders and the leaders of the committee that reported the bill at issue. They consult interested Senators, but it would be impractical to consult every Senator about every bill scheduled for floor action. For this reason, individual Senators and their staffs take the initiative to protect their own interests by advising the leaders of their preferences and intentions. Negotiations sometimes take place on the floor and on the public record, but at least the preliminary discussions and consultations usually occur in meetings during quorum calls or off the floor.

Senators prefer to expedite the conduct of legislative business whenever possible, and so normally cooperate in reaching time agreements. However, when Senators have special concerns—for instance, when they are intent on offering particular amendments or guaranteeing themselves ample time for debate—their interests must be accommodated. Any Senator who is dissatisfied with the terms of a proposed time agreement has only to object when it is propounded on the floor; so long as any one Senator objects, the standing rules remain in force with all the rights and opportunities they provide. As a result, time agreements may include exceptions to their general provisions in order to satisfy individual Senators. For example, a comprehensive agreement that generally limits debate on each first degree amendment to an hour and prohibits non-germane amendments may identify one or more specific amendments that are exempted from the germaneness requirement, and also may provide different amounts of time for debating them.

In these ways, time agreements can be less restrictive than the one quoted earlier. There may be no agreement at all if one or more Senators decide to fully preserve their rights to debate and offer amendments. On other occasions, however, agreements have been even more restrictive— for example, by prohibiting all amendments to a bill except for a few that are identified specifically in the agreement itself (and perhaps also prohibiting amendments to those amendments). If the Senate does accept a unanimous consent agreement, whatever its terms, it may be changed at a later time only by unanimous consent.

Other Unanimous Consent Agreements

In current practice, the Senate usually begins consideration of most bills without first having reached a time limitation agreement. In some cases, the floor managers expect few amendments and relatively little debate, making an elaborate agreement unnecessary. In other cases, the Majority Leader and committee chairman seek an agreement unsuccessfully, but proceed with the bill anyway because of its timeliness and importance. After the Senate has debated such a bill and controversial amendments for many hours or even days, the leaders often renew their attempts to reach an overall agreement limiting debate on each remaining amendment or setting a time for the Senate to vote on passage of the bill.

In the absence of a time agreement covering all amendments and other questions, the Majority Leader and the majority floor manager often try to arrange unanimous consent agreements for more limited purposes while the Senate is debating a bill. During consideration of a controversial amendment, either Senator may propose to limit—by unanimous consent—further debate on it. Senators also may agree to time limits on individual amendments before offering them. By unanimous consent, the Senate may set aside one amendment temporarily in order to consider another one. Other agreements may define the order in which Senators will offer their amendments, postpone roll call votes until a later time that is more convenient for Senators, or even set a super-majority threshold for the adoption of a particular amendment.

These examples only begin to illustrate the many ways in which the Senate relies every day on unanimous consent arrangements. From routine requests to end a quorum call or waive the reading of an amendment to extremely elaborate and complicated procedural "treaties," the Senate depends on unanimous consent requests and the willingness of Senators to agree to them.

The Daily Order of Business

The extent to which the Senate uses unanimous consent arrangements to supplement or supplant operation of its standing rules makes it difficult to predict with confidence what will actually take place on the Senate floor each day. This report already has mentioned some of the problems that can arise in scheduling legislation and in anticipating the time that will be consumed (and the amendments that Senators will offer) during consideration of each bill. In addition, the other proceedings that occur each day also depend on whether the Senate decides to operate under or outside of its rules.

The time at which the Senate convenes each day is set by a resolution the Senate adopts at the beginning of each Congress, but that time is often changed from day to day by unanimous consent—at the request of the Majority Leader—to suit changing circumstances. When the Senate does convene, and after the opening prayer and the Pledge of Allegiance, a brief period of "leader time" is set aside for the Majority Leader and for the Minority Leader, under a standing order also established at the beginning of the Congress. During this time, the two party leaders may discuss the legislative schedule as well as their views on policy issues, and they also may conduct non-controversial business by unanimous consent.

What happens thereafter depends on whether the Senate is beginning a new legislative day. A legislative day begins when the Senate convenes after an adjournment, and it continues until the next adjournment. When the Senate recesses at the end of a day, as it often does, a legislative day continues for two or more calendar days. Standing Rules VII and VIII prescribe what the Senate should do at the beginning of each new legislative day, and one of the reasons the Senate frequently recesses from day to day is to set aside the requirements imposed by these rules.

Under the two standing rules, the first two hours of session on each new legislative day are called the Morning Hour. They are a period for conducting routine business at a predictable time each day that does not interfere with the consideration of major legislation. The Morning Hour begins with the transaction of "morning business," which includes the introduction of bills and joint resolutions and the submission of Senate and concurrent resolutions and committee reports. During the remainder of the Morning Hour, the Senate can act on bills on the Calendar of Business, and may even vote to consider them by non-debatable motions to proceed. At the end of the Morning Hour, the Senate resumes consideration of the unfinished business—whatever bill, if any, was the pending business when the Senate adjourned.

In practice, the Senate very often recesses at the end of the day, so there is no Morning Hour on the following day of session. Instead, the Majority Leader usually arranges by unanimous consent that "a period for transacting routine morning business" follow "leader time." Senators make brief statements on whatever subjects they like during this period, the length of which can change from day to day, depending on the legislative schedule. Also by unanimous consent, there may be other periods for transacting morning business during the course of the day when time is available and Senators wish to speak on subjects unrelated to the pending bill.

After the Morning Hour or the period for transacting routine morning business, the Senate normally resumes consideration of the bill that is either the unfinished business (if the Senate had adjourned on the preceding day) or the pending business (if the Senate had recessed instead). However, this bill may be set aside—temporarily or indefinitely—in favor of other legislative or executive business if the Senate agrees to motions or unanimous consent requests made for that purpose by the Majority Leader. Before the end of the day, the Majority Leader also makes arrangements for the following day—establishing a meeting time by unanimous consent and commenting on the expected legislative program.

The Amending Process

The amending process is at the heart of the Senate's floor deliberations. If the Senate reaches a final vote on passing or defeating a bill, the bill is very likely to pass. It is through the amending process that Senators have an opportunity to influence the content of the bill before the vote on final passage occurs; this is an especially important opportunity for Senators who do not serve on the committee that marked up the bill and reported it.

When a bill is called up for floor consideration, opening statements usually are made by the two floor managers—the chairman and ranking minority member of the committee (or sometimes the subcommittee) that reported the bill—and often by other Senators as well. These statements lay the groundwork for the debate that follows, describing the purposes and provisions of the bill, the state of current law and the developments that make new legislation desirable or necessary, and the major points of controversy. These opening statements are a matter of custom and practice, however; the bill is open to amendment as soon as it is before the Senate.

The first amendments to be considered are those recommended by the committee reporting the bill, and so designated in the printed version of the bill "as reported." As each committee amendment is being debated, Senators may propose amendments to it and to the part of the bill the committee amendment would change. The Senate votes on any such amendments before it votes on the committee amendment itself. Thereafter, Senators may offer amendments in any order to any part of the bill that has not already been amended. The order in which amendments are offered depends largely on the convenience of the Senators proposing them, not on requirements imposed by standing rules or precedents. As a general rule, a Senator cannot propose an amendment to a bill while first degree (and possibly second degree) amendments to the bill are pending. It is not unusual, however, for the Senate to agree by unanimous consent to lay aside pending amendments temporarily in order to consider another amendment that a Senator wishes to offer at that time.

After a Senator offers an amendment, it must be read unless the Senate dispenses with the reading by unanimous consent. The Senate then debates the amendment and may dispose of it either by voting "up or down" on the amendment itself or by voting to table it. However, the amending process can become far more complicated. Bills are amendable in two degrees, so before the Senate votes on a first degree amendment, it is subject to second degree amendments that propose to change its text. After voting on any second degree amendments, the Senate votes on the first degree amendment as it may have been amended. Third degree amendments—amendments to second degree amendments—are not in order.

Additional complications are possible, depending on whether the first degree amendment proposes: (1) to insert additional language in the bill without altering anything already in the bill; (2) to strike out language from the bill without inserting anything in its place; (3) to strike out language from the bill and insert different language instead; or (4) to strike out the entire text of the bill (everything after the enacting or resolving clause at the very beginning of the measure) and replace it with a different text. In the case of a motion to insert, for example, Senators can offer as many as three first and second degree amendments before the Senate votes on any of them; in the case of an amendment that is a complete substitute for the text of the bill, Senators can propose six or more first and second degree amendments to the substitute and to the original text of the bill before any votes must occur.

These possibilities depend on several principles of precedence among amendments—principles governing the amendments that may be offered while other amendments are pending and also governing the order in which the Senate votes on the amendments that have been offered. Complicated amendment situations do not arise very often, but they are most likely to occur when the policy and political stakes are high.

Once a Senator has offered an amendment, the conditions for debating it depend on whether or not there is a time limitation for considering that particular amendment or all amendments to the bill. If there is no such limitation, each Senator may debate the amendment for as long as he or she pleases, subject only to the rule limiting each Senator to two speeches on a question during each legislative day. However, any Senator who has been recognized may move to table the amendment, and that motion is not debatable. If there is a time limitation, the time provided is both a minimum and a maximum. Senators may not make motions or points of order, propose other amendments, or move to table, until all the time for debating the amendment has been used or until all remaining time has been yielded back. After the time has expired, on the other hand, the amendment can be debated further only by unanimous consent or if the Senators controlling time for debating the bill as a whole choose to yield part of that time.

A number of general principles govern the amending process. For example, an amendment that has been defeated may not be offered again without substantive change. An amendment should not make changes in two or more different places in the bill, nor may it propose only to amend a part of the bill that already has been amended. If an amendment consists of two or more parts that could each stand as separate and independent propositions, any Senator may demand that the amendment be divided and each division treated as if it were a separate amendment (except that a motion to strike out and insert is not divisible). Generally speaking, Senators may not propose amendments to their own amendments, but they can modify or withdraw their amendments instead. If the Senate takes some "action" on an amendment (such as ordering the yeas and nays on it), the Senator who offered the amendment loses his right to modify it, but now gains the right to offer an amendment to his or her own amendment.

As mentioned before, floor amendments to most bills need not be germane unless a germaneness requirement is part of the unanimous consent agreement under which a particular bill is being considered. Alternatively, the Senate may, by unanimous consent, require that amendments to a bill be relevant to it; relevancy is a somewhat less restrictive standard that seeks to ensure that unrelated issues will not be raised in the form of amendments.

The amending process continues until Senators have no other amendments they wish to offer or until the entire bill has been changed by amendments. At either point, the Senate orders the bill engrossed and read a third time—a formal stage that precludes further amendments—and then votes on final passage.

Quorum Calls and Rollcall Votes

The Constitution requires that a quorum—that is, a majority of all Senators—be present to conduct business on the floor. Even though Senators have many responsibilities that frequently keep them from the floor, the Senate presumes that a quorum is present unless a quorum call demonstrates that it is not.

A Senator who has been recognized may suggest the absence of a quorum at almost any time; a clerk then begins to call the roll of Senators. Senators may not debate or conduct business while a quorum call is in progress. If a majority of Senators do not appear and respond to their names, the Senate can only adjourn or recess, or attempt to secure the attendance of additional Senators. However, quorum calls usually are ended by unanimous consent before the clerk completes the call of the roll and the absence of a quorum is demonstrated. The reason is that most quorum calls are not really intended to determine if a quorum is present.

The purpose of a quorum call usually is to suspend floor activity temporarily. If a Senator is coming to the floor to speak, a colleague may suggest the absence of a quorum until the expected Senator arrives. If the Senate finds itself confronted with unexpected procedural complications, if the Majority Leader needs to meet with several Senators on the floor about a possible unanimous consent agreement, or if the floor manager of a bill wants to discuss a compromise alternative to an amendment another Senator has offered—for any of these or many other reasons—a Senator may suggest the absence of a quorum to permit time for informal consultations. The time consumed by many quorum calls permits intensive and productive discussions that would be far more difficult to hold under the rules of formal Senate debate.

The Constitution also provides that one-fifth of the Senators on the floor (assuming that a quorum is present) can demand a rollcall vote. Since the smallest possible quorum is 51 Senators, the support of at least 11 Senators is required to order a rollcall vote. A Senator who has been recognized can ask for "the yeas and nays" at any time that the Senate is considering a motion, amendment, bill, or other question. Agreement to this request does not terminate debate. Instead, if a rollcall is ordered, that is how the Senate will vote on the question whenever the time for the vote arrives. Thus, the Senate may order a rollcall vote on an amendment as soon as it is offered, but the vote itself may not take place for several hours or more, when Senators no longer wish to debate the amendment.

The alternative to a rollcall vote usually is a voice vote in which the Senators favoring the bill or amendment (or whatever question is to be decided) vote "aye" in unison, followed by those voting "no." Although a voice vote does not create a public record of how each Senator voted, it is an equally valid and conclusive way for the Senate to reach a decision.

Sources of Additional Information

The standing rules of the Senate are published periodically in a separate Senate document and in the *Senate Manual*, which contains other related documents as well. The most recent compilation of the Senate's precedents is the *Riddick's Senate Procedure*, named in honor of Floyd M. Riddick, Parliamentarian Emeritus of the Senate (Senate Document No. 101-28; 101st Congress, second session).

The parliamentarian and his assistants welcome inquiries about Senate procedures, and offer expert assistance compatible with their other responsibilities.

The Congressional Research Service has prepared a variety of other reports on the Senate and its procedures, including CRS Report RL30788, *Parliamentary Reference Sources: Senate*, by

Megan Suzanne Lynch and Richard S. Beth, CRS Report 98-311, *Senate Rules Affecting Committees*, by Betsy Palmer, CRS Report RL30360, *Filibusters and Cloture in the Senate*, by Richard S. Beth and Stanley Bach, CRS Report 98-853, *The Amending Process in the Senate*, by Betsy Palmer, CRS Report 98-306, *Points of Order, Rulings, and Appeals in the Senate*, by Valerie Heitshusen, and CRS Report 96-708, *Conference Committee and Related Procedures: An Introduction*, and CRS Report 98-696, *Resolving Legislative Differences in Congress: Conference Committees and Amendments Between the Houses*, both by Elizabeth Rybicki.

The staff of CRS are available to consult with individual Senators and staff; they also present periodic staff seminars and institutes on legislative procedures.

Author Contact Information

Valerie Heitshusen
Analyst on the Congress and Legislative Process
vheitshusen@crs.loc.gov, 7-8635

Acknowledgments

This report was originally written by Stanley Bach, former senior specialist in the Legislative Process at CRS. The report has been updated by the listed author, who is available to respond to inquiries on the subject.

Procedural Distinctions between the House and the Committee of the Whole

Judy Schneider
Specialist on the Congress

May 7, 2008

Congressional Research Service

7-5700

www.crs.gov

98-143

CRS Report for Congress ——————————————

Prepared for Members and Committees of Congress

The Committee of the Whole House on the State of the Union, generally referred to as the Committee of the Whole, is a parliamentary device provided for under House rules to allow the House to operate as a committee on which every Member of the House serves. Through this practice, dating to colonial and English antecedents, the House is able to realize a procedural benefit from having established two somewhat different sets of rules to govern consideration of various types of measures. Measures placed on the Union Calendar must be considered in the Committee of the Whole before the House officially completes action on them, although the committee may also be used to consider other major bills as well.

Some of the chief distinctions between consideration in the House operating as the House and consideration in Committee of the Whole are shown in the table presented below. See http://www.crs.gov/products/guides/guidehome.shtml for more information on legislative process.

In most cases, the House resolves into the Committee of the Whole under authority granted to the Speaker in a special rule in accordance with House Rule XVIII, clause 2(b). Rule XVIII, clause 2 (a) also provides that for certain privileged measures, such as general appropriation bills, the majority floor manager may move that the House resolve into Committee of the Whole to consider the measure. The Committee of the Whole is used to facilitate consideration of legislation because its procedural differences may be used to permit more members to offer amendments and participate in the debate on a measure than is normally possible when a measure is considered in the House under the hour rule. When the Committee of the Whole finishes its consideration of a measure, it rises and reports back to the House, recommending that the bill be passed by the House with whatever amendments the committee has approved. For more on the Committee of the Whole, see CRS Report RS20147, *Committee of the Whole: An Introduction.*

Table 1. Procedural Distinctions between the House and Committee of the Whole

House	Committee of the Whole
Established by the Constitution	Established anew by the House for consideration of each specific measure
Mace raised	Mace lowered
Presided over by the Speaker of the House	Presided over by a chairman of the Committee of the Whole (appointed by the Speaker)
Operates under the one-hour rule with no separate procedure for consideration of amendments	Typically operates under the terms of a special rule with amendments considered under the five-minute rule
Quorum established under the Constitution as a majority of Members (218 with no vacancies)	Quorum established by House rules as 100 Members
1/5 of the Members present (44 with a minimum quorum) considered a sufficient second to trigger a recorded vote	25 Members considered a sufficient second to trigger a recorded vote
Motion for the previous question is in order	Motion for the previous question is not in order, although a motion to limit or end debate may be offered
Motion to recommit is in order	Motion to recommit is not in order
Motion to reconsider is in order	Motion to reconsider is not in order
Routine business of the House is in order	Routine business of the House is not in order

Congressional Research Service

Congressional Research Service

Committee of the Whole: Stages of Action on Measures

Richard S. Beth
Specialist on the Congress and Legislative Process

December 8, 2006

Congressional Research Service

7-5700

www.crs.gov

98-564

CRS Report for Congress ─────────────
Prepared for Members and Committees of Congress

The House gives initial floor consideration to most major legislation in Committee of the Whole, a parliamentary device that is technically a committee of the House to which all Members belong. This report describes seven chief stages that occur in considering a measure under this procedure: resolving into committee, general debate, amendment under the five-minute rule, reporting to the House, House vote on amendments, motion to recommit, and final passage. For more information on legislative process, see http://www.crs.gov/products/guides/guidehome.shtml.

House Rule XVIII prescribes procedures in Committee of the Whole, but these may be modified by a rule for considering a specific measure, reported by the Committee on Rules. Clause 3 of the Rule requires that revenue, appropriation, and authorization measures be considered initially in Committee of the Whole. Other measures may be considered there pursuant to a rule.

Resolving into Committee of the Whole

The House usually takes up a measure in Committee of the Whole when the Speaker, acting pursuant to a rule for consideration, declares the House resolved into Committee of the Whole for the purpose (Rule XVIII, clause 2(b)). For certain privileged measures, such as general appropriation bills, the majority floor manager may instead move that the House resolve into Committee of the Whole to consider the measure (clause 2(a)). In either case, the Speaker then leaves the chair and appoints a chair of the Committee of the Whole (clause 1(a)), usually a senior Member of the majority party not serving on a committee that handled the measure.

General Debate

A rule for considering a measure normally specifies a time limit for general debate, often one hour, equally divided and controlled by majority and minority floor managers. Otherwise, the majority manager obtains unanimous consent for similar arrangements before the House resolves into committee. If a measure is reported from several committees, a pair of managers from each usually controls a separate period for general debate. Each manager yields specified amounts of time to Members, usually in his or her own party, whom the chair then recognizes for debate. General debate ends when this time is consumed or the managers yield it back.

Amendment Under the Five-Minute Rule

After general debate, the measure normally is considered for amendment by section (by paragraph, for appropriation bills). The rule governing consideration normally provides that each section, when reached, be considered as read. Pursuant to the rule, or by unanimous consent, the measure may instead be considered for amendment by title, or may be considered as read and open to amendment at any point. Each amendment must be offered while the part of the measure it would amend is pending for amendment.

When an amendment is offered, its reading is often dispensed with by unanimous consent. Any point of order against it must be made or reserved before debate begins. The sponsor of the amendment is entitled to open the debate. A Member (often the majority manager) may then be recognized in opposition. Others may speak by offering a *pro forma* amendment to "strike the last word" (or the "requisite number of words"). Each speaker on an amendment may be recognized once, for five minutes (which may be extended by unanimous consent). Time for debate on an amendment or section may be limited by a motion (or unanimous consent) to close debate. Even after debate is closed, any amendment printed in advance in the *Record* may be debated for five minutes on each side (Rule XVIII, clauses 5, 8).

Committee of the Whole Reports

After all portions of a measure have been considered for amendment, the Committee of the Whole rises and reports the measure (with any adopted amendments) back to the House. It does so pursuant to either the rule for consideration or a motion offered by the majority manager. The Speaker then returns to the chair, and the chair of the Committee of the Whole reports the measure and any amendments recommended by Committee of the Whole.

House Vote on Amendments

Because it is technically a committee, the Committee of the Whole can only recommend amendments. When it reports a measure, the previous question is routinely ordered, either automatically by the terms of the rule, or by unanimous consent, thereby precluding the offering of any further amendment in the House. The chair then puts the amendments recommended by Committee of the Whole to a voice vote *en gros*. Any Member, however, may obtain a separate vote on any of these amendments. By this means, the House may reject an amendment adopted in Committee of the Whole. It may not vote to adopt amendments defeated in Committee of the Whole, however, for these are not reported back to the House.

Motion to Recommit

Next, the House routinely orders the measure engrossed (that is, printed as amended) and read a final time (by title). An opponent then has preference, usually exercised by the minority manager or floor leader, to move to recommit the measure (Rule XIX, clause 2(b)). No rule governing consideration may prevent such a motion by the minority leader (Rule XIII, clause 6(c)). A motion to recommit with instructions that the committee re-report forthwith with specified amendments is debatable for 10 minutes or, upon demand of the majority floor manager, for one hour. In the rare case when the House adopts this motion, the committee chairman immediately reports the measure back to the House with the amendments specified, on which the House then votes.

Vote on Final Passage

As on other matters, the Speaker initially puts the question on final passage to a voice vote, but a record vote may take place if requested from the floor with a sufficient second. After the vote, the chair routinely states that a motion to reconsider is tabled without objection. This action forecloses any later attempt to have the House reverse its decision.

House Committee Markup: Vehicle for Consideration and Amendment

Judy Schneider
Specialist on the Congress

July 17, 2008

Congressional Research Service
7-5700
www.crs.gov
98-188

CRS Report for Congress
Prepared for Members and Committees of Congress

Summary

The markup begins with the chair calling up a particular measure for consideration by the committee. The next action depends on the nature of the "markup vehicle" (i.e., the text that the chair intends for the committee to amend and report), which may be different from the measure laid before the panel for consideration. The vehicle can come before the committee in several different forms, each of which has its own procedural and political consequences.

The chair may lay before the committee either a bill that has been previously introduced and referred, or the text of a draft measure that has not been formally introduced. In each case, the text laid before the committee is itself the markup vehicle, but, in the second case, at the end of the markup process, the text must be incorporated or converted into a measure for reporting to the House. Alternatively, the markup vehicle may be placed before the committee as an amendment in the nature of a substitute for the bill or text initially called up. For more information on legislative process, see http://www.crs.gov/products/guides/guidehome.shtml.

Contents

Contacts

The markup begins with the chair calling up a particular measure for consideration by the committee. The next action depends on the nature of the "markup vehicle" (i.e., the text that the chair intends for the committee to amend and report), which may be different from the measure laid before the panel for consideration. The vehicle can come before the committee in several different forms, each of which has its own procedural and political consequences.

The chair may lay before the committee either a bill that has been previously introduced and referred, or the text of a draft measure that has not been formally introduced. In each case, the text laid before the committee is itself the markup vehicle, but, in the second case, at the end of the markup process, the text must be incorporated or converted into a measure for reporting to the House. Alternatively, the markup vehicle may be placed before the committee as an amendment in the nature of a substitute for the bill or text initially called up. For more information on legislative process, see http://www.crs.gov/products/guides/guidehome.shtml.

Introduced Measure

Using an introduced measure as both the bill for consideration and the vehicle requires no special motion or unanimous consent. The chair notifies committee members that the vehicle for the markup will be the introduced bill, identifying the bill number and, often, the original sponsor. If this option is selected, the bill is normally read for amendment by section (unless by unanimous consent the bill is open for amendment at any point), and each section can be amended in two degrees. The measure would then be reported to the House "as amended," if amended, or alternately as a clean bill, incorporating the changes made in markup into a new measure that would be introduced, referred, and reported back to the House without change.

Subcommittee Reported Version/Committee Print

Most measures considered at the full committee have already received prior subcommittee action. When a subcommittee reports its version of a text to the full committee, the product is often printed and referred to as a "committee print." This committee print can then be laid before the committee for consideration and used as the markup vehicle. Most committees in choosing this approach will notify their members of their intention to use the subcommittee reported version. With this approach, the chair will traditionally ask unanimous consent that the committee print "be considered as an original bill for the purpose of amendment," so that the measure will be read for amendment by section (or by unanimous consent for amendment at any point) and will be amendable in two degrees. At the end of the process, this text could either be offered as an amendment in the nature of a substitute to a previously introduced bill or reported as a clean bill.

An alternative is for the subcommittee chairman to offer the subcommittee reported version as an "amendment in the nature of a substitute" for the measure initially laid before the committee. This approach limits amendments and allows the chair the option to terminate the process by moving the previous question on the amendment in the nature of a substitute. That option is not available on measures open for amendment by section until the final section has been read for amendment.

A third approach is for the subcommittee chairman to introduce a new measure in the House reflecting the subcommittee's changes to the earlier measure. This new bill, which would carry the subcommittee chairman's name as sponsor, is referred to committee and then called up for consideration. The committee would use it as the markup vehicle, as a bill as introduced.

Congressional Research Service 1

Staff Draft/Chairman's Mark

Another option is for the full committee to mark up a text that incorporates both changes made in subcommittee markup and additional changes negotiated afterward, yet prior to full committee markup. Members from other subcommittees are often included in these negotiations; the party leadership and other Members may also be consulted. The product resulting from these negotiations is incorporated into a "committee print" and is often referred to as a "staff draft." A variant process occurs when the chairman prepares his own markup document, typically with collaboration only from majority members of the committee. That text is often referred to as a "chairman's mark." These kinds of documents usually are circulated to committee members prior to the markup. At the end of the process, the text would either be converted into an amendment in the nature of a substitute for a previously introduced measure or reported as a clean bill.

Amendment in the Nature of a Substitute

Oftentimes, the chairman prefers to offer an amendment in the nature of a substitute to the measure laid before the committee, usually an introduced bill. Such an amendment need not be distributed in advance, and usually is not provided prior to the markup. The amendment may only be offered at the outset of the amendment process, after the first section of the measure is read and can be amended in only one degree, unless unanimous consent is granted to consider it as "original text." (An amendment in the nature of a substitute may also be offered at the very end of the amendment process, but this is a less common occurrence.) Debate and additional amendments to the amendment in the nature of a substitute can be cut off by moving the previous question. At the reporting stage, the committee can report either the introduced bill with the committee substitute or a clean bill.

House Committee Markup: Reporting

Judy Schneider
Specialist on the Congress

July 17, 2008

Congressional Research Service

7-5700

www.crs.gov

98-267

CRS Report for Congress ————————————————————

Prepared for Members and Committees of Congress

Summary

At the end of the amendment process, the chair normally entertains a motion to report a measure favorably to the House. By House rule, a majority of a committee must be physically present. Once agreed to, a bill is "ordered reported;" it is actually "reported" when the committee report is filed in the House. When the committee orders a bill reported, it is incumbent upon the chair, pursuant to House rule, to report it "promptly" and take all other steps necessary to secure its consideration by the full House.

Reporting reflects the committee's actions in markup. However, the forms in which committees report have procedural consequences on the floor. Discussions of the ramifications of what to report often occur with the leadership prior to the vote on reporting. This report addresses the procedural options committees have regarding the form of reporting, such as what happens to amendments adopted in markup, as well as other considerations at the time of reporting. For more information on legislative process, see http://www.crs.gov/products/guides/guidehome.shtml.

Contents

Contacts

At the end of the amendment process, the chair normally entertains a motion to report a measure favorably to the House. By House rule, a majority of a committee must be physically present. Once agreed to, a bill is "ordered reported;" it is actually "reported" when the committee report is filed in the House. When the committee orders a bill reported, it is incumbent upon the chair, pursuant to House rule, to report it "promptly" and take all other steps necessary to secure its consideration by the full House.

Reporting reflects the committee's actions in markup. However, the forms in which committees report have procedural consequences on the floor. Discussions of the ramifications of what to report often occur with the leadership prior to the vote on reporting. This report addresses the procedural options committees have regarding the form of reporting, such as what happens to amendments adopted in markup, as well as other considerations at the time of reporting. For more information on legislative process, see http://www.crs.gov/products/guides/guidehome.shtml.

Options for Reporting Amendments

- Reporting a bill without amendment means a committee has made no changes to the text of the bill as introduced. This is usually quite rare.

- Reporting a bill with an amendment or amendments shows that a committee is recommending a single amendment, or multiple, so-called "cut and bite" amendments, which could be considered individually or adopted *en bloc* on the floor.

- Reporting a clean bill means that a new bill is introduced, the text of which incorporates amendments that were adopted in markup. This new bill is reintroduced in the House, assigned a new number, and referred back to the committee, which immediately and automatically reports it back to the House. This option is often selected because it protects the committee against procedural problems, such as questions about the germaneness of committee amendments. Clean bills may imply extensive changes during the markup, but that is not always the case.

- Reporting an introduced bill with an amendment in the nature of a substitute reflects recommending a new text developed in the same manner as a clean bill, but reported instead as a full-text substitute for the measure considered.

Options on How to Report

- Reporting favorably means that a majority of a committee is recommending the full House to consider and pass a measure.

- Reporting unfavorably or adversely usually implies that the party leadership believes that a majority on the floor supports a measure even though a majority of a committee does not. However, a bill reported adversely is laid on the table in the House unless the reporting committee or an individual Member requests its reference to a calendar. Adverse reports are rare because committees do not normally report bills without support by a majority of a committee's members.

- Reporting without recommendation generally means that a committee believes legislation should receive floor consideration although the committee could not find a majority opinion on what to report. In this case, the committee report could include a statement that the committee was unable to agree on a recommendation or the committee report could include minority views alone. Reports without recommendation are rare.

Other Reporting Actions and Considerations

- Committees report recommendations by motion. Some committee chairs recognize a senior majority member to make the motion to report, others recognize the ranking minority member, especially in the case of bipartisan support for a bill. Most committees request a recorded vote on the motion to report.

- Members of a committee are entitled under House rules to file supplemental, minority, or additional views in a committee report. The request to file such views is usually made following the vote on a motion to report.

- Many committees allow staff to make "technical and conforming" changes to the measure reported. Some panels grant this authority by unanimous consent, others grant it by motion. The authority is often included in the motion to report.

- Many chairs recognize a senior majority member to make a motion, pursuant to Rule XXII, clause 1, to authorize the chairman to offer such motions as may be necessary in the House to go to conference with the Senate if the measure being reported ultimately passes the House.

- If a markup was contentious, some committee chairs entertain a motion to reconsider the vote and then recognize another member to offer a motion to table the motion to reconsider. Agreeing to the tabling motion precludes future reconsideration of the committee's action.

Author Contact Information

Judy Schneider
Specialist on the Congress
jschneider@crs.loc.gov, 7-8664

Provisions of Special Rules in the House: An Example of a Typical Open Rule

Judy Schneider
Specialist on the Congress

April 15, 2008

Congressional Research Service

7-5700

www.crs.gov

98-334

CRS Report for Congress

Prepared for Members and Committees of Congress

Provisions of Special Rules in the House: An Example of a Typical Open Rule

Summary

This report includes a typical example of a simple open rule that the House Committee on Rules may report to govern House floor action on a bill that is not otherwise privileged for consideration. This resolution has been divided into five parts. See http://www.crs.gov/products/ guides/guidehome.shtml for more information on legislative process.

Congressional Research Service

This report includes a typical example of a simple open rule that the House Committee on Rules may report to govern House floor action on a bill that is not otherwise privileged for consideration. This resolution has been divided into five parts. See http://www.crs.gov/products/guides/guidehome.shtml for more information on legislative process.

The first part of the rule makes the bill in order for floor consideration by authorizing the Speaker to transform the House into the Committee of the Whole to consider that bill. Without this authority, a motion for the same purpose would not be in order; it would not be privileged to interrupt the regular daily order of business on the House floor.

The second part waives a reading of the bill. It also governs general debate on the bill by setting the amount of time for the debate, by dividing control of this time, usually between the chairman and ranking minority member of the committee that reported the bill, and by requiring that all general debate be relevant to the subject of the bill.

The third part merely states that the bill shall be read for amendment and that each Member may speak for five minutes on each amendment. By implication, this part also means that the bill is to be read for amendment one section at a time. Further, as each section is read, Members may offer to it whatever amendments they wish, so long as those amendments satisfy the House's rules and precedents—for example, the requirement that amendments must be germane. This part is what makes this special rule an open rule; it leaves the bill fully open to amendments that otherwise would be in order.

The fourth part provides for the Committee of the Whole, after disposing of the last amendment, to transform itself back into the House, and report the bill to the House with whatever amendments the Committee of the Whole adopted. This provision eliminates the need for the House to vote on a motion to achieve the same result. The Committee of the Whole does not vote on the bill as a whole, and the committee may not actually amend the bill; it only makes recommendations to the House about amendments.

The fifth and final part of the rule expedites final House passage of the bill by precluding almost all debate in the House and all other actions except those necessary for the House to vote on the amendments the Committee of the Whole recommended and to dispose of one motion to recommit the bill to a standing committee. That motion to recommit may include instructions containing a proposed amendment to the bill.

A Typical Open "Rule"
RESOLUTION

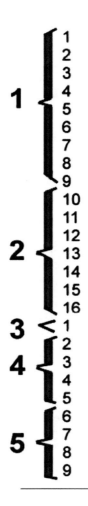

Resolved, That at any time after the adoption of this resolution the Speaker may, pursuant to clause 2(b) of rule XVIII, declare the House resolved into the Committee of the Whole House on the State of the Union for the consideration of the bill (H.R. 2230) to amend the Civil Rights Act of 1957 to extend the life of the Civil Rights Commission, and for other purposes, and the first reading of the bill shall be dispensed with. After general debate, which shall be confined to the bill and shall continue not to exceed one hour, to be equally divided and controlled by the chairman and ranking minority member of the Committee on the Judiciary, the bill shall be read for amendment under the five-minute rule. At the conclusion of the consideration of the bill for amendment, the Committee shall rise and report the bill to the House with such amendments as may have been adopted and the previous question shall be considered as ordered on the bill and amendments thereto to final passage without intervening motion except one motion to recommit.

Author Contact Information

Judy Schneider
Specialist on the Congress
jschneider@crs.loc.gov, 7-8664

Bills and Resolutions: Examples of How Each Kind Is Used

Richard S. Beth
Specialist on the Congress and Legislative Process

November 26, 2008

Congressional Research Service

7-5700

www.crs.gov

98-706

CRS Report for Congress ———————————————————
Prepared for Members and Committees of Congress

Contents

Contacts

W hen Congress seeks to pass a law, it uses a bill or joint resolution, which must be passed by both houses in identical form, then presented to the President for his approval or disapproval. To regulate its own internal affairs, or for other purposes where authority of law is not necessary, Congress uses a concurrent resolution (requiring adoption by both houses) or a simple resolution (requiring action only in the house of origin). More detailed descriptions appear in CRS Report 98-728, *Bills, Resolutions, Nominations, and Treaties: Characteristics, Requirements, and Uses*, by Richard S. Beth.

Congress may use each of the four forms of measure it employs for a variety of purposes. This report identifies the most prevalent uses of each and, as appropriate, gives brief explanations of these uses. For more information on legislative process, see http://www.crs.gov/products/guides/guidehome.shtml.

Bills (H.R. or S.)

- Authorization or reauthorization of federal policies, programs, and activities

- Amendment of existing law (sometimes also by joint resolution)

- Establishment of federal departments and agencies, or alteration of their structure

- Revenue (tax) legislation (originates in House only)

- Regular annual general appropriations

- Supplemental appropriations (sometimes also by joint resolution)

- Reconciliation bill (alters spending authority pursuant to instructions in a congressional budget resolution)

- Private bill (provides specified benefits to named individuals)

Joint Resolutions (S.J.Res. or H.J.Res.)

- "Incidental, inferior, or unusual purposes of legislation" (*House Manual*, section 397)

- Proposed constitutional amendment (requires two-thirds vote in each house)

- Declaration of war

- Continuing resolution (extends appropriations for specified purposes until regular appropriations are enacted)

- Transfer of appropriations

- Adjustment of debt limit

- Abrogation of treaty

- Alteration of date for convening of Congress

- Resolution of disapproval or approval (of specified executive action pursuant to a statute making a contingent delegation of authority)

- Extension of expiration or reporting dates under existing law (e.g., date for President to submit budget)

- Congratulations, condolences, welcomes, thanks, etc. (also by simple or concurrent resolution)

Concurrent Resolutions (S.Con.Res. or H.Con.Res.)

- Congressional budget resolution (sets targets for spending and revenue, procedurally enforceable against subsequent legislation; may set instructions to committees for reconciliation bill)

- Adjournment *sine die*

- Recess of either or both houses of more than three days

- Providing for a joint session of Congress

- Creation of a joint committee

- Correction of conference reports or enrolled bills

- Request for return of measures presented to the President

- "Sense of Congress" resolution (expresses "fact, principles, opinions, and purposes of the two houses," *House Manual*, section 396. "Sense of Congress" provisions may also appear in lawmaking measures)

Simple Resolutions (H.Res. or S.Res.)

- Adoption or amendment of chamber rules

- Special rule (for considering a measure) or other "order of business resolution" (House)

- Establishment of a standing order (principally Senate)

- Privileges of the House resolution (principally House; to secure a chamber's rights, safety, dignity, or integrity of proceedings, House Rule IX);

- "Blue slip resolution" (House; returns a Senate tax measure as violating House privilege to originate revenue measures)

- Personal privilege of individual Member

- Disposition of contest to a Member's election

- Expulsion of a Member (requires two-thirds vote)

- Censure or other discipline of a Member

- Citation for contempt of Congress

- Authorization of response to subpoena by Members or employees

- Resolution of ratification (advice and consent to treaty; Senate)

- Election of committee members or chamber officers

- Committee funding

- Expenditures from chamber's contingent fund (e.g., printing House and Senate documents, also by concurrent resolution)

- Creation of a special or select committee (e.g., investigating committee)

- Resolution of inquiry (requests factual information from executive branch; principally House)

- Providing notifications to other house, President, etc.

- Request for other house to return a measure (for technical corrections)

- Discharge of committee from a measure, nomination, or treaty (Senate)

- Instructions to conferees already appointed (Senate)

- Commemorative periods (formerly by joint resolution)

- "Sense of the Senate" or "sense of the House" resolution (expresses fact, principles, opinions, or purposes of one house, *House Manual*, section 395; such provisions may also appear in lawmaking measures)

Author Contact Information

Richard S. Beth
Specialist on the Congress and Legislative Process
rbeth@crs.loc.gov, 7-8667

Floor Consideration of Conference Reports in the House

James V. Saturno
Specialist on the Congress and Legislative Process

November 5, 2004

Congressional Research Service

7-5700

www.crs.gov

98-736

CRS Report for Congress ——————————————————————————
Prepared for Members and Committees of Congress

Contents

Contacts

Filing Conference Reports

When a committee of conference approves its report, the next step in the legislative process is for the report, along with a joint explanatory statement of the managers, to be presented to the House and Senate for consideration. A conference report must be filed and considered in one chamber at a time, when a chamber is in possession of the official conference papers. The high privilege accorded to conference reports in the House under Rule XXII, clause 7(a) allows them to be presented or filed at almost any time the House is in session, provided that it is in possession of the conference papers. Exceptions to this procedure include a time when the *Journal* is being read, during a quorum call, or when the House is conducting a record or division vote. This privilege applies in the House, so that conference reports may not be filed while the chamber is resolved into Committee of the Whole. See http://www.crs.gov/products/guides/guidehome.shtml for more information on legislative process.

House Rule XXII, clause 8(a)(1) provides that it is not in order to consider a conference report until the third calendar day (excluding Saturdays, Sundays, or holidays, unless the House is in session) after the report has been filed. A conference report may be considered only if it has been printed in the *Congressional Record* of the day on which it was filed. These requirements are not in force during the last six days of a session, and may be waived by unanimous consent, or, more commonly, by adopting a special rule.

Copies of the conference report and joint explanatory statement must be available to Members at least two hours before the beginning of floor consideration. This requirement may also be waived by unanimous consent or special rule, allowing for the consideration of a conference report immediately after it is filed. None of these requirements would apply to a conference report considered under suspension of the rules.

Debating Conference Reports

A conference report is highly privileged and may be called up for consideration at almost any time another matter is not pending. A conference report that meets the layover and availability requirements does not need to be read when it is called up. If it does not meet these requirements, the report must be read unless the reading is dispensed with by unanimous consent. Typically, majority managers of a conference call up a conference report, even when they do not sign or support it, although the Speaker may recognize another Member for this purpose.

Once called up, conference reports are normally considered in the House under the one-hour rule. A conference report may also be considered under a special rule from the Rules Committee or suspension of the rules. House Rule XXII, clause 8(d)(1) requires that the time allotted for debate on a conference report be equally divided and controlled by the majority and minority parties. However, if managers from both parties support the report, the rule also provides that a Member who opposes it may claim and control one-third of the hour. Recognition of a Member in opposition does not depend on party affiliation, but priority is given to a member of the conference committee. Debate may be extended beyond one hour by unanimous consent, by special rule, or by defeating the previous question on the conference report. The House may choose to accept or reject a conference report, but amendments are not in order.

The chamber that *agrees to a request* for a conference is normally the one that considers the report *first*. This is significant because the first chamber to act can agree or disagree to a conference report, or it can agree to a preferential motion to recommit the report to conference. (A motion to recommit to conference may be made after the previous question is ordered on the conference report, and may include non-binding instructions to the conferees.) However, after one chamber has acted on a conference report, its conferees are discharged, and the other chamber may only accept or reject the conference report.

If the second house rejects the conference report, the measure is left in the procedural situation it was in before the conference was requested. Under such a circumstance, one house could propose a new position to the other house as an amendment between the houses, or it could ask for a new conference. In the event that a report is recommitted or rejected and the measure submitted to a new conference committee, all of the matters originally sent to conference are again before the conferees *de novo* for consideration.

Points of Order

In the House, any point of order against a conference report must be made or reserved before debate on it has begun (or before a joint explanatory statement is read). If a report is required to be read because it has not met the layover and availability requirements, a point of order cannot be made or reserved until after the reading. A point of order may only be made against the conference report, and not against the language in the joint explanatory statement. If a point of order is sustained against a conference report, it falls and any further consideration of the measure must follow some alternate route in the same manner as if the report had been defeated. Rule XXII, clause 10 establishes a procedure for points of order against a conference report due to the inclusion of Senate matter not germane to the House-passed bill.

A special rule may be used to protect a conference report from one or more points of order, and all points of order are implicitly waived when a conference report is considered under suspension of the rules.

Author Contact Information

James V. Saturno
Specialist on the Congress and Legislative Process
jsaturno@crs.loc.gov, 7-2381

The House Amendment Tree

Walter J. Oleszek
Senior Specialist in American National Government

May 19, 2008

Congressional Research Service

7-5700

www.crs.gov

98-777

CRS Report for Congress ————————————————
Prepared for Members and Committees of Congress

Summary

The House amendment "tree" is a chart that depicts the maximum number and types of amendments that may be offered to a measure before any amendment is voted upon. This diagram is outlined in various sources, including the 2003 summary compilation of House precedents, titled *House Practice: A Guide to the Rules, Precedents, and Procedures of the House*. The amendment tree generally indicates, for instance, the relationship of one amendment to another and the sequence of voting on amendments. For further detail about amendments, such as first degree or second degree, and the amending process in general, see CRS Report 98-613, *Amendments in the House: Types and Forms*, by Christopher M. Davis, and CRS Report 98-439, *Amendment Process in the Committee of the Whole*, by Judy Schneider.

Congressional Research Service

The House amendment "tree" is a chart that depicts the maximum number and types of amendments that may be offered to a measure before any amendment is voted upon. This diagram is outlined in various sources, including the 2003 summary compilation of House precedents, titled *House Practice: A Guide to the Rules, Precedents, and Procedures of the House*. The amendment tree generally indicates, for instance, the relationship of one amendment to another and the sequence of voting on amendments. For further detail about amendments, such as first degree or second degree, and the amending process in general, see CRS Report 98-613, *Amendments in the House: Types and Forms*, by Christopher M. Davis, and CRS Report 98-439, *Amendment Process in the Committee of the Whole*, by Judy Schneider.

The amendment tree and its accompanying "limbs" grow from various parliamentary principles and precedents. House Rule XVI, clause 6, identifies the four amendments (or motions) that characterize the basic amendment tree; it is portrayed in the chart on the next page. Under Rule XVI, four amendments may be pending simultaneously to the text of a measure: (1) an amendment to the pending bill; (2) a perfecting amendment to that amendment; (3) a substitute amendment, which strikes all of amendment #1 and replaces it with different language; and (4) a perfecting amendment to the substitute.

Three other aspects of the amending process merit mention:

- The amendment to the original measure is offered first; thereafter, there is no rule that regulates what amendment is to come next. It could either be a perfecting amendment or a substitute amendment. The substitute, of course, must be proposed before an amendment to it is in order.

- As stated in Rule XVI, only one amendment to an amendment and one amendment to a substitute is in order at any one time. However, once an amendment to the original amendment or to the substitute is disposed of either by rejection or incorporation, both generally remain open to further perfecting amendments.

- Amendments are voted on in a definite order. Amendments to the original amendment are voted on first; amendments to the substitute are voted on next; then the substitute is voted on; and, finally, the original amendment is voted on. If the substitute is agreed to, the last vote is on the amendment, as amended.

Figure 1. The Basic Amendment Tree

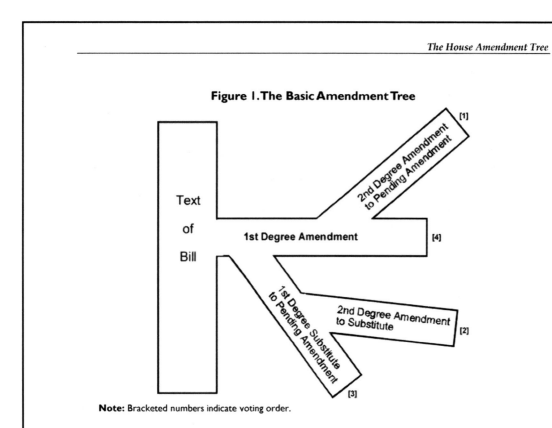

Note: Bracketed numbers indicate voting order.

Author Contact Information

Walter J. Oleszek
Senior Specialist in American National Government
woleszek@crs.loc.gov, 7-7854

Congressional
Research
Service

Commonly Used Motions and Requests in the House of Representatives

Betsy Palmer
Analyst on the Congress and Legislative Process

May 22, 2008

Congressional Research Service

7-5700

www.crs.gov

RL32207

CRS Report for Congress ————————————————

Prepared for Members and Committees of Congress

Summary

This report identifies the most commonly used motions and requests available to Members during proceedings in the House of Representatives. This report does not identify motions and requests used when the House is in the Committee of the Whole House on the State of the Union. (See CRS Report RL32200, *Debate, Motions, and Other Actions in the Committee of the Whole*, by Bill Heniff Jr. and Elizabeth Rybicki. For a discussion of motions and requests used in committees see CRS Report RS20308, *House Committee Markups: Commonly Used Motions and Requests*, by Judy Schneider.)

The report divides the motions and requests into seven broad categories, based on when the motion or request is in order and who can make the motion or request. Daily Business is the category that includes items that are routine to the conduct of business in the House each day, such as the motion to adjourn. Decorum and Privilege covers issues of the rights and privileges of Members and the House and how Members conduct themselves on the floor. In Parliamentary Tools, motions and requests are identified that Members may use to get information about the parliamentary situation or to object to the pending proposal. Proceedings on Legislation includes motions and requests available to Members that are related to bringing up and considering legislation. Closing Debate and Voting identifies motions and requests used to bring debate to a close and obtain a vote. Commit, Recommit and Refer looks at the motions and requests used to send a bill to committee. Finally, Resolving Differences identifies motions and requests used to facilitate amendments between the chambers or to set up a conference between the chambers on differing versions of legislation.

This report will be updated as needed.

Contents

Contacts

Congressional Research Service

Introduction

Members of the House of Representatives have an array of options available to them to participate in the activities of the House. Those options allow Members to ask questions about the parliamentary situation, object to proceedings in the House, or ask for a recorded vote, among other things.

This report identifies the motions and requests Members may use to exercise these options during House proceedings. It describes only procedures used in the House proper. It does not identify motions and requests used when the House is in the Committee of the Whole House on the State of the Union.[1]

For the purposes of this report, a motion is a formal proposal by a Member to institute any one of a broad array of procedural actions as provided for under House rules. Motions must be agreed to by the House to take effect. Motions include the motion to adjourn and the motion to table.

Also, for the purposes of this report, requests are efforts by a Member to accomplish some action that is disposed of not by a vote, but by an act of the Speaker or with the consent of the House. An example of a request is a unanimous consent request or a parliamentary inquiry. The former would be accomplished with the consent of the House, the latter is answered by the Speaker.

The following discussion divides the motions and requests into seven categories, based on when the motion or request is in order and who is most likely to make the motion or request. Those categories are

- **Daily Business** includes motions and requests that are routinely made in the House;

- **Decorum and Privilege** covers motions and requests that deal with Members' rights and conduct;

- **Parliamentary Tools** identifies motions and requests that Members may use to get information about, or challenge, the parliamentary situation or pending proposals;

- **Proceedings on Legislation** includes motions and requests related to bringing up a measure for consideration;

- **Closing Debate and Voting** consists of motions and requests to conclude consideration and proceed to a vote on a measure or matter;

- **Commit, Recommit and Refer** deals with motions that may send a bill to committee; and

- **Resolving Differences** identifies motions and requests used to set up a conference between the House and Senate or to facilitate the exchange of amendments between the chambers.

---

[1] See CRS Report RL32200, *Debate, Motions, and Other Actions in the Committee of the Whole*, by Bill Heniff Jr. and Elizabeth Rybicki; also CRS Report RS20308, *House Committee Markups: Commonly Used Motions and Requests*, by Judy Schneider.

Unless otherwise noted, a motion or request that is in order may be made by any Member if he or she has the floor or is recognized by the Speaker for that purpose. On motions that are debatable, as noted in the report, the debate begins after the reading of the motion. Debatable motions are considered under the hour rule[2], unless otherwise noted. Any Member may demand that any motion be reduced to writing. Many motions are customarily presented in writing, especially those incident to consideration of a measure; others, like the motion to adjourn, are customarily not. Requests are typically not presented in writing.

Only the key features and conditions applicable to the motions and requests are covered in this report. More detailed analysis is available in the *House Manual* and other printed sources, from the House Parliamentarian, or from CRS analysts and specialists. Terms in italic have their own entries in the report. Some descriptions also provide typical language used to invoke the motion or request.[3]

Daily Business

A number of motions and requests are routinely made in the House each day as a part of its daily business.

Adjourn

A motion to adjourn is not debatable and must be considered before all other motions. It is not in order to *table* this motion. Generally, it is not in order to repeat the motion to adjourn immediately after one such motion has been defeated.

A Member would say: *Mr. Speaker, I move that the House do now adjourn.*

Adjourn to a Date and Time Certain

A motion that the House adjourn to a date and time certain may not be *tabled*, is not debatable, and may not be amended.

Approve the Journal

At the start of each day that the House is in session, the Speaker declares his approval of the *Journal* of the previous day's proceedings. A Member may request a vote on the question of the Speaker's approval of the *Journal*. These votes are generally used by the House leadership to see

---

[2] The "hour rule" is the default rule for consideration of measures or matters in the House. Under the rule, each Member could be granted one hour of debate. In practice, however, the first Member recognized under the hour rule moves the previous question at the end of the first hour of debate, which, if approved by the House, has the effect of ending debate and bringing the underlying measure or matter to a vote.

[3] For complete, official information on House Rules, see *U.S. Congress, House, Constitution, Jefferson's Manual, and Rules of the House of Representatives*, One Hundred Ninth Congress, H..Doc. 109-157, 109th Cong., 2nd sess.. [compiled by] John V. Sullivan, Parliamentarian (Washington: GPO, 2007), sec. 714, pp. 428-540 . Hereafter cited as *House Manual.* See also Congressional Quarterly's *American Congressional Dictionary*, (Washington: Congressional Quarterly, 2001); an updated version of the book is found at http://www.crs.gov/products/guides/glossary/a.shtml.

---

who is in town and available to vote. The *Journal* is the official record of the proceedings of the House.

Insert Material in the Congressional Record

A Member may ask to insert material into the *Congressional Record* only by *unanimous consent*. There is no motion to be made if unanimous consent is not given.

Morning Hour Debate

Since the 103rd Congress, the House, by *unanimous consent*, has set aside a period on Mondays and Tuesdays for the purpose of conducting "morning hour debates." On those days, the House convenes 90 minutes earlier than normal for the purpose of recognizing Members to speak, with 30 minutes controlled by each party. After mid-May of each year, the time set aside for morning hour debate on Tuesdays is reduced to one hour, with 25 minutes allocated to each party. Members must reserve time in advance with their respective leadership, speeches are limited to five minutes, and the chair alternates recognition between the majority and minority parties.

One-Minute Speeches

A Member may ask *unanimous consent* to address the House for one minute. After being recognized by the Speaker, the Member may speak for one minute on any topic. The Speaker has discretion to decide how many "one-minutes" (if any) will be permitted each day and when in the day they will take place (typically, they are at the beginning of a day's session). At the beginning or end of a one-minute speech, a Member may ask *unanimous consent* to revise and extend his or her remarks.

Recess

Unlike an adjournment of the House, a recess is a temporary interruption or suspension of a meeting of the House, generally proposed by a member of the leadership. The Speaker may entertain a nondebatable motion authorizing him to declare a recess, and that motion will be considered before any other motion, except a motion to adjourn. In addition, the Speaker is authorized to declare a recess "for a short time" when no question is pending before the House.

Special Order Speeches

Special order speeches are normally in order after legislative business has concluded in the House for the day, and they can be on any topic the Member chooses. Members are granted permission to speak from five minutes up to one hour, and generally are placed on a list to obtain the time by their party's leadership. Members are recognized for special order speeches at the discretion of the Speaker, and the practice is allowed by *unanimous consent* of the body—no standing rules provide for special order speeches.

Decorum and Privilege

Members may act to protect their privileges, or those of the House, or to respond to a break in the decorum of the House by using these motions and requests, which involve the rights and privileges of a Member or of the House or deal with Member conduct in the House.

Personal Privilege, Question of

Members can raise a question of personal privilege when they believe that their rights, reputation, or conduct as a Representative have been called into question. When a Member raises a question of personal privilege, the Speaker must determine whether the question qualifies under the rules and precedents of the House. If it does, the Speaker would recognize the Member for one hour to talk about the question. Unlike a *question of privileges of the House*, a question of personal privilege does not need to be in the form of a House resolution.

A Member would say: *Mr. Speaker, I rise to a question of personal privilege.*

Privileges of the House, Question of

Questions of the privileges of the House are defined as those affecting the rights of the House and the safety, dignity, and integrity of its proceedings. Questions of privilege have priority of consideration above all other motions, except the motion to adjourn. A question of the privileges of the House must be presented in the form of a House resolution. After a Member has presented the question in the form of a resolution, the Speaker determines when the House will consider it. If the question is raised by the Majority or Minority leader, has been reported from a committee, or concerns the House's right to originate revenue bills, the question must be considered immediately. On other questions, the Speaker has the discretion to postpone consideration for up to two days. Once such a question has been raised and called up, the Speaker then determines whether it qualifies as a question of the privileges of the House under House rules and precedents. If so, the Speaker then recognizes the Member who made the motion for debate for half of the one hour allotted. The second half hour would be controlled by the Majority Leader, the Minority Leader or a designee, as determined by the Speaker. The question, in the form of a resolution, is subject to the motion to *table*. See also *Personal Privilege*.

A Member would say: *Mr. Speaker, I rise to a question of the privileges of the House, and offer a resolution ....*

Words Taken Down (Take Down the Words)

A Member may demand that the words of another Member be taken down. This typically takes place during debate when one Member believes another Member has violated the rules of decorum in the House. The request requires that the Member's remarks be read to the House so that the Speaker may determine whether they are offensive or otherwise violate the rules of the House. If the Speaker determines that the words are out of order, the violator is customarily given a chance to withdraw or amend them, and the Member may ask the House for *unanimous consent* to strike the words from the *Congressional Record*. If there is objection, a motion may be offered to strike the words from the debate. Upon the demand that the words be taken down, the alleged violator must immediately sit down and await the Speaker's decision. A Member whose words have been ruled out of order may not speak again on the same day without the House's permission, but the Member can vote.

A Member would say: *Mr. Speaker, I rise to a point of order, and ask that the gentleman's (or gentlelady's) words be taken down.*

Parliamentary Tools

The following are motions and requests that are available to all Members during proceedings of the House that allow Members to gain an understanding of the parliamentary situation or allow a Member to register his or her disapproval of the conduct of business, or try to stop it. They can be seen as parliamentary tools.

Appeal the Ruling of the Chair

With this request, a Member formally protests a ruling, or decision, made by the presiding officer of the House. The appeal must be made immediately after the ruling or decision. A motion to appeal the ruling from the chair is debatable and can be followed by a motion by another Member to *table* the appeal or to order the *previous question*, which, if approved, would end debate on the matter. Some decisions by the Speaker are not subject to an appeal, such as a decision about whom to recognize to speak. The appeal of the ruling of the chair is decided by the Speaker; Members may request a vote to sustain the ruling or overturn the ruling.

A Member would say: *Mr. Speaker, I respectfully appeal the ruling of the Chair.*

Objection

By objecting to a *unanimous consent* request, a Member may prevent the occurrence of an action, not otherwise in order under the rules, for which unanimous consent has been requested, but that he or she would prefer the House not take. See also "Reserve the Right to Object."

Parliamentary Inquiry

A Member may ask the Speaker to explain the existing parliamentary situation by raising a parliamentary inquiry, or a Member may use the parliamentary inquiry to question whether something taking place is permitted by, or in violation of, the rules. A parliamentary inquiry may be used to ascertain information only about procedural questions—the Speaker will not provide information about substantive policy questions. After the Speaker has responded to the parliamentary inquiry, Members may ask additional questions to clarify the situation further, or may proceed to challenge the pending action through a *point of order*.

A Member would say: *Mr. Speaker, I have a parliamentary inquiry.*

Point of Order

A point of order is a claim by a Member from the floor that a pending proceeding violates the rules of the House. A point of order may not be made after debate on the matter being challenged begins; a Member desiring to raise a point of order receives preference in recognition from the

Speaker. Once the Member is recognized to make a point of order, he or she must specifically cite which House rule is being violated and why. No further action may take place until the Speaker rules on the point of order. In order to make a ruling, the Speaker may ask Members to argue for and against a point of order, but any debate is at the discretion of the Speaker. If the Speaker sustains the point of order, the proposed action falls from consideration. A Member may *appeal the ruling of the chair* on a point of order. See also "Reserve a Point of Order."

A Member would say: *Mr. Speaker, I make a point of order against ... on the grounds that ...*

Regular Order

A Member may demand "regular order" to request that the House return to the pending business. For example, if a Member had *reserved a point of order*, a demand for regular order would force that Member to either make the *point of order* or withdraw the reservation. Similarly, a demand for regular order would require a Member who had *reserved the right to object* to state his or her objection or withdraw the reservation.

Reserve a Point of Order

If a Member is unsure whether an amendment or other action would violate House rules, the Member may reserve a point of order against the action at the time it is proposed. Debate on the proposal would then proceed. By reserving a point of order when an action is initially proposed, a Member may preserve the right to make the *point of order* against the action at some later point, after debate has occurred (but before the House disposes of the proposed action). For example, if a Member offers an amendment, another Member may reserve a point of order against the amendment to gain time to examine it. Subsequently, if the reserving Member finds that the amendment violates no rule, or is substantively acceptable, he or she may withdraw the reservation. Otherwise, the Member also may insist on the point of order. A Member is allowed to reserve a point of order at the Speaker's discretion—once the Speaker desires to hear the point of order, the Member must make it or withdraw it. Similarly, if there is a demand for *regular order*, the Member reserving a point of order must make it or withdraw it.

A Member would say: *Mr. Speaker, I reserve a point of order.*

Reserve the Right to Object

A Member may "reserve the right to object" to a *unanimous consent* request. As *unanimous consent* requests are not debatable, a Member may reserve the right to object, to allow the proponent of the request time to explain the proposal. For example, if a Member asks unanimous consent to bring up a bill, another Member may reserve the right to object, and then yield to the original Member to allow an explanation of what is proposed. If, in light of the explanation, the reserving Member is not satisfied with the proposed action, he or she may then object to the unanimous consent request; if satisfied, he or she may withdraw the reservation of objection. See also "Objection, Regular Order."

Table, Lay on the Table

If agreed to, a motion to table disposes of the pending matter adversely and without a direct vote on its substance. The motion is not debatable, and is adopted by majority vote or without objection. If adopted, the tabling motion is the same as defeating the underlying proposition. If the tabling motion is defeated, the situation reverts to where it was when the motion to table was made. The House does not allow the tabling motion against the motion to *recommit*, but it is in order against some other motions, such as the motion to *reconsider a vote* or *appeal the ruling of the chair*. A motion to table an amendment, if successful, also would table the underlying proposition to which the amendment was proposed.

A Member would say: *Mr. Speaker, I move to lay the [proposition] on the table.*

Unanimous Consent

A Member may make a unanimous consent request to ask permission to allow an action to take place, even if it is contrary to House rules or practice. Although Members rarely object to routine unanimous consent requests, they have the right to do so and thereby force full compliance with the rules. A Member might ask unanimous consent to address the House for *one minute*. Or a Member might ask unanimous consent that all Members have five legislative days in which to revise and extend their remarks on a measure. See "Reserve the Right to Object."

A Member would say: *Mr. Speaker, I ask unanimous consent that...*

Proceedings on Legislation

These are motions and requests that allow a Member to participate in proceedings on legislation, such as the consideration and disposition of legislation on the House floor.

Consideration, Question of

A Member may raise the question of consideration, literally whether the House should take up a measure, only if the measure being called up is being debated without a special rule to govern its consideration, and the measure does not need to be considered in the Committee of the Whole. The question is in order at the point when the measure is called up but before debate begins. The question also may be raised on some motions, such as the motion to *recommit*. The question is not debatable. Once the question has been raised, the House must vote on whether to consider the measure.

A Member would say: *Mr. Speaker, I raise the question of consideration.*

Postpone Indefinitely

A pending matter may be subject to a motion to postpone indefinitely, which kills it. The motion to postpone indefinitely is not amendable, it is debatable and may also be *tabled*, which, if successful, would kill the motion to postpone indefinitely, but not the underlying matter or measure.

A Member would say: *Mr. Speaker, I move that the [further] consideration of ____ be postponed indefinitely.*

Postpone Until a Day Certain

The motion to postpone to a day certain postpones consideration of specified business and brings it back for consideration on the specified day. The motion to postpone until a day certain is amendable, and it is debatable. The motion may not specify a time when the matter will be considered. It is in order to offer a motion to *table* this motion, which, if successful, would kill the motion to postpone to a date certain but not the underlying matter or measure.

A Member would say: *Mr. Speaker, I move that the [further] consideration of ____ be postponed until Friday next.*

Suspend the Rules

Noncontroversial measures can be considered by moving that the House suspend the rules and pass a bill, adopt a resolution or conference report, or concur in amendments of the Senate. Typically, the motion to suspend the rules is offered by the committee or subcommittee chair of the committee of jurisdiction. A measure considered under suspension of the rules must pass by a two-thirds vote of those Members present and voting. Debate on a motion to suspend the rules and pass a measure is limited to 40 minutes; the time is evenly divided between proponents and opponents of the measure. Members may not offer amendments from the floor, but the motion itself can include an amendment, typically a committee amendment.

A Member would say: *Mr. Speaker, I move that the House suspend the rules and pass...*

Take from the Speaker's Table

The Speaker is required to dispose of certain communications received by the House from the executive branch and from the Senate (such as Senate-passed bills), and until he does so, these communications are said to be on his table. He can refer them to appropriate committees. Customarily, a floor manager of legislation may make a *unanimous consent* request or a motion that the House act on an item at the Speaker's table, such as to motion to *concur in the Senate amendments* to a bill.

Closing Debate and Voting

There are a variety of motions and requests available to Members who want to bring debate to a close or get to a vote on a measure or matter.

Previous Question

The previous question is a nondebatable motion to close consideration and bring a pending matter to an immediate vote. If the motion is agreed to by a majority vote, it generally cuts off further debate and prevents the offering of additional amendments or motions. If the previous question is ordered on a debatable proposal before any debate has occurred, the proposal may be debated after the previous question is ordered for 40 minutes. When the House considers a special rule from the Rules Committee, the majority floor manager usually moves the previous question on the resolution when time for debate has been used or yielded back. If the motion fails, the Speaker recognizes a Member who opposed ordering the previous question to offer and debate an amendment. After debate on the amendment, that Member typically then moves the previous question on the resolution and the amendment to it. Once a special rule has been approved and the House considers the matter governed by it, typically in the Committee of the Whole, the special rule normally directs that the previous question is ordered as soon as the Committee of the Whole reports the measure back to the House.

A Member would say: *Mr. Speaker, I move the previous question on ....*

Quorum Call

Also known as the Call of the House. A Member may make a point of order that a quorum is not present. Under the Constitution, a majority of House Members (218) must be present to conduct business, but the House typically assumes it has a quorum present (a "presumptive quorum"). In general, Members may make this point of order only when the Speaker has put the question on a pending matter.

A Member would say: *Mr. Speaker, I object to the vote on the grounds that a quorum is not present and make a point of order that a quorum is not present.*

Reconsider (a Vote)

A Member who has voted with the prevailing side may make a motion that the House reconsider a vote. This motion allows the House one opportunity to review its decision on a motion, amendment, measure, or any other proposition on which it has voted. The motion to reconsider must be offered on the same day as the original vote, or on the next legislative day. The motion is debatable only when offered to a proposal that was debatable. If the motion to reconsider a vote succeeds, it brings the original question back before the House. Immediately after the result of a vote has been announced, the Speaker usually declares, "Without objection, a motion to reconsider is laid on the table." Any Member can object and force a vote on the motion to reconsider, or on a motion to table the motion to reconsider. Those who oppose reconsidering the vote may move to *table* the motion, which would kill the move to reconsider the vote and block any future attempt to reopen the issue.

A Member would say: *I move to reconsider the vote by which the [proposition] was passed [or rejected].*

Recorded Vote

A vote in which Members are recorded by name. The House uses an electronic voting system, where a Member can record his or her vote in one of three ways: yea, nay or present. To obtain a recorded vote in the House requires support from 44 Members (one-fifth of a quorum), but a Member can usually obtain a vote without the requisite quorum if the Member notes the absence of a *quorum* when asking for the vote. Recorded votes may be requested in both the House and the Committee of the Whole.

A Member would say: *Mr. Speaker, on that I demand a recorded vote.*

Separate Vote

After a bill has been reported back to the House from the Committee of the Whole, any Member may demand a separate vote on any amendments that were agreed to in the Committee of the Whole. A separate vote is not in order on amendments that were defeated in the Committee of the Whole. Typically, the Speaker will inquire: "Is a separate vote demanded on any amendment? If not, the Clerk will put them *en gros*."

A Member would say: *Mr. Speaker, I demand a separate vote on....*

Yea-and-Nay Vote

Under the Constitution, any Member, with the support of one-fifth of those present, may request a Yea-and-Nay vote when in the House. These votes are typically taken by the electronic voting system. The Constitution as well as some laws and House rules require that specific questions pending before the House be decided by the yeas and nays. A Yea-and-Nay vote is required, for example, to override a presidential veto.

A Member would say: *Mr. Speaker, I demand the yeas and nays.*

Commit, Recommit, Refer

Although the formal purpose of these motions is to send to committee legislation being considered by the House, they are in practice used principally to bring amendments to the measure before the House. These motions are most likely offered by an opponent of the pending legislation towards the end of House consideration (except for *Refer*, which is used earlier in the process). Only one such motion is in order; the parliamentary situation would determine which of these very similar motions is in order in a given circumstance.

Commit

The motion to commit sends a measure or matter to a committee or committees. It is in order only on measures or matters that have not been previously referred to and reported from committee. When the measure or motion was reported by committee, the motion to *recommit* is used. Agreement to the motion to commit sends the measure or matter to a committee or committees. If the motion is on a bill or joint resolution and contains instructions (essentially telling the committee how to handle it), it is debatable. It may be *tabled*. It is in order only after the motion for the *previous question* has been moved or ordered.

Recommit

A motion to recommit, to send the bill back to committee, may be offered with or without instructions. The motion to *recommit with instructions* is discussed below. The motion to recommit without instructions, sometimes called a "straight" motion to recommit, sends the pending matter back to committee and can effectively kill the measure. The motion is offered just before the vote on final passage or adoption, and only one such motion (*commit*, *recommit* or either of those with *instructions*) is permitted. The Speaker gives priority of recognition for offering the motion to recommit, in order, to minority members of the reporting committee, to any other minority party member, to majority members of the committee, and finally to any other majority party member, but only to a member who declares that he or she opposes the measure. The Rules Committee may not report a special rule that prevents the motion from being offered. The motion to recommit may not be *tabled*. The straight motion to recommit is not subject to debate, but it may be amended to include instructions, so long as the amendment is germane to the underlying measure. A conference report may be subject to a motion to recommit, with or without instructions, if the House is the first chamber to act on the conference agreement.

Recommit with Instructions

The motion to recommit with instructions sends the pending matter back to committee to take some action which may include reporting it back to the House, but may also include holding hearings or studying the matter further. In this form, the motion can be, essentially, an attempt to amend the bill before final passage. If the instructions call for the committee to report back "forthwith," and the motion to recommit is successful, then the committee is presumed to have acted upon the bill in the manner included in the instructions and it is immediately before the House with the instructed amendment pending. If the instructions do not explicitly state the term "forthwith," or use terms such as "promptly," the effect is to place the measure again before committee, not before the House. The motion is offered just before the vote on final passage or adoption, and only one such motion (*commit*, *recommit* or either of those with *instructions*) is permitted. The motion to recommit with instructions is subject to the same priority for recognition as the motion to *recommit* (see above). A House rule precludes the Rules Committee from reporting a special rule that prevents the motion from being offered. When offered on a bill or a joint resolution, the motion is debatable for 10 minutes, equally divided between proponents and opponents, although the majority floor leader may extend debate to one hour. This motion may not be *tabled* and the instructions are amendable. An amendment must be germane to the underlying bill and may not violate the right of the minority to offer the motion to recommit (by, for example, completely changing the intent of the original motion). A conference report may be subject to a motion to recommit, with or without instructions, if the House is the first chamber to act on the conference agreement.

Refer

The motion to refer sends a measure or matter to a committee or committees. It is in order only on measures or matters that have not been referred to a committee and are being considered under the general rules of the House. It is a debatable motion that may contain instructions (see "Recommit with Instructions"), and it may be *tabled*. It is in order only before the *previous question* has been moved or ordered.

Resolving Differences

The actions discussed in this section are used to resolve differences on legislation that has been considered by both chambers and passed in differing versions. The requests and motions described below represent the two methods Congress has of resolving differences between the two chambers' versions of legislation. One method is called amendments between the chambers. Under this method, the bill is amended by one chamber and then sent over to the second chamber, either for its approval or for further amendment. Differences also can be resolved if the two chambers agree to go to conference on a measure. The House and Senate can disagree to each other's positions and then agree to create a conference committee to propose a package of settlements to all their disagreements. The motions described below can be used to send amendments back and forth or to get to a conference between the chambers. The majority of these requests and motions are typically made by the majority floor manager of the legislation. The motions discussed below are debatable under the hour rule.

Concur in the Senate Amendment(s), Concur in the Senate Amendment(s) with an Amendment

The motion to concur in the Senate amendment or any of its variations is associated with the method of resolving differences known as amendments between the chambers. If the House concurs in a Senate amendment, it clears the measure for the President. If the House concurs in the amendment with a further amendment, the action sends the matter back to the Senate for action on the House amendment to the Senate amendment. This motion can only be used when the last amendments were those of the Senate.

A Member would say: *Mr. Speaker, I ask unanimous consent to take _____ from the Speaker's table and a Senate amendment thereto, and concur in the Senate amendment.*

Disagree to the Senate Amendment(s)

The motion to disagree to the Senate amendments is associated with setting up a conference. The House must first formally disagree to the Senate amendments to be able to request a conference with the Senate to work out those differences. This motion puts the House on record as disagreeing to an amendment or amendments from the Senate and may initiate action to go to conference between the two chambers on the measure. This motion is used when the Senate was the latter chamber to amend the measure.

A Member would say: *Mr. Speaker, I ask unanimous consent to take _____ from the Speaker's table with the Senate amendment thereto, disagree to the Senate amendment and agree to the conference asked by the Senate.*

Insist on House Amendment(s)

The motion to insist on House amendments is associated with setting up a conference. Essentially, it is a motion that the House reiterate a position it already has taken during the process of amendments between the houses. The House may insist on its amendment before or after the Senate has disagreed to it, or the House may insist on its previous disagreement to an amendment of the Senate. The motion is typically accompanied by a request for a conference or agreement to a conference requested by the Senate.

A Member would say: *Mr. Speaker, I ask unanimous consent to take _____ from the Speaker's table, insist on the House amendment and request a conference with the Senate thereon.*

Instruct Conferees

The result of a motion to instruct conferees is a formal vote of the House to tell its conference committee members how they should resolve an issue. Under House precedents, the right to offer a motion to instruct conferees is the prerogative of the minority. There are three situations where such a motion may be offered: 1) after the House decides to go to conference but before House conferees are named (only one such motion is in order); 2) 20 calendar days and 10 legislative days after conferees have been named if a conference report has not been filed; and 3) as a part of a motion to recommit a conference report with instructions. This last opportunity does not exist if the Senate has already acted on the conference report. Motions to instruct conferees are not binding. There is no point of order against a conference report that does not follow a House-passed motion to instruct. Motions to instruct are debated under the hour rule.

A Member would say: *Mr. Speaker, I offer a motion to instruct.*

Recede and Concur, Recede and Concur with an Amendment

The motion to recede and concur and its variations are associated with amendments between the houses, after the House has already previously disagreed to Senate amendments or insisted on House amendments, so as to go to conference. It can only be used when the last amendments are those of the Senate. These are motions that allow the House to go back to the method of amendments between the chambers after having disagreed or insisted on its position and possibly gone to conference. If used in this situation or in any situation which the House had already insisted on House amendments, the motion would have to propose that the House recede from insistence on its own amendment as well as receding from the amendment itself. These steps are typically taken when items are reported from a conference in disagreement or when a conference report has been defeated.

A Member would say: *Mr. Speaker, I move that the House recede from its disagreement to the amendment of the Senate and agree to the same, with an amendment.*

Recede from House Amendment(s)

The motion to recede from House amendments is also associated with amendments between the houses. This is a motion that the House withdraw from its previous position during the process of amendments between the houses. The House would use this to recede from its amendments if it was the last chamber to act. This step is typically taken when items are reported from a conference in disagreement or when a conference report has been defeated. The motion to recede from House amendments would typically be followed by a motion to concur in Senate amendments with a new and different House amendment.

A Member would say: *Mr. Speaker, I move that the House recede from its amendment.*

Author Contact Information

Betsy Palmer
Analyst on the Congress and Legislative Process
bpalmer@crs.loc.gov, 7-0381

Amendments Between the Houses

Elizabeth Rybicki
Analyst on the Congress and Legislative Process

June 27, 2008

Congressional Research Service

7-5700

www.crs.gov

98-812

CRS Report for Congress ————————————————————

Prepared for Members and Committees of Congress

Summary

The House and Senate must approve an identical version of a measure before it may be presented for the President's approval or veto. If the House and Senate approve differing versions of a measure, the differences must first be resolved. One way to do this is through an exchange of amendments between the houses.

When the House or Senate passes a measure, it is sent to the other chamber for further consideration. If the second chamber passes the measure with one or more amendments, it is then sent back to the originating chamber. In modern practice, the second chamber often substitutes its version of a measure as a single amendment to the measure as passed by the first chamber. The first chamber then may accept the amendment or propose its own further amendment. In this way, the measure may be messaged back and forth between the House and Senate in the hope that both houses will eventually agree to the same version of a measure.

Contents

Contacts

The House and Senate must approve an identical version of a measure before it may be presented for the President's approval or veto. If the House and Senate approve differing versions of a measure, the differences must first be resolved. One way to do this is through an exchange of amendments between the houses.[1]

When the House or Senate passes a measure, it is sent to the other chamber for further consideration. If the second chamber passes the measure with one or more amendments, it is then sent back to the originating chamber. In modern practice, the second chamber often substitutes its version of a measure as a single amendment to the measure as passed by the first chamber. The first chamber then may accept the amendment or propose its own further amendment. In this way, the measure may be messaged back and forth between the House and Senate in the hope that both houses will eventually agree to the same version of a measure.

The House and Senate may use this method in an attempt to resolve their differences in a variety of circumstances: prior to a conference, instead of a conference, or even after a conference (as amendments in either true or technical disagreement). As an alternative to conference, this procedure can be useful in a variety of circumstances, particularly when the measure is not controversial or the differences between the House and Senate are relatively small. It is also used occasionally when time pressures or other circumstances make the requirements for a formal conference undesirable.[2] In addition, while conference reports receive a single vote, resolving differences by exchanging more than one amendment allows for separate votes on different elements of a bicameral compromise.

When the House or Senate considers an amendment of the other chamber, it does not yet formally disagree to that amendment. At this stage, the House or Senate may concur in the amendment, thus ending the process, or concur in the amendment with a further amendment of its own, proposing a new text to the other chamber. At any point, either house may choose not to act or it may insist on its own position and formally disagree with the amendment posed by the other. If a chamber insists on its position and formally disagrees with the amendment, it reaches the "stage of disagreement" necessary to allow the two chambers to proceed to conference.

This procedure allows two degrees of amending. The amendment of the second chamber to the measure is considered the text that is subject to amendment. Each chamber thus has one opportunity to propose an amendment to the amendment from the other. The House may extend the amendment exchange to another degree, however, by unanimous consent, a motion to suspend the rules, or under the terms of a special rule reported by the Rules Committee. The Senate can extend the amendment exchange to another degree by unanimous consent, or, if the House has already amended the text in the third degree, by motion. Generally, however, the provisions of an amendment between the houses are the subject of informal negotiations, and an extended exchange of amendments is rare.

---

[1] This report was written by James V. Saturno. The analyst listed as the author is available to answer questions on the topic.

[2] For information on the potentially time-consuming steps required to arrange for a conference committee in the Senate, see CRS Report RS20454, *Going to Conference in the Senate*, by Elizabeth Rybicki. For information on other procedural requirements in connection with conference committees, see CRS Report 98-696, *Resolving Legislative Differences in Congress: Conference Committees and Amendments Between the Houses*, by Elizabeth Rybicki.

Congressional Research Service   *1*

Consideration of Senate Amendments by the House

When the Senate passes a House bill with one or more amendments, it is messaged back to the House, where it is normally held at the Speaker's table. The bill may be referred to a committee at the Speaker's discretion, but this would be likely only if the Senate has included substantial nongermane matters in its amendment that would fall in the jurisdiction of a committee different from the one that considered the original matter in the bill.

One limitation on the use of amendments between the houses is that, before reaching the stage of disagreement, Senate amendments generally are not privileged in the House. This means a Member cannot interrupt the regular order of business to move that the House consider a measure with a Senate amendment if the subject of the amendment would normally need to be considered in Committee of the Whole (generally matters related to appropriations, or authorizations, appropriations, or revenues). The only motion that can be made on the House floor at this stage is a motion to go to conference with the Senate if made at the direction of the committee(s) with jurisdiction over the subject of the measure.

The House, however, may choose to consider Senate amendments by one of several methods that overcome this limitation. The House floor manager may ask unanimous consent to concur in the Senate amendments or concur with an amendment. Either case would normally only occur when the provisions in question are noncontroversial since objection by any Member would cause the request to fail. (This procedure does not allow for any debate, although another Member will often reserve the right to object, allowing the floor manager to clarify the purpose and content of the request.) As an alternative, or if an objection is made to a unanimous consent request, the House may also consider Senate amendments either by a motion to suspend the rules (when such a motion is in order) or under the terms of a special rule.

Consideration of House Amendments by the Senate

Senate consideration of House amendments is less restricted by chamber rules. Senate Rule VII provides that a motion to proceed to consideration of such an amendment is privileged, and, therefore, decided without debate. The rule also provides that any question pending when the motion is made be suspended (but not displaced). Under Senate precedents, before reaching the stage of disagreement, a motion to concur in House amendments has precedence over a motion to disagree and go to conference, and a motion to concur with an amendment has precedence over either.

If the Senate agrees to a motion to concur or concur with a further amendment, the amendment itself would be debatable and amendable under the regular rules of the Senate. As a result, the Senate typically takes action on an amendment of the House after negotiations that lead to the expectation that the amendment will be disposed of readily, often by unanimous consent. In the absence of such an expectation, the Senate would typically proceed to conference in order to negotiate a resolution to any serious disagreements within the Senate or with the House. In the 109th (2005-2006) and 110th (2007-2008) Congresses, the Majority Leader has, on occasion, attempted to restrict both Senate floor amendments and debate by offering all the motions available in connection with the disposition of House amendments (sometimes referred to as "filling the tree") and filing cloture on the base motion.[3] If a sufficient number of Senators (60 under most circumstances) agree to invoke cloture, then after a maximum of 30 hours of consideration, the Senate votes on any pending motions.

---

[3] See, for example. *Congressional Record*, daily edition, vol. 152, September 27, 2006, pp. S10616-10618; *Congressional Record*, daily edition, vol. 152, December 8, 2006, pp. S11658-11659; *Congressional Record*, daily edition, vol. 153, July 31, 2007, pp. S10400-10401; *Congressional Record*, daily edition, vol. 153, September 26, 2007, pp. S12122-12123; *Congressional Record*, daily edition, vol. 153, December 12, 2007, p. S15218, *Congressional Record*, daily edition. vol. 154, May 20, 2008, p. S4475.

Congressional
Research
Service

Parliamentary Reference Sources: Senate

Megan Suzanne Lynch
Analyst on the Congress and Legislative Process

Richard S. Beth
Specialist on the Congress and Legislative Process

April 21, 2008

Congressional Research Service

7-5700

www.crs.gov

RL30788

CRS Report for Congress ——————————————
Prepared for Members and Committees of Congress

Summary

The Senate's procedures are determined not only by its standing rules, but also by its standing orders, published precedents, committee rules, and informal practices. Constitutional mandates and rule-making statutes also impose procedural requirements on the Senate, and rules of Senate party conferences can sometimes affect committee and floor action. Parliamentary reference sources set forth the text of these authorities or provide information about how and when they govern different parliamentary situations. This report discusses the coverage, format, and availability of three types of Senate parliamentary reference sources: official sources such as the *Senate Manual* and *Riddick's Senate Procedure*; publications of committees and offices of the Senate; and rules of party conferences. The report also reviews some key principles of Senate parliamentary procedure that bear on appropriate use of these sources. Summaries and appendices provide citations to print and electronic versions, and list related Congressional Research Service (CRS) products.

The Senate sets forth its chief procedural authorities in the *Senate Manual*, a new edition of which appears periodically as a Senate Document and is distributed to Senators' and committee offices. Among these authorities, the Senate also publishes its Standing Rules as a separate document, and the Constitution is available in an annotated edition prepared by CRS. The *Manual* also contains more specialized authorities, such as permanent standing orders, rules for impeachment trials, and a manual of procedures related to House-Senate conferences. Other Senate procedural authorities include *Riddick's Senate Procedure*, last published in 1992 but with online updates, which offers a topically ordered digest of precedents interpreting Senate procedures and standard forms for procedural action.

The Senate also often regulates itself through orders entered by unanimous consent, either as standing orders or for the consideration of individual measures; these can often most readily be found in the *Congressional Record*. Some statutes contain "rule-making" provisions that act as procedural authorities, though no Senate source compiles all of them. Each committee adopts its own written rules, which are published in the *Record* and compiled, in each Congress, in *Authority and Rules of Senate Committees*, a print of the Committee on Rules and Administration. Other Senate committee prints, which provide supporting information on elements of Senate procedure, include *Budget Process Law Annotated*, the *Senate Cloture Rule*, and *Treaties and Other International Agreements*. The parliamentarians in both chambers have prepared concise summary documents on procedure in the legislative process. In the Senate, currently only the Republican Conference appears to have adopted written rules.

This report assumes a basic familiarity with Senate procedures. It will be updated to reflect the appearance of new editions of the documents discussed and to address substantial changes in their content and availability. Information about House parliamentary reference sources is provided in CRS Report RL30787, *Parliamentary Reference Sources: House of Representatives*, by Richard S. Beth and Megan Suzanne Lynch.

Contents

Figures

Appendixes

Contacts

Introduction

The Senate's procedures are not based solely on its standing rules. The foundations of Senate procedure also include the body's standing orders, published precedents, rule-making statutes, committee rules, and informal practices. Constitutional mandates also impose procedural requirements on the Senate, and rules of the Senate's party conferences can sometimes affect committee and floor action.

Various reference sources provide information about how and when these foundations of Senate procedures govern specific parliamentary situations. This report discusses the contents, format, and availability of reference sources that provide information about contemporary procedures in the Senate. It covers three types of parliamentary reference authority:

- official documents that set forth Senate rules, precedents, or other sources parliamentary authority, such as the *Senate Manual*, *Riddick's Senate Procedure*, rule-making statutes, and the rules adopted by Senate committees;

- publications on procedure from committees and offices of the Senate (e.g., *Enactment of a Law*, a document prepared by the Senate Parliamentarian); and

- rules of the Senate's party conferences.

Before describing the individual parliamentary reference sources that fall into each of these groups, this report reviews some principles of Senate parliamentary procedure that are applicable when using and evaluating information from these sources.

The report next takes up the Senate's official parliamentary reference sources. These are documents that set forth authoritative statements of Senate rules, procedures, and precedents. Senators often cite these official reference sources when raising a point of order or defending against one. This report discusses the following procedural authorities:

- *Senate Manual*;

- *Standing Rules of the Senate*;

- Permanent standing orders of the Senate;

- Rules for Regulation of the Senate Wing of the Capitol;

- Rules for Impeachment Trials;

- Cleaves' Manual on Conferences;

- Laws Relating to the Senate;

- the Constitution;

- *Riddick's Senate Procedure*;

- rule-making statutes;

- Standing orders of the Senate adopted by unanimous consent;

- unanimous consent agreements; and

- committee rules.

Following the description of each authority, a box presents information on how to consult the source, including any versions available through the Internet. Names of websites are listed in bold type. Many of the descriptions are also accompanied by sample pages excerpted from the printed version of the official source documents in which they appear, which show the format of the document and are annotated to indicate special features and components. Although some of these excerpts are not drawn from the most recent edition of the source in question, they illustrate the same format and other features retained in the current editions.

A number of additional publications of committees and other offices of the Senate, which do not themselves constitute parliamentary authorities of the Senate, nevertheless provide background information on those parliamentary authorities and guidance on their use. Those discussed in this report include:

- *Budget Process Law Annotated*;

- *Senate Cloture Rule*;

- *Treaties and Other International Agreements*;

- *Enactment of a Law*; and

- *How Our Laws Are Made*

The rules of the party conferences are also included within the scope of the report because, although they do not themselves govern Senate proceedings, their provisions may nevertheless have effects on those proceedings. The report presents a description of each parliamentary reference source in these groups, and each description is, again, followed by a box presenting information on how to consult the source, including its availability on the Internet.

Two appendices summarize the information on access presented in the boxes throughout the report. **Appendix A** furnishes citations for each reference source described in this report and for relevant Congressional Research Service (CRS) products. A summary of Senate parliamentary reference information available through the Internet is provided in **Appendix B**.

Official guidance on Senate procedure is available from the Office of the Senate Parliamentarian (4-6128). CRS staff (7-5700) also can assist with clarifying Senate rules and procedures.

Principles of Senate Parliamentary Practice

The Senate applies the regulations set forth in its various parliamentary authorities in accordance with several principles that remain generally applicable across the entire range of parliamentary situations: Among these principles may be listed the following: (1) Senate procedures derive from multiple sources; (2) the Senate has the constitutional power to make its own rules of procedure; (3) Senators often must initiate enforcement of their rules; (4) the Senate conducts much of its business by unanimous consent; (5) the Senate usually follows its precedents; and (6) the Senate adheres to many informal practices. Each of these principles is discussed below.

Multiple Sources of Senate Procedure

The standing rules of the Senate may be the most obvious source of Senate parliamentary procedure, but they are by no means the only one. Other sources of Senate procedures include

- requirements imposed by the Constitution, particularly those in Article I, Section 5;

- standing orders of the Senate;

- precedents of the Senate;

- statutory provisions that establish procedural requirements (hereafter referred to as "rule-making statutes");

- rules of procedure adopted by each committee;

- rules of the Senate's party conferences;

- procedural agreements entered into by unanimous consent; and

- informal practices that the Senate adheres to by custom.

In order to answer a question about Senate procedure, it often is necessary to take account of several of these sources. For example, Rule XIX of the Senate's standing rules provides that "the presiding officer shall recognize the Senator who shall first address him."[1] When several Senators seek recognition at the same time however, there is precedent that "priority of recognition shall be accorded to the majority leader and minority leader, the majority manager and minority manager, in that order."[2] This precedential principle sometimes can have significant consequences on the Senate floor. For example, it gives the majority leader the opportunity to offer the debate-ending motion to table, or to propose second-degree amendments to "unfriendly" first-degree amendments.

Constitutional Rule-Making Authority of the Senate

Article I of the Constitution gives the Senate the authority to determine its rules of procedure. There are two dimensions to the Senate's constitutional rule-making authority. First, the Senate can decide what rules should govern its procedures. The Senate exercises this rule-making power when it adopts an amendment to the standing rules, or creates a new standing rule, by majority vote. The Senate also uses its rule-making power when it creates standing orders, and when it enacts rule-making provisions of statutes such as the Congressional Budget and Impoundment Act of 1974. Standing orders and rule-making provisions of law have the same standing and effect as the Senate's standing rules because all are created through an exercise of the Senate's constitutional rule-making authority.

The second dimension to the Senate's rule-making authority is that the chamber can decide when its rules of procedure should not govern. In practical terms, this means the Senate can waive its rules by unanimous consent. Under a provision of Senate Rule V, the body can also suspend its rules by a two-thirds vote, although this course is procedurally difficult and rarely taken. The Senate has no established means to supersede its rules by majority vote, an option that is available to the House through the adoption of a "special rule."[3] The Senate can achieve the effect of

---

[1] Rule XIX, in U.S. Congress, Senate, *Senate Manual*, S. Doc. 107-1, 107th Cong., 1st sess., prepared by Committee on Rules and Administration (Washington: GPO, 2002), sec. 19.

[2] Floyd M. Riddick and Alan S. Frumin, *Riddick's Senate Procedure: Precedents and Practices*, S.Doc. 101-28, 101st Cong., 2nd sess. (Washington: GPO, 1992), p. 1098.

[3] Special rules are resolutions reported by the House Rules Committee that usually specify how a measure is to be (continued...)

waiving a rule if a majority votes to overrule a decision of the presiding officer to sustain a point of order, or not to sustain a point of order that the presiding officer has submitted to the full body for decision.[4] Action of this kind, however, not only sets the rule aside for the immediate situation, but thereby establishes a precedent that will govern subsequent rulings of the presiding officer interpreting the meaning and applicability of that rule. In some cases, decisions of the Senate on points of order have had the effect of rendering a rule unenforceable in its previous generally accepted sense.

Enforcing the Senate Rules and Precedents

The Senate's presiding officer (whether it is the Vice President or a Senator of the majority party) does not always call to the chamber's attention that a violation of Senate rules is taking place.[5] The Senate often can violate its procedures unless a Senator makes a point of order, at the right moment, that the proposed action violates the standing rules or precedents, a constitutional provision, or a source of procedure that has the same authority as a standing rule (i.e., standing order, rule-making statute, or unanimous consent agreement).

When a point of order is raised, the presiding officer usually makes a ruling without debate. Under Rule XX, the presiding officer has the option of submitting "any question of order for the decision of the Senate." He rarely does this, but may do so if the existing rules and precedents do not speak clearly on the parliamentary question at hand. In such cases, the presiding officer will often invite debate on the question of order.

The presiding officer must submit two types of questions of order to the Senate for it to decide. First, under Rule XVI, paragraph 4, the Senate decides questions concerning the germaneness or relevance of most amendments to appropriations bills, and does so without debate. Second, according to the Senate's precedents, the Senate is to decide all constitutional questions, with debate usually allowed.[6] This practice rests on the principle that the presiding officer possesses authority only over the interpretation of procedures established by the Senate, and only the Senate itself possesses any such authority in relation to the Constitution.

Any Senator can appeal the ruling of the presiding officer on a question of order. The Senate then decides, usually by majority vote, to uphold or overturn the presiding officer's decision. This vote usually establishes a precedent that guides the presiding officer in deciding future questions of order, unless and until this precedent is overturned by another decision of the Senate or by a rules change. Some rulemaking statutes require a super-majority vote to overturn on appeal the presiding officer's ruling on a point of order.[7]

(...continued)

considered on the floor. Once the House adopts a special rule by a majority vote, it governs consideration of the measure. Special rules often waive procedural requirements imposed by the rules of the House or rule-making statutes.

[4] Section 904 of the Congressional Budget Act establishes a procedure by which the Senate can vote to waive certain budget-related prohibitions and requirements in an individual case by majority vote or by a three-fifths vote of all Senators.

[5] An important exception occurs when the Senate is operating under cloture. When this happens, the precedents provide that the presiding officer has the authority to rule all dilatory motions out of order on his own initiative. See Senate Rule XXII, paragraph 2, in *Senate Manual*, sec. 22.2.

[6] *Riddick's Senate Procedure*. pp. 989 and 1491-1492.

[7] For examples of provisions that would require such a super-majority, see Section 904(d) of the Congressional Budget (continued...)

Senators are much more likely than Representatives to appeal decisions of their presiding officer. This difference in the practices of the two chambers arises largely because the officer who presides over the proceedings of the House of Representatives is either the Speaker of the House, who is the elected leader of the majority party, or her designee. An appeal of the decision of the chair on a point of order could thus be viewed as a vote against the Speaker's leadership. This situation does not arise in the Senate, because the constitutional presiding officer of the Senate is the Vice President, who is not elected as a leader of a Senate majority.

Parliamentary actions taken on the basis of an informal practice, or a rule of one of the Senate's party conferences, are not enforceable on the Senate floor. While informal practices and party conference rules can affect Senate committee and floor action, they are not invoked through an exercise of the Senate's constitutional rule-making authority; hence, they do not have the same authority as Senate rules and procedures. Informal practices evolve over the years as custom, and party conference rules are adopted and enforced by each party.

The Senate's Reliance on Unanimous Consent

The Senate's Standing Rules emphasize the rights of individual Senators, in particular by affording each Senator the right to debate at length and the right to offer amendments even if they are not relevant to the bill under consideration. It would be impossible for the Senate to act on legislation in a timely fashion if Senators always exercised these two powerful rights. For this and other reasons, the Senate often agrees by unanimous consent to operate outside its standing rules.

In practice, Senate business is frequently conducted under unanimous consent agreements, known as "time agreements" when they include limits on the time for debating measures, amendments, motions or other questions. These agreements also may structure the amendment process and require the germaneness or relevance of amendments. Unanimous consent agreements may be used to bring up a measure,[8] to define how the measure will be considered on the floor, and to control how the Senate will consider individual amendments.

Given the fact that it takes only one Senator to object to a unanimous consent agreement, each agreement is carefully crafted by the majority leader, in consultation with the minority leader, leaders of the committee that reported the bill in question, and other Senators who have indicated a particular interest in the legislation. The agreement is then formally propounded on the floor, usually again by the majority leader, and takes effect if no Senator objects. Once entered into, a consent agreement has the same authority as the Senate's standing rules and is enforceable on the Senate floor. Consent agreements have the effect of changing "all Senate rules and precedents that are contrary to the terms of the agreement."[9] One could argue that these agreements are even stronger than the standing rules because once entered into, they can be altered only by a further unanimous consent; this is a more rigorous threshold than the majority vote requirement for changing the Senate's standing rules.

(...continued)

Act, P.L. 93-344 as amended, (2 U.S.C. 621 note)

[8] A body of precedents has developed on how unanimous consent agreements are to be interpreted and applied in different procedural situations. These precedents are covered in *Riddick's Senate Procedure*, pp. 1311-1369. The majority leader often calls up a measure by unanimous consent rather than by offering a motion to proceed to consideration of the measure. The motion to proceed is usually debatable, and hence open to a filibuster.

[9] *Riddick's Senate Procedure*, p. 1311.

The Importance of Precedents

The published precedents of the Senate expound the ways in which the Senate has interpreted and applied its rules. The precedents both complement and supplement the rules of the Senate. As illustrated earlier by the example of according priority recognition to the majority leader, the close interplay between the precedents and the standing rules often makes it necessary to consult the precedents for guidance on how rules are to be understood. The brevity of the Senate's standing rules often makes the body's precedents particularly important as a determinant of proceedings.

Precedents are analogous to case law in their effect. Just as attorneys in court will cite previous judicial decisions to support their arguments, Senators will cite precedents of the Senate to support a point of order, or defend against one, or to argue for or against an appeal of the presiding officer's ruling on a point of order. Similarly, the presiding officer will often support his or her ruling by citing the precedents. In this way, precedents influence the manner in which current Senate rules are applied by relating past decisions to the specific case before the chamber.

Precedents usually are established when the Senate votes on questions of order (i.e., on a point of order that the presiding officer has submitted to the body, or on whether to uphold or overturn a ruling of the presiding officer), or when the presiding officer decides a question of order and this ruling is not appealed. Historically, the Senate follows such precedents until "the Senate in its wisdom should reverse or modify that decision."[10] Precedents also can be created when the presiding officer responds to a parliamentary inquiry.

Precedents do not carry equal weight. Inasmuch as the Senate itself has the ultimate constitutional authority over its own rules, precedents reflecting the judgment of the full Senate are considered the most authoritative. Accordingly, precedents based on a vote of the Senate have more weight than those based on rulings of the presiding officer. Responses of the presiding officer to parliamentary inquiries have even less weight, because they are subject to no process of appeal through which the full Senate could confirm or contest them. In addition, more recent precedents generally have greater weight than earlier ones, and a precedent that reflects an established pattern of rulings will have more weight than a precedent that is isolated in its effect. All precedents also must be evaluated in the historical context of the Senate's rules and practices at the time the precedents were established. Senators seeking precedents to support or rebut an argument may consult the Senate Parliamentarian's Office (4-6128).

The Senate's Unofficial Practices

Some Senate procedural actions are based on unofficial practices that have evolved over the years and become accepted custom. These practices do not have the same standing as the chamber's rules, nor are they compiled in any written source of authority. Although these unofficial practices cannot be enforced on the Senate floor, many of them are well established and customarily followed. Some contemporary examples of unofficial practices include respecting "holds" that individual Senators sometimes place on consideration of specific measures, and giving the majority leader or his designee the prerogative to offer motions to proceed to the consideration of a bill, to recess, or to adjourn.

---

[10] *Riddick's Senate Procedure*, p. 987.

The *Senate Manual* and Authorities it Contains

Senate Manual

The *Senate Manual* compiles in a single document many of the chief official parliamentary authorities of the Senate, several of which are not readily available in any other current publication.[11] The publication, prepared under the auspices of the Senate committee on Rules and Administration, appears periodically in a new edition as a Senate Document. The current edition, which was issued in the 107th Congress, contains the text of the following parliamentary authorities (the titles given are those used in the Manual):[12]

- The Standing Rules of the Senate, with its own table of contents and index;

- Non-Statutory Standing Orders Not Embraced in the Rules, and Resolutions Affecting the Business of the Senate;

- Rules for Regulation of the Senate Wing of the United States Capitol and Senate Office Buildings;

- Rules of Procedure and Practice in the Senate When Sitting on Impeachment Trials;

- Cleaves' Manual of the Law and Practice in Regard to Conferences and Conference Reports, with its own index;

- General and Permanent Laws Relating to the U.S. Senate, with its own table of contents; and

- The Constitution of the United States of America, as well as the amendments to the Constitution, with its own index.

The following sections of this part discuss each of these authorities in more detail, with references, where appropriate, to other available sources in which the authority is also presented.

The *Manual* also contains a general table of contents and an index, which are less detailed in their references to the respective components than are the special tables of contents and indexes, when present. Individual provisions of each procedural authority are assigned section numbers that run throughout the *Manual* in a single sequence, often with gaps between the end of one section and the start of the next, and that always appear in bold type. The section numbers assigned to the Standing Rules correspond to the numbers of the rules themselves. For example, paragraph 2 of Senate Rule XXII, which sets forth the cloture rule, is found at section 22.2 of the *Manual*. All the indexes to the *Manual* direct readers to these section numbers. For example, the indexes indicate that the motion to adjourn is covered in *Manual* sections 6.4, 9, and 22.1. For this reason, the document is generally cited by section number rather than by page. The indexes should be examined thoroughly to find all pertinent citations.

---

[11] The Senate Manual also includes a variety of historical and statistical information; this report describes only those materials included in the *Manual* that constitute procedural authorities.

[12] The excerpts from the *Senate Manual* that appear later in this part of this report were taken from the 103rd Congress edition, S. Doc. 103-1 (Washington: GPO, 1993). These excerpts illustrate the same format and other features retained in the most recent edition (S.Doc. 107-1).

Senate Manual

U.S. Congress, Senate, *Senate Manual*, S.Doc. 107-1, 107th Cong., 1st sess., compiled by the Senate Committee on Rules and Administration, (Washington: GPO, 2002).

Print: When published, the *Senate Manual* is distributed to offices of Senators and committees; limited copies are available from Senate Printing and Document Services (4-7701). The *Senate Manual* also can be consulted at the CRS Senate Research Center (7-5978) in B-07, Russell Senate Office building.

Internet: The Senate Manual

GPO Access, a website of the Government Printing Office: The full text of the *Senate Manual* can be searched online at http://www.gpoaccess.gov/smanual/index.html.

Standing Rules of the Senate

The Senate does not re-adopt its code of Standing Rules at the beginning of each new Congress, but instead has always regarded its rules as continuing in effect without having to be re-adopted.[13] The Senate follows this practice on grounds that it is a continuing body, inasmuch as only one-third of its membership enters on new terms of office after every biennial election, so that a quorum is continuous. Changes to the standing rules are proposed in the form of Senate resolutions, which can be adopted by majority vote. At the start of the 110th Congress, there were 44 standing rules of the Senate.

The Standing Rules of the Senate are set forth both in the *Senate Manual* and in a free-standing Senate Document periodically issued by the Senate Committee on Rules and Administration, the most recent edition of which is *Standing Rules of the Senate* (Senate Document 110-9). This free-standing print reflects changes made to the rules since the last edition of the *Manual*.

In both the *Manual* and the separate print, the Standing Rules appear with footnotes indicating amendments adopted since their last general revision in 1979. These footnotes cite the resolution adopted by the Senate to make the rules change. The *Manual* and the separate print each present the Standing Rules with an itemized table of contents and a detailed, separate index.

---

[13] This principle is now embodied in paragraph 2 of Senate Rule V.

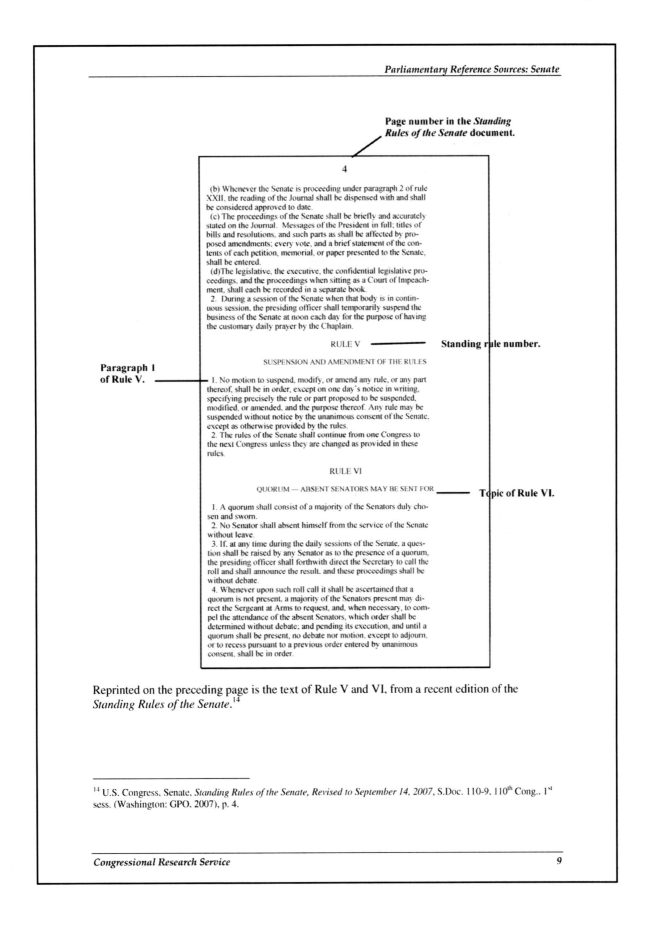

Reprinted on the preceding page is the text of Rule V and VI, from a recent edition of the *Standing Rules of the Senate*.[14]

---

[14] U.S. Congress, Senate, *Standing Rules of the Senate, Revised to September 14, 2007*, S.Doc. 110-9, 110th Cong., 1st sess. (Washington: GPO, 2007), p. 4.

Standing Rules of the Senate

U.S. Congress, Senate, *Standing Rules of the Senate, Revised to September 14, 2007*, S.Doc. 110-9, 110th Cong., 1st sess. (Washington: GPO, 2007).

Print: When published, the *Standing Rules of the Senate* document is distributed to the offices of Senators and committees. Copies also are available from Senate Printing and Document Services (4-7701). The Standing Rules of the Senate also appear in the *Senate Manual*, secs. 1-50.

Internet: The Senate's standing rules (with no footnotes or index) are available through the following:

Senate home page
http://rules.senate.gov/senaterules/

CRS, the Congressional Research Service Guide to "Congressional Processes" at
http://www.crs.gov/products/guides/guidehome.shtml

THOMAS, the public access website of the Library of Congress
http://thomas.loc.gov/home/legbranch/legbranch.html

Permanent Standing Orders

From time to time, the Senate adopts a resolution or agrees to a unanimous consent request to create a standing order of the Senate. A standing order, while not embraced in the Standing Rules, operates with the same authority as a standing rule, and is enforceable on the Senate floor in the same way. A standing order remains in effect until repealed by the Senate, unless otherwise specified in the order itself.

The standing orders that the Senate has created by the adopting resolutions and that remain in effect are compiled in the *Senate Manual* under the heading "Nonstatutory Standing Orders Not Embraced in the Rules, and Resolutions Affecting the Business of the Senate." This is the only readily available compilation of permanent standing orders currently in effect. In addition to setting forth the text of these standing orders, the *Senate Manual* provides: (1) a heading stating the subject matter of each; and (2) a citation to the Senate resolution(s) that created and amended it (especially for older standing orders, a citation to the *Senate Journal* is sometimes provided). Footnotes provide supplementary information, such as noting when references in the standing order (e.g., the name of a committee) were changed. Reprinted below is a standing order dealing with the authority of the Committee on Appropriations, as it appears in the *Senate Manual*.[15]

Sources for standing orders adopted by unanimous consent and effective only for a single Congress or other limited period of time are covered below in the section "Standing Orders by Unanimous Consent."

Standing Orders

A compilation of standing orders adopted by resolution and currently in effect appears in the *Senate Manual*, sections 60-114.

---

[15] "Standing Orders of the Senate", in *Senate Manual*, S.Doc. 103-1, p. 106.

Senate Manual —— [70]
section number.

STANDING ORDERS OF THE SENATE

70   COMMITTEE ON APPROPRIATIONS AUTHORITY —— Standing order's
subject matter.

Resolved, That for the purpose of obtaining and laying
factual data and information before the Senate Committee
on Appropriations, or any subcommittee thereof, for its
consideration in the discharge of its functions, the chair-

Text of standing order. —— man or acting chairman of said committee is hereby authorized and directed, within the limit of funds made
available by resolutions of the Senate, to appoint and
employ such experts as he may deem necessary to obtain
such data and information, and such experts, upon the
written authority of the chairman or acting chairman,
shall have the right to examine the books, documents,
papers, reports, or other records of any department,
agency, or establishment of the Federal Government in
the District of Columbia and elsewhere; be it further
Resolved, That the said committee through its chairman
is hereby authorized, within the limit of funds made available by resolutions of the Senate, to appoint additional
clerical help and assistants.

(S. Res. 193, 78-1, Oct. 14, 1943; S. Res. 261, 95-2, Mar. 11, 1978.) —— Citation to the adopted
Senate resolutions that
created and amended
this standing order.

72   CLOSING THE OFFICE OF A SENATOR OR SENATE LEADER WHO
DIES OR RESIGNS

Resolved, That (a)(1) In the case of the death or resignation of a Senator during his term of office, the employees
in the office of such Senator who are on the Senate payroll on the date of such death or resignation shall be
continued on such payroll at their respective salaries for a
period not to exceed sixty days, or such greater number of
days as may, in any particular case, be established by the
Senate Committee on Rules and Administration as being
required to complete the closing of the office of such Senator. Such employees so continued on the payroll of the
Senate shall, while so continued, perform their duties
under the direction of the Secretary of the Senate, and
such Secretary shall remove from such payroll any such
employees who are not attending to the duties for which
their services are continued.

(2) If an employee of a Senator continued on the Senate
payroll pursuant to paragraph (1) resigns or is terminated
during the period required to complete the closing of the
office of such Senator, the Secretary of the Senate may
replace such employee by appointing another individual.
Any individual appointed as a replacement under the au-

106 —— Senate Manual page number.

Rules for Regulation of the Senate Wing

Senate Rule XXXIII authorizes the Senate Committee on Rules and Administration to make
"rules and regulations respecting such parts of the Capitol ... as ... may be set apart for the use of
the Senate." The rule is so framed as to extend this authority to the entire Senate side of the
Capitol complex, and explicitly includes reference to the press galleries and their operation.[16]
Several of the regulations adopted by the Committee on Rules and Administration under this
authority have a bearing on floor activity, including ones addressing: (1) the floor duties of the
secretaries for the majority and for the minority; (2) the system of "legislative buzzers and signal
lights;" and (3) the "use of display materials in the Senate chamber."[17]

---

[16] Senate Rule XXXIII, paragraph 2, in *Senate Manual,* sec. 33.2.

[17] Rules II, XV, and XVII for Regulation of the Senate Wing, *in Senate Manual,* secs. 121, 134, and 136, respectively.

These regulations are carried in the *Senate Manual* under the heading "Rules for Regulation of the Senate Wing of the United States Capitol and Senate Office Buildings." (Before 1998, the title used was "Rules for Regulation of the Senate Wing of the United States Capitol.")[18] Footnotes in this section include citations to the date when various regulations were adopted, identification of amendments adopted and citations to their dates, and references to related authorities.

Rules for Regulation of the Senate Wing

Current regulations adopted by the Senate Committee on Rules and Administration for Regulation of the Senate portion of the Capitol complex are presented in the *Senate Manual*, secs. 120-136.

Internet: The full text of the Senate Manual can be searched online at

GPO Access, a website of the Government Printing Office
http://www.gpoaccess.gov/smanual/index.html.

Rules for Impeachment Trials

The Senate has adopted a special body of rules to govern its proceedings when sitting as a Court of Impeachment to try impeachments preferred to it by the House of Representatives. The Senate treats these rules, like its Standing Rules, as remaining permanently in effect unless altered by action of the Senate. On occasion, usually when the trial of an impeachment is in prospect, the Senate has adopted amendments to these rules. Significant changes occurred in 1974, when an impeachment of President Richard Nixon was impending, and the most recent amendments were adopted in 1986, pursuant to S.Res. 479 of the 99th Congress, in preparation for the trial of the impeachment of Federal District Judge Harry E. Claiborne.

The *Senate Manual* presents these rules for impeachment trials, as most recently revised in 1986, under the heading "Rules of Procedure and Practice in the Senate When Sitting on Impeachment Trials." Otherwise, these rules were most recently printed in 1999 as part of a volume (S.Doc. 106-2) containing the articles of impeachment against President William J. Clinton in 1999, the President's response, and the replication of the House. Previously, the Senate in 1986 published a document, entitled *Procedure and Guidelines for Impeachment Trials in the United States Senate* (S.Doc. 99-33), which contains not only these rules for trying impeachments, but also a variety of additional materials concerning procedure in impeachments. These materials included pertinent excerpts from the Constitution and the Standing Rules of the Senate, descriptions of the "Sequence of events at the beginning of a trial" and "Sequence of events at the close of a trial," and a summary of "Precedents and practices for impeachment trial." This summary is arranged alphabetically by topic, with citations to the *Congressional Record*, *Senate Journal*, or other documents for each precedent cited, in much the same format used in *Riddick's Senate Procedure* (discussed below).

---

[18] See U.S. Congress, Senate, *Senate Manual*, S. Doc. 104-1, 104th Cong., 1st sess., prepared by the Senate Committee on Rules and Administration (Washington: GPO, 1995), sec. 80.

Rules for Impeachment Trials

The "Rules of Procedure and Practice in the Senate When Sitting on Impeachment Trials" appear in the *Senate Manual* at secs. 140-165.

Print: Other than in the *Senate Manual*, these rules were most recently printed in: U.S. Congress, Senate, *Impeachment of President William Jefferson Clinton*, (S. Doc. 106-2), 106th Cong., 1st sess., printed at the direction of Gary Sisco, Secretary of the Senate (Washington: GPO, 1999), pp. 3-13. This document is available from Senate Printing and Document Services (4-7701).

These rules also appear in: U.S. Congress, Senate, *Procedure and Guidelines for Impeachment Trials in the United States Senate (Revised Edition)*, S.Doc. 99-33, 99th Cong., 2nd sess., prepared pursuant to Senate Resolution 439, 99th Congress. 2nd session, submitted by Senator Robert C. Byrd and Senator Robert Dole, by Floyd M. Riddick, Parliamentarian Emeritus of the United States Senate and Robert B. Dove, Parliamentarian of the United States Senate (Washington: GPO, 1986), pp. 2-8.

Internet: Both of the Senate Documents cited can be accessed, in both text and in PDF format, through:

GPO Access, a website of the Government Printing Office
http://www.access.gpo.gov/congress/senate/miscspub.html

Cleaves' Manual on Conferences

Cleaves' Manual presents a digest of the rules, precedents, and other provisions of parliamentary authorities governing Senate practice in relation to the functioning of House-Senate conference committees and conference reports, as they stood at the end of the 19th century. Although rules and practices governing conferences have since altered in many respects, and many of the precedents now applicable to conferences have been established since Cleaves' Manual was prepared, many of the principles compiled and set forth in Cleaves' Manual are still applicable to current practice.

The document, which was "collated and prepared" at the direction of the Senate in 1900, is carried in the *Senate Manual* under the heading "Cleaves' Manual of the Law and Practice in Regard to Conferences and Conference Reports." It includes excerpts from the *Manual of Parliamentary Practice* prepared by Thomas Jefferson as Vice President at the turn of the 19th century, as well as pertinent statements by other Vice Presidents and by Speakers, excerpts from Senate Rules, statements of principles established by precedent, and explanatory notes. In addition, a section at the end sets forth forms for conference reports and joint explanatory statements.

The material presented in Cleaves' Manual is arranged in numbered paragraphs under a series of topical headings. Each entry includes a citation to the source of the excerpt or to the rules and precedents on which the stated principles are based. These citations often reference the record of proceedings in the *Congressional Record*, its predecessors, or the *Senate Journal* that established pertinent precedent. The *Senate Manual* also includes a separate index to this compilation.

Cleaves' Manual on Conferences

The text of Cleaves' Manual, together with its index, is carried in the *Senate Manual* at sections 170-231.

Laws Relating to the Senate

The most voluminous component of the *Senate Manual* presents a compilation of "General and Permanent Laws Relating to the U.S. Senate." The statutory excerpts appear in their codified version (i.e., organized under the relevant title, chapter and section of the United States Code). The *Manual* provides a separate table of contents to the provisions included, but it sets forth the provisions themselves without citation or commentary.

Although most of the selected provisions address the administration and operations of the Senate, some of them bear on questions related to Senate procedure, such as those concerning Senators' oaths of office, officers of the Senate, and investigative procedure in Senate committees. The compilation includes, as well, some "rule-making statutes," or statutory provisions that establish procedures for Senate action on specified measures. The provisions included here are specifically those associated with the congressional budget process and the Trade Act. Rulemaking provisions of statute are discussed more comprehensively in the section on **Error! Reference source not found.**," below, and the statutes regulating the budget process are treated further in the section on "Budget Process Law Annotated."

General and Permanent Laws Relating to the U.S. Senate

The selected excerpts from statute, together with their own table of contents, are carried in the *Senate Manual* at secs. 250-1227.

Constitution

The Constitution imposes several procedural requirements on the Senate. For example, Article I, section 5 requires the Senate to keep and publish an official *Journal* of its proceedings, requires a majority quorum for the conduct of business on the Senate floor, and mandates that a yea and nay vote take place upon the request of one-fifth of the Senators present. The Constitution also bestows certain exclusive powers on the Senate: Article II, section 2 grants the Senate sole authority to advise and consent to treaties and executive nominations; and Article I, section 3 gives the Senate the sole power to try all impeachments.[19]

The *Senate Manual* presents the text of the Constitution, followed by that of its amendments. The *Manual* places bold brackets around text that has been amended, and a citation directs readers to the *Manual* section containing the amendment. The *Manual* also provides historical footnotes about the ratification of the Constitution and each amendment, as well as a special index to the text.

Reprinted on the next page is an excerpt from Article I of the Constitution, as it appears in the *Senate Manual*.[20]

[19] The Senate's "Rules for Impeachment Trials" are discussed above, in the section with that title. The Senate's advice and consent role is addressed in the section on "Treaties and Other International Agreements," below.

[20] Constitution of the United States, in *Senate Manual*, S.Doc. 103-1, p. 825.

Parliamentary Reference Sources: Senate

CONSTITUTION OF THE UNITED STATES   【761.17】 — Senate Manual section number.

Clause 4 of Article 1, Section 3 of the Constitution.

elected, be an Inhabitant of that State for which he shall be chosen.

⁴ The Vice President of the United States shall be President of the Senate, but shall have no Vote, unless they be equally divided.   761.10 — Each constitutional clause is assigned a Senate Manual number.

⁵ The Senate shall chuse their other Officers, and also a President pro tempore, in the absence of the Vice President, *or when he shall exercise the Office of President of the United States.*   761.11

⁶ The Senate shall have the sole Power to try all Impeachments. When sitting for that Purpose, they shall be on Oath or Affirmation. When the President of the United States *is tried, the Chief Justice shall preside:* And no Person shall be convicted without the Concurrence of two-thirds of the Members present.   761.12

⁷ Judgment in Cases of Impeachment shall not extend further than to removal from Office, and disqualification to hold and enjoy any Office of honor, Trust, or Profit under the United States: but the Party convicted shall nevertheless be liable and subject to Indictment, Trial, Judgment, and Punishment, according to Law.   761.13

Section 4 of Article 1 of the Constitution.

SECTION 4. ¹ The Time, Places and Manner of holding Elections for Senators and Representatives, shall be prescribed in each State by the Legislature thereof; but the Congress may at any time by Law make or alter such Regulations, except as to the Places of chusing Senators.   761.14

² The Congress shall assemble at least once in every Year, and such Meeting shall 【be on the first Monday in December,】 unless they shall by Law appoint a different Day.*   761.15

Text enclosed in the bold brackets was changed by an Amendment to the Constitution.

SECTION 5. ¹ Each House shall be the Judge of the Elections, Returns, and Qualifications of its own Members, and a Majority of each shall constitute a Quorum to do Business; but a smaller Number may adjourn from day to day, and may be authorized to compel the Attendance of absent Members, in such Manner, and under such Penalties as each House may provide.   761.16

² Each House may determine the Rules of its Proceedings, punish its Members for disorderly Behavior, and, with the Concurrence of two thirds, expel a Member.   761.17

*The part included in heavy brackets was changed by Section 2 of amendment XX, Senate Manual section 790.2.

Directs reader to Senate Manual section where amended text for Section 4, clause 2 is located.

825 — Senate Manual page number.

The Constitution

The Constitution and its amendments, together with a separate index, are printed in the *Senate Manual* at secs. 760-797.5.

Print: The text of the Constitution and amendments, with annotations prepared by CRS that include references to decisions of the Supreme Court, is printed in: U.S. Congress, Senate, *The Constitution of the United States of America: Analysis and Interpretation,* S.Doc. 108-17, 108th Cong., 2nd sess., prepared by the Congressional Research Service, Library of Congress, Johnny H. Killian, George A. Costello, Kenneth R. Thomas, co-editors (Washington: GPO, 2004). This document is often referred to as *The Constitution Annotated.*

Between comprehensive revisions, *The Constitution Annotated* is supplemented by "pocket parts" also prepared by CRS. The current supplement is: U.S. Congress, Senate, *The Constitution of the United States of America: Analysis and Interpretation: 2006 Supplement,* S.Doc. 110-6, 110th Cong., 1st sess., prepared by the Congressional Research Service, Library of Congress, Kenneth R. Thomas, editor-in-chief (Washington: GPO, 2007).

Internet: *The Constitution of the United States of America: Analysis and Interpretation* is available through the following websites:

CRS, the Congressional Research Service
http://www.crs.gov/products/conan/.

GPO Access, a website of the Government Printing Office:
http://www.gpoaccess.gov/constitution/index.html.

The Constitution, with its amendments, is available through:

THOMAS, the public access website of the Library of Congress,
http://lcweb2.loc.gov/const/const.html

Other Official Senate Parliamentary Authorities

Riddick's Senate Procedure

Riddick's Senate Procedure, often referred to simply as *Riddick's Procedure,* is the most comprehensive reference source covering Senate rules, precedents, and practices. Its principal purpose is to present a digest of precedents established in the Senate; the current edition, published in 1992, covers significant Senate precedents established from 1883 to 1992. It was written by Floyd M. Riddick, Parliamentarian of the Senate from 1964 to 1974, and Alan S. Frumin, Parliamentarian of the Senate from 1987 to 1995 and Senior Assistant Parliamentarian since 1995. This edition is an updated and revised version of the 1981 edition, written by Riddick. Earlier editions of this and predecessor documents appeared under the names of earlier Parliamentarians of the Senate, such as Charles J. Watkins, or Chief Clerks of the Senate, such as Henry H. Gilfry, extending back in the 19th century.

As implied by its full title, *Riddick's Senate Procedure: Precedents and Practices,* the document also presents discussions of the practice of the Senate on the basis of on its rules and customary practices as well as its precedents. It is organized around procedural topics, which are presented in alphabetical order. For each procedural topic, the volume first presents a summary of the general principles governing that topic, followed by the text of relevant Standing Rules, constitutional provisions, or rulemaking provisions of statute. Summaries of the principles established by individual precedents are then presented under subject headings organized in alphabetical order. The summaries rarely exceed one sentence. Many of the subject headings are further divided into more detailed topics, which are also presented in alphabetical order, and some of which may be further divided into subtopics. For example, the topic "Cloture Procedure" has a subject heading "Amendments After Cloture" which is further divided into 18 topics, such as "Drafted Improperly" and "Filing of Amendments."

Footnotes provide citations to the date, the Congress, and the session when each precedent was established, and to the *Congressional Record* or *Senate Journal* pages where readers can locate the pertinent proceedings (e.g., "July 28, 1916, 64-1, *Record*, pp. 11748-50"). Footnote citations beginning with the word "*see*" indicate precedents based on presiding officers' responses to parliamentary inquiries; citations without "*see*" indicate precedents created by ruling of the presiding officers or by votes of the Senate.

An appendix to *Riddick's Procedure* contains sample floor dialogues showing the terminology that Senators and the presiding officer use in different parliamentary situations. Examples of established forms used in the Senate (e.g., for various types of conference reports, the motion to invoke cloture) also are provided. Useful supplementary information appears in brackets throughout the appendix.

The publication's main index is useful for locating information on specific topics of Senate procedure; the table of contents lists only the main procedural topics covered in the book. The appendix has a separate index.

Reprinted on the following pages are excerpts from the "Cloture Procedure" sections in the body of *Riddick's Senate Procedure* and on the motion for "Reconsideration" from the appendix.

Riddick's Senate Procedure

Floyd M. Riddick and Alan S. Frumin, *Riddick's Senate Procedure: Precedents and Practices*, S.Doc. 101-28, 101st Cong., 2nd sess., with a foreword by Robert C. Byrd, [then] President pro tempore (Washington: GPO, 1992).

Print: *Riddick's Senate Procedure* is automatically distributed to new Senators. The publication also can be consulted in the CRS Senate Research Center (7-5978) in B-07, Russell Senate Office building. Copies are no longer available from GPO.

Internet: A browseable version of *Riddick's Senate Procedure* is available through:

GPO Access, a website of the Government Printing Office http://www.gpoaccess.gov/riddick/index.html.

There are no chapters in Riddick's Senate Procedure. The publication is organized around procedural topics such as "Cloture Procedure."

CLOTURE PROCEDURE

Cloture is the means by which the Senate limits debate on a measure or matter. A cloture motion "to bring to a close the debate on any measure, motion or other matter pending before the Senate, or the unfinished business" must be signed by at least sixteen Senators, and (with few exceptions) may be presented at any time. It may even be presented over the objections of the Senator who has the floor, but such presentation is merely an interruption and does not remove the Senator from the floor. When a cloture motion is presented, it is immediately reported by the Clerk at the direction of the Chair. The motion is applicable to the pending measure or matter or amendment pending thereto, or the unfinished business.

Under Rule XXII, the vote occurs on the motion on the second day of session after it is filed, and by precedent this is the case even if the consideration of the matter to which the motion applies had been suspended or displaced in the interim. One hour after the Senate convenes on the second day of session after the motion is presented, the Presiding Officer lays the motion before the Senate and directs the Clerk to call the roll to ascertain the presence of a quorum. If a quorum is present, a roll call vote occurs on the motion without debate. Adoption of the motion requires an affirmative vote of three-fifths of the Senators duly chosen and sworn, unless it applies to an amendment to the Senate rules, in which case an affirmative vote of two-thirds of the Senators voting (a quorum being present) is necessary.

If cloture is invoked, total consideration of the measure or matter to which it applies is limited to 30 hours, and a vote occurs on the clotured matter at the expiration of that time to the exclusion of all amendments not actually pending, and all motions except a motion to reconsider and table, and one quorum call (and motions required to establish a quorum). All time used for debate, votes, quorum calls, points of order and inquiries addressed to the Chair and responses thereto, the reading of amendments and for anything else that occurs while the Senate is considering the clotured matter, is charged against the allotted 30 hours. However, the time may be extended by a vote of three-fifths of the Senators duly chosen and sworn, and any such additional time is controlled by the two Leaders. Only one motion to extend time is in order on any calendar day.

For most procedural topics, the publication first discusses general principles governing the procedure.

Each Senator may speak for no more than one hour on the clotured matter and all amendments and motions affecting such matter. The Majority and Minority Leaders and the managers of the measure or matter may each be yielded up to two hours by other Senators, and the recipient of such time may yield time to other Senators. No other yielding of time is permitted except by unanimous consent. Any Senator who did not use or yield 10 minutes before the expiration of the 30 hours may thereafter speak only for the balance of the guaranteed 10 minutes.

Once cloture is invoked, no first degree amendment may be offered if it had not been filed with the Journal Clerk while the Senate was in session by 1:00 p.m. on the day following the day

282 — Page number in Riddick's Senate Procedure.

CLOTURE PROCEDURE   283

Continued discussion of general principles governing cloture.

the cloture motion was filed, and no second degree amendment may be offered if it had not been so filed at least 1 hour prior to the beginning of the cloture vote. Amendments must be correctly drafted, and may not be modified (except to conform page and line designations to a reprinted matter). Amendments which have been available in printed form on Senators' desks for at least 24 hours need not be read. No Senator may call up more than two amdendments until every Senator has had the opportunity to do likewise.

Nongermane amendments are out of order, as are all dilatory motions, quorum calls or amendments, and the Chair is authorized to make such determinations on its own initiative or in response to a point of order. The Chair is also authorized to count a quorum. Appeals are decided without debate.

Page number.

Paragraph of Senate standing rule that sets forth cloture procedure.

Rule XXII, Paragraph 2

[Procedure To Invoke Cloture]

Notwithstanding the provisions of rule II or rule IV or any other rule of the Senate, at any time a motion signed by sixteen Senators, to bring to a close the debate upon any measure, motion, other matter pending before the Senate, or the unfinished business, is presented to the Senate, the Presiding Officer, or clerk at the direction of the Presiding Officer, shall at once state the motion to the Senate, and one hour after the Senate meets on the following calendar day but one, he shall lay the motion before the Senate and direct that the clerk call the roll, and upon the ascertainment that a quorum is present, the Presiding Officer shall, without debate, submit to the Senate by a yea-and-nay vote the question:

"Is it the sense of the Senate that the debate shall be brought to a close?"

Full text of paragraph.

And if that question shall be decided in the affirmative by three-fifths of the Senators duly chosen and sworn—except on a measure or motion to amend the Senate rules, in which case the necessary affirmative vote shall be two-thirds of the Senators present and voting—then said measure, motion, or other matter pending before the Senate, or the unfinished business, shall be the unfinished business to the exclusion of all other business until disposed of.

Thereafter no Senator shall be entitled to speak in all more than one hour on the measure, motion, or other matter pending before the Senate, or the unfinished business, the amendments thereto, and motions affecting the same, and it shall be the duty of the Presiding Officer to keep the time of each Senator who speaks. Except by unanimous consent, no amendment shall be proposed after the vote to bring the debate to a close, unless it had been submitted in writing to the Journal Clerk by 1 o'clock p.m. on the day following the filing of the cloture motion if an amendment in the first degree, and unless it had been so submitted at least one hour prior to the beginning of the cloture vote if an amendment in the second degree. No dilatory motion, or dilatory amendment, or amendment not germane shall be in order. Points of order, including questions of relevancy, and appeals from the decision of the Presiding Officer, shall be decided without debate.

Page number. —— 286   SENATE PROCEDURE

Summaries of precedents—
are grouped together
under subject headings.
The heading for these
precedents, "Amends
Measure in Two or More
Places -- Out of Order on
Its Face," appears on
page 285.

in fact more than one amendment and is not in order.
Amendments consisting of two provisions and amending a
bill at two different points or in more than one place is in
fact two amendments and not in order,[6] and is subject to a
point of order. An amendment that hits a bill in more
than one noncontiguous place is technically out of order
as being more than one amendment, and if the Senate is
operating under cloture the Presiding Officer is required
to hold such a purported "amendment" out of order on his
or her own initiative.[7] In 1977, the Vice President on his
own initiative ruled out of order 26 such amendments
when the Senate was operating under cloture.[8]

One-sentence summary
of a precedent established
in 1977. Each summary
ends with a footnote number.

The Chair during the consideration of a measure under
cloture sustained a point of order against an amendment
which proposed to add a new section to a bill and at the
same place in the bill specified that succeeding sections be
renumbered accordingly,[9] but several days later reversed
itself during the consideration of an amendment which
was drafted in the same manner, and stated further that
"amending the bill in two places, where the second one is
simply redesignating another section, does not hit in two
places".[10] The Chair has ruled amendments out of order,
which hit the bill in two or more places, before they were
read holding the reading of such amendments was not
necessary prior to a ruling by the Chair thereon.[11]

Subject heading used to ——
group together relevant
precedents.

Chair Takes Initiative To Rule Amendments Out of Order:

The Vice President took "judicial notice of the fact that
we have now been for some 13 days, I believe, on this
measure, well over 100 votes having been taken" and sustained a point of order made by the Majority Leader that
required the Chair to take the initiative to rule out of
order amendments which were dilatory or out of order on
their face. An appeal was taken and laid upon the table,
sustaining the ruling of the Vice President.[12] Soon thereafter, the Vice President took the initiative to rule out of
order 33 consecutive amendments (26 of which hit the bill

Congressional Record
citations beginning with
"see" designate precedents
based on Presiding Officer's
response to a parliametary
inquiry.

Congressional Record citation—
for 1977 precedent highlighted
above. Citations without "see"
designate precedents created
by Presiding Officer's ruling, or
by a Senate vote.

[6] Oct. 19, 1978, 95-2, *Record*, p. 35262; Sept. 26, 1977, 95-1, *Record*, p. 30828; Sept. 27, 1977, 95-1, *Record*, pp. 31241-42, 31246-47; Sept. 28, 1977, 95-1, *Record*, p. 31432, *see*
Apr. 22, 1982, 97-2, *Record*, pp. 7450-51.
[7] Sept. 15, 1984, 98-2, *Record*, p. 25291.
[8] Sept. 27, 1977, 95-1, *Record*, pp. 31243-45.
[9] Oct. 3, 1977, 95-1, *Record*, pp. 31827-31.
[10] Oct. 1, 1977, 95-1, *Record*, pp 31860-62.
[11] Sept. 28, 1977, 95-1, *Record*, pp. 31297-82.
[12] Oct. 3, 1977, 95-1, *Record*, pp. 31916-30.

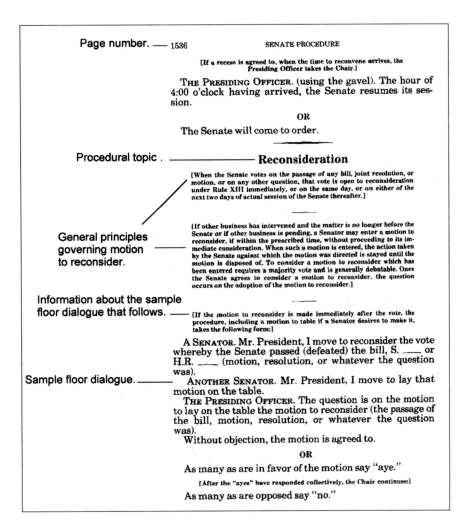

Page number. —— 1536   SENATE PROCEDURE

[If a recess is agreed to, when the time to reconvene arrives, the Presiding Officer takes the Chair.]

THE PRESIDING OFFICER. (using the gavel). The hour of 4:00 o'clock having arrived, the Senate resumes its session.

OR

The Senate will come to order.

Procedural topic. ——————— **Reconsideration**

[When the Senate votes on the passage of any bill, joint resolution, or motion, or on any other question, that vote is open to reconsideration under Rule XIII immediately, or on the same day, or on either of the next two days of actual session of the Senate thereafter.]

General principles governing motion to reconsider. ——

[If other business has intervened and the matter is no longer before the Senate or if other business is pending, a Senator may enter a motion to reconsider, if within the prescribed time, without proceeding to its immediate consideration. When such a motion is entered, the action taken by the Senate against which the motion was directed is stayed until the motion is disposed of. To consider a motion to reconsider which has been entered requires a majority vote and is generally debatable. Once the Senate agrees to consider a motion to reconsider, the question occurs on the adoption of the motion to reconsider.]

Information about the sample floor dialogue that follows. ——

[If the motion to reconsider is made immediately after the vote, the procedure, including a motion to table if a Senator desires to make it, takes the following form:]

A SENATOR. Mr. President, I move to reconsider the vote whereby the Senate passed (defeated) the bill, S. ___ or H.R. ___ (motion, resolution, or whatever the question was).

Sample floor dialogue. ——

ANOTHER SENATOR. Mr. President, I move to lay that motion on the table.

THE PRESIDING OFFICER. The question is on the motion to lay on the table the motion to reconsider (the passage of the bill, motion, resolution, or whatever the question was).

Without objection, the motion is agreed to.

OR

As many as are in favor of the motion say "aye."

[After the "ayes" have responded collectively, the Chair continues:]

As many as are opposed say "no."

Rulemaking Statutes and Budget Resolutions

As already noted, the constitutional grant to each chamber of Congress of authority over its own rules permits the Senate to establish procedural regulations through simple resolutions, which are adopted through action of the originating chamber alone. In certain cases, nevertheless, the Senate institutes procedures through provisions included in statutory measures (bills and joint resolutions), which can become effective only through agreement between both houses and presentation to the President, or through concurrent resolutions, which require agreement between both houses. Given that these procedures are created through an exercise of each chamber's constitutional rule-making authority, they have the same standing as Senate and House rules. A statute or concurrent resolution that contains "rule-making provisions," in this sense, usually also incorporates a section titled "Exercise of Rule-Making Power," which asserts the rulemaking authority of each chamber by declaring that the pertinent provisions "shall be considered as part of the rules of each House," and are subject to being changed "in the same manner ... as in the case of any other rule of such House"[21]—that is, for example, by adoption of a simple resolution of the Senate.

In the Senate, statutory rulemaking provisions are principally of three kinds: (1) those derived from Legislative Reorganization Acts; (2) those establishing expedited procedures for consideration of specific classes of measure; and (3) those derived from the Congressional Budget Act and related statutes governing the budget process. In addition, provisions regulating action in the Senate (or House of Representatives, or both) in the congressional budget process are often contained in congressional budget resolutions, which are concurrent resolutions adopted pursuant to the Congressional Budget Act. Rule-making provisions of most of these kinds are not comprehensively compiled in any document of the Senate, and where no such compilation exists, the provisions applicable to the Senate can most readily be found only by referring to the statutes (or concurrent resolutions) themselves.

Legislative Reorganization Acts

The Legislative Reorganization Act of 1946 (P.L. 79-601, 60 Stat. 812) and the Legislative Reorganization Act of 1970 (P.L. 91-510, 84 Stat. 1140) are important rulemaking statutes that affected legislative procedures. Many rulemaking provisions in these statutes were later incorporated into the Senate's Standing Rules, and some others appear in the compilation of Laws Relating to the Senate presented in the *Senate Manual*, as discussed earlier.

Expedited Procedures

The term "rule-making statute" is most often used in connection with laws that include provisions specifying legislative procedures to be followed in the Senate or the House, or both, in connection with the consideration of a class of measure also specified by the statute. This type of rulemaking statute, commonly referred to as "expedited procedures" or "fast track" provisions, defines special procedures for congressional approval or disapproval of specified actions proposed to be taken by the executive branch or independent agencies. Well-known examples include (1) the "trade authorities procedures" for considering legislation approving trade agreements, which were originally established by the Trade Act of 1974;[22] (2) the procedures for congressional consideration of the recommendations of a base closure commission under the Defense Base Closure and Realignment Act of 1990;[23] and (3) the procedures for Senate action on resolutions disapproving of agency regulations under the Congressional Review Act.[24] Many of these rulemaking provisions are set forth under the heading "Legislative Procedures Enacted in Law" in the *House Manual*.[25] This House compilation, however, does not include certain statutes that establish procedures for the Senate alone, and presents some statutes in a form that omits procedural provisions pertaining only to the Senate.

---

[21] For example, sec. 904(a)(1) and 904(a)(2) of the Congressional Budget and Impoundment Act of 1974, P.L. 93-344.

[22] 19 U.S.C. 2191-2194.

[23] 10 U.S.C. 2687.

[24] 5 U.S.C. 801-804.

[25] U.S. Congress, House, *Constitution, Jefferson's Manual, and Rules of the House of Representatives of the States, One Hundred Tenth Congress*, H.Doc. 109-157, 109th Cong., 2nd sess., [compiled by] John V. Sullivan, Parliamentarian (Washington: GPO, 2007), secs. 1130-1130(31).

Budget Process Statutes

Three of the most important rulemaking statutes define specific procedures for considering budgetary legislation: the Congressional Budget and Impoundment Act of 1974 (commonly known as the Congressional Budget Act), the Balanced Budget and Emergency Deficit Control Act (the so-called "Gramm-Rudman-Hollings Act"), and the Budget Enforcement Act of 1990. For example, Section 305(b) of the Congressional Budget Act defines Senate floor procedures for considering the annual congressional budget resolution. An excerpt from Section 305(b) appears on the following page. In general, rulemaking provisions of these statutes are set forth in *Budget Process Law Annotated,* discussed below.

Procedural Provisions in Budget Resolutions

The chief purpose of the concurrent resolution on the budget that the Congressional Budget Act requires Congress to adopt each year is to set spending, revenue, and deficit targets for the fiscal year and to allocate spending (budget authority and outlays) subject to those targets among budgetary functional categories. In recent years, however, the Senate has often also included in this congressional budget resolution supplementary procedural regulations to govern subsequent action on spending bills or other budget-related measures. The procedures established by these provisions may be made applicable only to the coming year's budgetary action, but are often established as permanent procedures, and are subsequently altered or abolished only by further action in a subsequent budget resolution. Nevertheless, they are not comprehensively compiled in any single source, and may best be identified by examining the texts of adopted congressional budget resolutions for successive years.

Many of the procedural provisions in congressional budget resolutions institute new points of order that, like those established by the Budget Act itself, are available against budgetary measures or provisions contained in these measures. For example, provisions appearing in various budget resolutions beginning in 1993 have established "pay-as-you-go" ("PAYGO") procedures for Senate consideration of legislation affecting direct spending and revenues. The current version of these procedures, which appears in the budget resolution for FY2008 (S.Con.Res. 21), establishes a point of order generally against direct spending and revenue legislation that is projected to increase the deficit or reduce the surplus over either of two specified time periods.[26] Budget resolutions have also extended to this point of order the requirement, applicable to many Budget Act points of order, that the Senate can waive it only by a three-fifths vote.

---

[26] For detail, see CRS Report RL31943, *Budget Enforcement Procedures: Senate Pay-As-You-Go (PAYGO) Rule,* by Bill Heniff Jr.

Rule-Making Provisions in Statutes and Budget Resolutions

No Senate source provides a comprehensive compilation of rule-making provisions in statutes or budget resolutions. Rule-making provisions of many statutes, especially those providing for expedited procedures. are presented in: U.S. Congress, House, *Constitution, Jefferson's Manual, and Rules of the House of Representatives of the States, One Hundred Tenth Congress*, H.Doc. 109-157, 109th Cong., 2nd sess., [compiled by] John V. Sullivan, Parliamentarian (Washington: GPO, 2007), sec. 1130. This compilation, however, omits some statutory expedited procedures applicable only to the Senate.

Rulemaking statutes related to the congressional budget process, together with relevant Senate precedents, are presented in *Budget Process Law Annotated* (discussed later in this report) and addressed in *Riddick's Senate Procedure* (discussed earlier in this report) at pages 502-642.

A discussion of statutory expedited procedures for "Congressional Approvals and Disapprovals" appears in *Riddick's Senate Procedure* at pages 496-501.

Procedural provisions in budget resolutions are best identified by examining the texts of the congressional budget resolutions themselves.

Internet: Congressional budget resolutions that contain procedural provisions are available in searchable form through:

LIS, the Legislative Information System of the U.S. Congress
http://www.congress.gov/crtext/110-advanced.html

Page number in Riddick's — 522
Senate Procedure.

SENATE PROCEDURE

PERMISSIBLE REVISIONS OF CONCURRENT RESOLUTIONS ON THE BUDGET

SEC. 304. (a) IN GENERAL.—At any time after the concurrent resolution on the budget for a fiscal year has been agreed to pursuant to section 301, and before the end of such fiscal year, the two Houses may adopt a concurrent resolution on the budget which revises or reaffirms the concurrent resolution on the budget for such fiscal year most recently agreed to.

(b) ECONOMIC ASSUMPTIONS.—The provisions of section 301(g) shall apply with respect to concurrent resolutions on the budget under this section (and amendments thereto and conference reports thereon) in the same way they apply to concurrent resolutions on the budget under such section 301(g) (and amendments thereto and conference reports thereon).

PROVISIONS RELATING TO THE CONSIDERATION OF CONCURRENT RESOLUTIONS ON THE BUDGET

SEC. 305.

· · · · · · ·

Text of Section 305(b) — (b) PROCEDURE IN SENATE AFTER REPORT OF COMMITTEE; DEBATE;
of the Congressional AMENDMENTS.—
Budget Act.

(1) Debate in the Senate on any concurrent resolution on the budget, and all amendments thereto and debatable motions and appeals in connection therewith, shall be limited to not more than 50 hours, except that with respect to any concurrent resolution referred to in section 304(a) all such debate shall be limited to not more than 15 hours. The time shall be equally divided between, and controlled by, the majority leader and the minority leader or their designees.

Clause 2 of Section 305(b). — (2) Debate in the Senate on any amendment to a concurrent resolution on the budget shall be limited to 2 hours, to be equally divided between, and controlled by, the mover and the manager of the concurrent resolution, and debate on any amendment to an amendment, debatable motion, or appeal shall be limited to 1 hour, to be equally divided between, and controlled by, the mover and the manager of the concurrent resolution, except that in the event the manager of the concurrent resolution is in favor of any such amendment, motion, or appeal, the time in opposition thereto shall be controlled by the minority leader or his designee. No amendment that is not germane to the provisions of such concurrent resolution shall be received. Such leaders, or either of them, may, from the time under their control on the passage of the concurrent resolution, allot additional time to any Senator during the consideration of any amendment, debatable motion, or appeal.

(3) Following the presentation of opening statements on the concurrent resolution on the budget for a fiscal year by the chairman and ranking minority member of the Committee on the Budget of the Senate, there shall be a period of up to four hours for debate on economic goals and policies.

(4) Subject to the other limitations of this Act, only if a concurrent resolution on the budget reported by the Committee on the Budget of the Senate sets forth the economic goals (as de-

Standing Orders by Unanimous Consent

In addition to the standing orders created by resolution, discussed above under "Permanent Standing Orders," the Senate also establishes standing orders by agreeing to unanimous consent requests. These agreements usually make the standing orders effective only for the duration of a Congress, or some other limited period. It has come to be the practice of the Senate to adopt an established package of these standing orders at the beginning of each successive Congress. Standing orders of this kind are not included in the *Senate Manual*, but appear only in the *Congressional Record* on the day they are adopted. For example, on the first day of the 110th Congress in 2007, the Senate adopted 12 unanimous consent agreements establishing (in most cases, re-establishing) standing orders. All 12 of these standing orders appear in the *Congressional Record* excerpt on the following page.[27] One of them established a period of

---

[27] *Congressional Record*, daily edition, vol. 153 (January 4, 2007), pp. S8.

"leader time" on each calendar day. During this time, the majority and minority leaders discuss matters such as the legislative schedule and policy views.

Standing Orders by Unanimous Consent

No Senate document comprehensively compiles standing orders the Senate has adopted by unanimous consent. They may be identified by searching the Congressional Record.

Print: The Congressional Record for each day of session of the Senate is delivered to Senate offices on the following day. The Senate's Calendar of Business is printed for each day of session of the Senate and delivered to Senate offices.

Internet: The Congressional Record for the 110th Congress is available in searchable form through:

LIS, the Legislative Information System of the U.S. Congress
http://www.congress.gov/crtext/110-advanced.html

The Senate's Calendar of Business is available in searchable form through:

GPO Access, a website of the Government Printing Office
http://www.gpoaccess.gov/calendars/senate/index.html

S8   CONGRESSIONAL RECORD — SENATE   *January 4, 2007*

UNANIMOUS-CONSENT AGREEMENT

Mr. REID. Mr. President, I send to the desk en bloc 12 unanimous consent requests. I ask unanimous consent that the requests be considered en bloc, that the requests be agreed to en bloc, and that they appear separately in the RECORD.

Before the Chair rules, I wish to point out that these requests are routine and are done at the beginning of every new Congress. They entail issues such as authority for the Ethics Committee to meet, authorizing the Secretary to receive reports at the desk, establishing leader time each day and floor privileges for House parliamentarians.

The PRESIDING OFFICER. Without objection, it is so ordered.

The requests read as follows:

Mr. President, I ask unanimous consent that for the duration of the 110th Congress, the Ethics Committee be authorized to meet during the session of the Senate.

Mr. President, I ask unanimous consent that for the duration of the 110th Congress, there be a limitation of 15 minutes each upon any rollcall vote, with the warning signal to be sounded at the midway point, beginning at the last 7½ minutes, and when rollcall votes are of 10-minute duration, the warning signal be sounded at the beginning of the last 7½ minutes.

Mr. President, I ask unanimous consent that during the 110th Congress, it be in order for the Secretary of the Senate to receive reports at the desk when presented by a Senator at any time during the day of the session of the Senate.

Mr. President, I ask unanimous consent that the majority and minority leaders may daily have up to 10 minutes each on each calendar day following the prayer and disposition of the reading of, or the approval of, the journal.

Mr. President, I ask unanimous consent that the Parliamentarian of the House of Representatives and his five assistants be given the privileges of the floor during the 110th Congress.

Mr. President, I ask unanimous consent that, notwithstanding the provisions of rule XXVIII, conference reports and statements accompanying them not be printed as Senate reports when such conference reports and statements have been printed as a House report unless specific request is made in the Senate in each instance to have such a report printed.

Mr. President, I ask unanimous consent that the Committee on Appropriations be authorized during the 110th Congress to file reports during adjournments or recesses of the Senate on appropriations bills, including joint resolutions, together with any accompanying notices of motions to suspend rule XVI, pursuant to rule V, for the purpose of offering certain amendments to such bills or joint resolutions, which proposed amendments shall be printed.

Mr. President, I ask unanimous consent that, for the duration of the 110th Congress, the Secretary of the Senate be authorized to make technical and clerical corrections in the engrossments of all Senate-passed bills and resolutions, Senate amendments to House bills and resolutions, Senate amendments to House amendments to Senate bills and resolutions, and Senate amendments to House amendments to Senate amendments to House bills or resolutions.

Mr. President, I ask unanimous consent that for the duration of the 110th Congress, when the Senate is in recess or adjournment, the Secretary of the Senate is authorized to receive messages from the President of the United States, and—with the exception of House bills, joint resolution, and concurrent resolutions—messages from the House of Representatives; and that they be appropriately referred; and that the President of the Senate, the President pro tempore, and the Acting President pro tempore be authorized to sign duly enrolled bills and joint resolutions.

Mr. President, I ask unanimous consent that for the duration of the 110th Congress, Senators be allowed to leave at the desk with the journal clerk the names of two staff members who will be granted the privilege of the floor during the consideration of the specific matter noted, and that the Sergeant-at-Arms be instructed to rotate such staff members as space allows.

Mr. President, I ask unanimous consent that for the duration of the 110th Congress, it be in order to refer treaties and nominations on the day when they are received from the President, even when the Senate has no executive session that day.

Mr. President, I ask unanimous consent that for the duration of the 110th Congress, Senators may be allowed to bring to the desk bills, joint resolutions, concurrent resolutions, and simple resolutions, for referral to appropriate committees.

Unanimous Consent Agreements

Unanimous consent agreements also include additional orders that function as parliamentary authorities in the Senate. These consent agreements establish conditions for floor consideration of specified measures, which, in relation to those measures, override the regulations established by the Standing Rules and other Senate parliamentary authorities. Commonly, for example, agreements of this kind may set the time for taking up or for voting on the measure, limit the time available for debate (in which case they are sometimes referred to as "time agreements"), or specify what amendments and other motions are in order.

These consent agreements constitute parliamentary authorities of the Senate because, once propounded and accepted on the Senate floor, they are enforceable just as are the Senate's Standing Rules and other procedural authorities. Unanimous consent agreements are set forth in the *Congressional Record* when propounded on the floor. Those that have been accepted, but not yet executed, so that they remain in effect, are printed at the front of the Senate's daily *Calendar of Business*.

Unanimous Consent Agreements

Although not comprehensively compiled, consent agreements that have been propounded on the Senate floor are set forth in the Congressional Record, and those that have been accepted and remain in effect are printed at the front of the Senate's daily *Calendar of Business* (legislative calendar).

Print: The *Congressional Record* for each day of session of the Senate is delivered to Senate offices on the following day. The Senate's *Calendar of Business* is printed for each day of session of the Senate and delivered to Senate offices.

Internet: The *Congressional Record* for the 110th Congress is available in searchable form through:

LIS, the Legislative Information System of the U.S. Congress
http://www.congress.gov/crtext/110-advanced.html

The Senate's *Calendar of Business* is available in searchable form through:

GPO Access, a website of the Government Printing Office
http://www.gpoaccess.gov/calendars/senate/index.html

Committee Rules of Procedure

Rule XXVI, paragraph 2, of the Senate's standing rules requires that each standing committee adopt written rules of procedure and publish these rules in the *Congressional Record* not later than March 1 of the first session of each Congress.[28] In addition, any amendments to committee rules do not take effect until they are published in the *Congressional Record*. Committee rules cover important aspects of the committee stage of the legislative process, such as referral of legislation to subcommittees, quorum and voting requirements, markups, and preparation of committee reports. Subcommittees also may have their own supplemental rules of procedure.

Committee rules of procedure do not supersede those established by the standing rules of the Senate. Rule XXV defines the jurisdiction of the standing committees, and Rule XXVI sets forth rules of procedure to be followed by standing committees. The full text of these rules is provided, and relevant Senate precedents are discussed, on pages 382-429 of *Riddick's Senate Procedure*. Committee rules can be enforced in the committee that has adopted them.

Each committee's rules appear in the *Congressional Record* on the day they are submitted for publication. Some committees also publish their rules in a committee print, or in the committee's interim or final "Legislative Calendar," and many post them on their website. In addition, the Senate Committee on Rules and Administration usually issues a document each Congress that compiles the rules of procedure adopted by all Senate committees. This document, entitled

---

[28] According to Rule XXVI, paragraph 2, the March 1 deadline does not apply to committees established on or after February 1. Such committees must publish their rules of procedure not later than 60 days after being established.

Authority and Rules of Senate Committees, also presents the jurisdiction statement for each committee from Rule XXV as well as related information, such as provisions of public law affecting committee procedures.

Reprinted on the following page is an excerpt from the rules of the Senate Committee on Finance for the 105th Congress.[29]

Rules of Senate Committees

U.S. Senate, Committee on Rules and Administration, *Authority and Rules of Senate Committees*, S.Doc. 109-8, 109th Cong., 1st sess., printed under authority of S.Res. 166, 109th Cong. (Washington: GPO, 2005).

Print: *Authority and Rules of Senate Committees* for the 110th Congress(SD-110-10) is available from Senate Printing and Document Services (4-7701), or the Office of Senate Legal Counsel (4-4435).

Internet: Rules of Senate committees are available through:

GPO Access, a website of the Government Printing Office
Legislative page at http://www.gpoaccess.gov/congress/index.html

Rules of individual Senate committees may be found by searching the *Congressional Record* through:

LIS, the Legislative Information System of the U.S. Congress
http://www.congress.gov/crtext/110-advanced.html

Committee websites:
Many Senate committees post their committee rules on their website.

---

[29] *Authority and Rules of Senate Committees, 1997-1998*, S.Doc. 105-4. (Washington: GPO, 1995), p. 84.

Page number. — **84** — **Authority and Rules of Senate Committees** — Title of print issued by Senate Rules and Administration Committee.

After the agenda for a committee meeting is published and distributed, no nongermane items may be brought up during that meeting unless at least two-thirds of the members present agree to consider those items.

(b) In the absence of the chairman, meetings of the committee may be called by the ranking majority member of the committee who is present, provided authority to call meetings has been delegated to such member by the chairman.

RULE 3. PRESIDING OFFICER.—(a) The chairman shall preside at all meetings and hearings of the committee except that in his absence the ranking majority member who is present at the meeting shall preside.

(b) Notwithstanding the rule prescribed by subsection (a) any member of the committee may preside over the conduct of a hearing.

Number and subject matter of committee rule. — RULE 4. QUORUMS.—(a) Except as provided in subsection (b) one-third of the membership of the committee, including not less than one member of the majority party and one member of the minority party, shall constitute a quorum for the conduct of business.

Paragraph b of Rule 4. — (b) Notwithstanding the rule prescribed by subsection (a), one member shall constitute a quorum for the purpose of conducting a hearing.

RULE 5. REPORTING OF MEASURES OR RECOMMENDATIONS.—No measure or recommendation shall be reported from the committee unless a majority of the committee is actually present and a majority of those present concur.

RULE 6. PROXY VOTING; POLLING.—(a) Except as provided by paragraph 7(a)(3) of Rule XXVI of the Standing Rules of the Senate (relating to limitation on use of proxy voting to report a measure or matter), members who are unable to be present may have their vote recorded by proxy. — Reference to Senate's Standing Rules.

(b) At the discretion of the committee, members who are unable to be present and whose vote has not been cast by proxy may be polled for the purpose of recording their vote on any rollcall taken by the committee.

RULE 7. ORDER OF MOTIONS.—When several motions are before the committee dealing with related or overlapping matters, the chairman may specify the order in which the motions shall be voted upon.

RULE 8. BRINGING A MATTER TO A VOTE.—If the chairman determines that a motion or amendment has been adequately debated, he may call for a vote on such motion or amendment, and the vote shall then be taken, unless the committee votes to continue debate on such motion or amendment, as the case may be. The vote on a motion to continue debate on any motion or amendment shall be taken without debate.

RULE 9. PUBLIC ANNOUNCEMENT OF COMMITTEE VOTES.—Pursuant to paragraph 7(b) of Rule XXVI of the Standing Rules of the Senate (relating to public announcement of votes), the results of rollcall votes taken by the committee on any measure (or amendment thereto) or matter shall be announced publicly not later than the day on which such measure or matter is ordered reported from the committee.

Publications of Committees and Offices of the Senate

Some publications prepared by committees and offices of the Senate provide valuable information about Senate parliamentary procedure and practices. While these publications are not official parliamentary reference sources, they often make reference to official sources such as the Senate's standing rules and published precedents. Publications developed by the Senate Parliamentarian, and by the Committees on Budget, Foreign Relations, and Rules and Administration, are described below.

Budget Process Law Annotated

Budget Process Law Annotated (Senate Print 103-49), a print of the Senate Committee on the Budget, provides the text of the Congressional Budget and Impoundment Control Act,[30] the "Gramm-Rudman-Hollings" Act,[31] the Budget Enforcement Act of 1990,[32] and other budget documents such as executive orders. Although no edition of the print has been issued since the 103rd Congress (1993-1994), its great value lies in its informative annotations, which were prepared by William G. Dauster, then Chief Counsel of the Committee on the Budget. These annotations provide summaries of, and citations to, important Senate precedents. For some precedents, the full text of the procedural exchange establishing the precedent is presented.

In addition, the annotations explain references made in the budgetary laws and include the legislative history of certain provisions in these laws. Throughout the print, symbols are used to indicate provisions that establish a point of order in the Senate, or a procedure for controlling time in the Senate.

Budget Process Law Annotated

U.S. Congress, Senate Committee on the Budget, *Budget Process Law Annotated*, committee print, S.Prt. 103-49, 103rd Cong., 1st sess., with annotations by William G. Dauster, Chief Counsel, Committee on the Budget (Washington: GPO, 1993).

Print: The 1993 edition of *Budget Process Law Annotated* is out of print. Photocopies are available from the Senate Budget Committee (621 Dirksen Senate Office Building, 4-0642). The print is 857 pages long.

Internet: Not available.

Senate Cloture Rule

Senate Cloture Rule, a print prepared for the Senate Committee on Rules and Administration by the Congressional Research Service, was last issued during the 99th Congress (1985-1986).[33] The print's coverage of the rule's history and application can be useful to those wanting a more detailed knowledge of how the cloture rule has developed and been used.

The print provides the text of standing rules affecting debate, a chronological history of efforts to limit debate in the Senate (the facts of each situation are provided), a list of selected filibusters throughout history, tables summarizing Senate votes on cloture motions, a bibliography of publications and articles on cloture and filibusters, and legislative histories of the original cloture rule and later amendments to the rule.

Senate Cloture Rule

U.,S. Congress, *Senate Committee on Rules and Administration, Senate Cloture Rule: Limitation of Debate in the Congress of the United States and Legislative History of Paragraph 2 of Rule XXII of the Standing Rules of the United States Senate*

---

[30] P.L. 93-344, 88 Stat. 298, as amended.

[31] Balanced Budget and Emergency Deficit Control Act of 1985, title II of P.L. 99-177, 99 Stat. 1037, as amended.

[32] Title XIII of P.L. 101-508, 104 Stat. 1388-573, as amended.

[33] U.,S. Congress, Senate Committee on Rules and Administration, *Senate Cloture Rule: Limitation of Debate in the Congress of the United States and Legislative History of Paragraph 2 of Rule XXII of the Standing Rules of the United States Senate (Cloture Rule),* committee print, S.Prt. 99-95, 99th Cong., 1st sess., prepared by the Congressional Research Service, Library of Congress (Washington: GPO, 1985).

(Cloture Rule), committee print, S.Prt. 99-95, 99th Cong., 1st sess., prepared by the Congressional Research Service, Library of Congress (Washington: GPO, 1985).

Print: The 1985 edition of the committee print is no longer available from GPO or the Committee, but copies can be obtained from CRS (7-5700).

Internet: Not available.

Treaties and Other International Agreements

Treaties and Other International Agreements: The Role of the United States Senate was designed, in part, to serve as a "reference manual" for the Senate's consideration of treaties and other international agreements.[34] It was prepared as a print for the Senate Committee on Foreign Relations by the Congressional Research Service. The latest edition (S.Prt.106-71) appeared in the 106th Congress.

The print provides detailed information about the Senate's advice and consent role and explains the steps involved in making treaties and executive agreements as well as the history of international agreements. Chapter 5 covers the procedures that govern all stages of Senate consideration of treaties and international agreements, from receipt and referral to committee to final action on the Senate floor. Chapter 10 discusses congressional oversight of treaties and other international agreements.

Treaties and Other International Agreements

U.S. Congress, Senate Committee on Foreign Relations, *Treaties and Other International Agreements: The Role of the United States Senate*, committee print S.Prt. 106-71, 106th Cong., 2nd sess., prepared by the Congressional Research Service, Library of Congress (Washington: GPO, 2001).

Print: *Treaties and Other International Agreements* is available from the Document Room of the Senate Committee on Foreign Relations (423 Dirksen Senate Office Building, 4-4620).

Internet: A link to Senate Print 106-71 is available through:

GPO Access, a website of the Government Printing Office
http://www.gpo.gov/congress/senate/senate11cp106.html

Enactment of a Law

The Senate has maintained a publication providing a concise summary of the legislative process under the title *Enactment of a Law: Procedural Steps in the Legislative Process*. This document, prepared by the Parliamentarian of the Senate under the direction of the Secretary of the Senate, explains Senate floor procedures and the functions of the various Senate officials, such as the Secretary of the Senate, the Sergeant at Arms, and the Senate Parliamentarian. Some information about House and conference procedures and presidential action also is provided. In addition, the document contains illustrations of some of the chief kinds of document used in the legislative process.

---

[34] U.S. Congress, Senate, *Treaties and Other International Agreements: The Role of the United States Senate*, committee print S.Prt. 106-71, 106th Cong., 2nd sess., prepared by the Congressional Research Service, Library of Congress (Washington: GPO, 2001), p. xi.

Enactment of a Law has not appeared in a new printed edition since 1981 and appears no longer to be readily available in print. An updated version, however, was prepared in February 1997 by Senate Parliamentarian Robert B. Dove, and is available on-line. This online version reflects changes made to the congressional budget process and Senate rules and procedures since the last printed edition.

Enactment of a Law

U.S. Senate, *Enactment of a Law: Procedural Steps in the Legislative Process* (S.Doc. 97-20, 97th Cong., 2nd sess., revised under the direction of William F. Hildenbrand, Secretary of the Senate, by Robert B. Dove, Parliamentarian of the Senate (Washington: GPO, 1982).

Print: *Enactment of a Law* is available in print from Senate Printing & Document Services (4-7701).

Internet: An online version of *Enactment of a Law* is available through:

THOMAS, the public access website of the Library of Congress
http://thomas.loc.gov/home/enactment/enactlawtoc.html

CRS, the Congressional Research Service Guides to "Congressional Processes" at
http://www.crs.gov/products/guides/legproc/parloverview/senate/SenateOverview.shtml

How Our Laws Are Made

How Our Laws Are Made was first published in 1953 by the House Committee on the Judiciary. The work provides a summary of the legislative process from the drafting of legislation to final approval and presidential action. While this document focuses on House procedures, it includes a review of Senate committee and floor procedures prepared by the Office of the Parliamentarian of the Senate. Although the document is intended for nonspecialists, its summary descriptions of House procedures serve as a useful reference source. Some earlier editions included sample documents from key stages of the process.

The 23rd edition of *How Our Laws Are Made*, published in 2003,[35] reflects the changes in congressional procedures since the 22nd edition, which was revised and updated in 2000. The new edition, which was prepared by the Office of the Parliamentarian of the House in consultation with the Office of the Parliamentarian of the Senate, also is available online.

How Our Laws Are Made

U.S. Congress, House, *How Our Laws Are Made*, H.Doc. 108-93, 108th Cong., 1st sess., (Washington: GPO, 2003).

Print: At the time this report was issued, the latest print version of *How Our Laws Are Made* was the 23rd edition (H.Doc. 108-93). It is available from the Government Printing Office.

Internet: The text of the 23rd edition of *How Our Laws Are Made* is available through the following websites:

LIS, the Legislative Information System of the U.S. Congress a link appears on the House page at
http://www.congress.gov/house.php

Clerk of the House
http://clerk.house.gov/

THOMAS, the public access website of the Library of Congress
http://thomas.loc.gov/home/lawsmade.toc.html

---

[35] U.S. Congress, House, *How Our Laws Are Made*, H.Doc. 108-93, 108th Cong., 1st sess., (Washington: GPO. 2003).

Rules of Senate Party Conferences

The rules of the conferences of the two parties in the Senate are not adopted by the Senate itself, and accordingly have no binding force in relation to the proceedings of the Senate itself; they cannot be enforced on the Senate floor. Conference rules may nevertheless affect proceedings of the Senate, for they may cover topics such as the selection of party leaders, meetings of the conference, and limitations on committee assignments for conference members. The Senate Republican Conference has adopted rules that it makes available both in printed form and online. It appears that the Senate Democratic Conference currently operates without formally adopted rules.

Rules of Senate Party Conferences

For the Senate Democratic Conference, no source makes available any formal rules.

Print: Copies of the Rules of the Senate Republican Conference are available from the office of the Senate Republican Conference (4-2764).

Internet: An online version of the Rules of the Senate Republican Conference for the 109th Congress can be accessed at http://src.senate.gov/public/. Select the link "About the SRC," then choose "Conference Rules."

Appendix A. Senate Parliamentary Reference Sources

Official Reference Sources

U.S. Congress. Senate. *Authority and Rules of Senate Committees, 2003-2004*. Usually issued each Congress by the Senate Committee on Rules and Administration. 108th Congress, 1st session. S.Doc. No. 108-6 (latest edition). Washington: GPO, 2003.

——*Senate Manual*. Compiled by the Senate Committee on Rules and Administration. 107th Congress, 1st session. S.Doc. No. 107-1 (latest edition). Washington: GPO, 2002.

——*Standing Rules of the Senate*. Prepared by the Senate Committee on Rules and Administration. 106th Congress, 2nd session. S.Doc. 106-15 (latest edition). Washington: GPO, 2000.

U.S. Congress. Senate. *Riddick's Senate Procedure*. 101st Congress, 2nd session. S.Doc. 101-28. Washington: GPO, 1992.

Publications of Committees and Offices of the Senate

U.S. Congress. Senate. *Budget Process Law Annotated*. 103rd Congress, 1st session. S.Prt. 103-49. Washington: GPO, 1993.

——Chapter 3 "Legislative Activity", in *U.S. Senate Handbook*. 104th Congress, 2nd session. S.Prt. 104-64. Washington: GPO, 1996.

——*Enactment of a Law*. 97th Congress, 2nd session. S.Doc. 97-20. Washington: GPO, 1982. An electronic version (February 1997) is available through THOMAS, a Web service of the Library of Congress; see **Appendix B** of this report.

U.S. Congress. House. *How Our Laws Are Made* (23rd edition). Prepared by the Office of the House Parliamentarian. 108th Congress, 1st session. H.Doc. 108-93. Washington: GPO, 2003. An electronic version (June 20, 2003) can be accessed through the Legislative Information System; see **Appendix B** of this report.

U.S. Congress. Senate. *Senate Cloture Rule*. 99th Congress, 1st session. S.Prt. 99-95. Washington: GPO, 1985.

——*Procedure and Guidelines for Impeachment Trials in the United States Senate*. 99th Congress, 2nd session. S.Doc. 99-33. Washington: GPO, 1986.

——*Treaties and Other International Agreements: The Role of the United States Senate*. 106th Congress, 2nd session. S.Prt. 106-71. Washington: GPO, 2001.

CRS Products

Most titles are available full-text from the CRS Home Page at http://www.crs.gov.

CRS Report 98-853, *The Amending Process in the Senate*, by Betsy Palmer.

CRS Report RL30862, *The Budget Reconciliation Process: The Senate's "Byrd Rule"*, by Robert Keith.

CRS Report RL30743, *Committee Assignment Process in the U.S. Senate: Democratic and Republican Party Procedures*, by Judy Schneider.

CRS Report 96-708, *Conference Committee and Related Procedures: An Introduction*, by Elizabeth Rybicki.

CRS Report RS20722, *The First Day of a New Congress: A Guide to Proceedings on the Senate Floor*, by Mildred Amer.

CRS Report RL30548, *Hearings in the U.S. Senate: A Guide for Preparation and Procedure*, by Betsy Palmer.

CRS Report 98-712, *"Holds" in the Senate*, coordinated by Walter J. Oleszek.

CRS Report RL30945, *House and Senate Rules of Procedure: A Comparison*, by Judy Schneider.

CRS Report RS20668, *How Measures Are Brought to the Senate Floor: A Brief Introduction*, by Christopher M. Davis.

CRS Report 96-548, *The Legislative Process on the Senate Floor: An Introduction*, by Valerie Heitshusen.

CRS Report RL30850, *Minority Rights and Senate Procedures*, by Judy Schneider.

CRS Report 98-503, *Publications of the U.S. Senate*, by Matthew Eric Glassman.

CRS Report 98-696, *Resolving Legislative Differences in Congress: Conference Committees and Amendments Between the Houses*, by Elizabeth Rybicki.

CRS Report 98-183, *Senate Committees: Categories and Rules for Committee Assignments*, by Judy Schneider.

CRS Report 98-308, *Senate Legislative Procedures: Published Sources of Information*, by Christopher M. Davis.

CRS Report RL34255, *Senate Policy on "Holds": Action in the 110th Congress*, coordinated by Walter J. Oleszek.

CRS Report 98-311, *Senate Rules Affecting Committees*, by Betsy Palmer.

CRS Report 98-470, *Senate Manual: A Guide to Its Contents*, by Lorraine H. Tong.

CRS Report 98-912, *Senate Rules and Practices on Committee, Subcommittee, and Chairmanship Assignment Limitations as of November 4, 2000*, by Judy Schneider.

CRS Report 96-452, *Voting and Quorum Procedures in the Senate*, by Betsy Palmer.

Appendix B. Senate Parliamentary Reference Information Available Through the Internet

Citations to Internet locations and websites at which electronic versions of various Senate parliamentary reference sources are available can be found throughout this report. This appendix lists these online resources in a single compendium for the convenience of the reader.

The vast majority of the referenced links can be accessed through one of two "gateway" websites maintained by legislative branch organizations: the Legislative Information System (LIS) and GPO Access. Each of these sites (detailed below) provides a good entry point for research into Senate procedures. Documents relating to Senate procedures can also be found on the CRS Guides to Congressional Processes website, as well as on other Library of Congress and U.S. Senate websites at the locations indicated.

Websites are provided for the documents cited. The list is current as of this report's publication date, but because information on the Internet is constantly changing, it should not be considered exhaustive.

Legislative Information System of the U.S. Congress (LIS)

http://www.congress.gov (Congress Only)
The Legislative Information System was released at the start of the 105th Congress. The information in the system is organized into six Web pages: Home, Senate, House, Government, News, and A-Z Index. Each page is accessible by clicking on one of the navigation tabs near the top of the page. The Senate and House pages include multiple links under the category "Rules, and Procedures." The "Government" page includes a link to GPO Access (Legislative), where many documents related to parliamentary procedure are located.

CRS Guides to Congressional Processes

http://www.crs.gov/products/guides/guidehome.shtml
The latest version of this CRS electronic guide provides a wide range of information relating to House and Senate procedures. It includes links to current versions of House and Senate rules and CRS reports on specific procedural topics. Electronic versions of *How Our Laws Are Made* and *Enactment of a Law* provide an overview of procedures in each chamber. Links within the fact sheets and procedural overviews take the user directly to pertinent House or Senate rules and to definitions in Congressional Quarterly's *American Congressional Dictionary*.

GPO Access

GPO Access Home Page
http://www.gpoaccess.gov/index.html

Links to rules of Senate committees
http://www.access.gpo.gov/congress/senate/sclinks.html

Searchable version of the *Senate Manual* (S.Doc. 107-1, 107th Congress, 1st session)
http://www.gpoaccess.gov/smanual/index.html

Browseable version of *Riddick's Senate Procedure* available from GPO
http://www.gpoaccess.gov/riddick/index.html

A searchable version of the 1992 edition of *The Constitution of the United States of America: Analysis and Interpretation)*, and the 1996, 1998, and 2000 supplements is available at http://www.gpoaccess.gov/constitution/index.html. A pdf version of a more recent edition of the main volume (S.Doc. 108-17) can be accessed at http://www.gpoaccess.gov/serialset/cdocuments/index.html. These documents are prepared by the Congressional Research Service, which also maintains an online version at http://www.crs.gov/products/conan/index.shtml.

Other Library of Congress Sites

Links to House and Senate rules via Thomas
http://thomas.loc.gov/home/legbranch/legbranch.html

Enactment of a Law, (online version, February 1997)
http://thomas.loc.gov/home/enactment/enactlawtoc.html

How Our Laws Are Made, (version dated June 20, 2003)
http://thomas.loc.gov/home/lawsmade.toc.html

Constitution
http://www.loc.gov/rr/program/bib/ourdocs/Constitution.html

Amendments 1-10, (Bill of Rights)
http://www.loc.gov/rr/program/bib/ourdocs/billofrights.html

Author Contact Information

Megan Suzanne Lynch
Analyst on the Congress and Legislative Process
mlynch@crs.loc.gov, 7-7853

Richard S. Beth
Specialist on the Congress and Legislative Process
rbeth@crs.loc.gov, 7-8667

*Congressional
Research
Service*

The Committee System in the U.S. Congress

Judy Schneider
Specialist on the Congress

March 21, 2007

Congressional Research Service

7-5700

www.crs.gov

RS20794

CRS Report for Congress
Prepared for Members and Committees of Congress

Summary

Due to the high volume and complexity of its work, Congress divides its tasks among committees and subcommittees. Both the House and Senate have their own committee systems, which are similar but not identical. Within chamber guidelines, however, each committee adopts its own rules; thus, there is considerable variation among panels. This report provides a brief overview of the organization and operations of House and Senate committees.

Contents

Contacts

Introduction

Decentralization is the most distinctive characteristic of the congressional committee system. Due to the high volume and complexity of its work, Congress divides its legislative, oversight, and internal administrative tasks among committees and subcommittees. Within assigned subject areas, committees and subcommittees gather information; compare and evaluate legislative alternatives; identify policy problems and propose solutions to them; select, determine the text of, and report out measures for the full chambers to consider; monitor executive branch performance of duties (oversight); and look into allegations of wrongdoing (investigation).

Although Congress has used committees since its first meetings in 1789, the 1946 Legislative Reorganization Act (60 *Stat.* 812) set the foundation of today's committee system. The House and Senate each have their own committees and related rules of procedure, which are similar but not identical. Within the guidelines of chamber rules, each committee adopts its own rules addressing organizational, structural, and procedural issues; thus, even within a chamber, there is considerable variation among panels.

Within their respective areas of responsibility, committees generally operate rather independently of each other and of their parent chambers. The difficult tasks of aggregating committees' activities, and of integrating policy in areas where jurisdiction is shared, fall largely to the chambers' party leaderships.

Structure and Organization

Types of Committees

There are three types of committees—standing, select, and joint.

Standing committees are permanent panels identified in chamber rules. The rules also list the jurisdiction of each committee. Because they have legislative jurisdiction, standing committees consider bills and issues and recommend measures for consideration by the respective chambers. They also have oversight responsibility to monitor agencies, programs, and activities within their jurisdictions, and in some cases in areas that cut across committee jurisdictions. Most standing committees recommend authorized levels of funds for government operations and for new and existing programs within their jurisdiction. Standing committees also have jurisdiction over appropriations (in the case of the Appropriations Committees), taxation (in the case of the House Ways and Means and Senate Finance Committees), various other revenues, and direct spending such as Social Security, veterans' pensions, and some farm support programs.

Select committees usually are established by a separate resolution of the parent chamber, sometimes to conduct investigations and studies, sometimes to consider measures. A select committee is established because the existing standing committee system does not address an issue comprehensively, or because a particular event sparks interest in an investigation. A select committee may be permanent or temporary. *Special committees* tend to be similar in constitution and function and that distinction from select committees is generally thought to be only semantic.

Joint committees are made up of Members of both chambers. Today, they usually are permanent panels that conduct studies or perform housekeeping tasks rather than consider measures. A *conference committee* is a temporary joint committee formed to resolve differences in Senate- and House-passed versions of a particular measure.

Subcommittees

Most committees form subcommittees with legislative jurisdiction to consider and report bills on particular issues within the purview of the full committee. Committees may assign their subcommittees such specific tasks as the initial hearings held on measures and oversight of laws and programs in their areas. Subcommittees are responsible to and work within guidelines established by their parent committees. Consequently, subcommittees' number, independence, and autonomy vary between committees.

Composition

Party leaders generally determine the size of committees and the ratio of majority to minority members on each of them. Each party is primarily responsible for choosing its committee leaders and assigning its Members to committees, and, once assigned to a particular committee, a Member often makes a career there. Each committee distributes its members among its subcommittees, on which only members of the committee may serve. There are limits on the number and type of committees and subcommittees on which each Member may serve. Members, especially in the House, tend to specialize in the issues of their assigned committees.

Leadership

A committee's authority is centered in its chair. In practice, a chair's prerogatives usually include determining the committee's agenda, deciding when to take or delay action, presiding during meetings, and controlling most funds allocated by the chamber to the committee. Several rules allow others a share in controlling a committee's business, such as one allowing a majority of members of a committee to call a meeting. The ranking minority member, usually the minority party member of longest committee service, often participates in the chair's regulation of the committee, in addition to leading on matters affecting a committee's minority members. Also, each subcommittee has a chair and a ranking minority member who oversee the affairs of their panel.

To distribute committee power, chamber and party caucus rules limit the number of full and subcommittee chair or ranking minority positions a single Member may hold. Only the Republicans have committee leadership term limits. No House Republican may serve as chair (or ranking minority member) of a committee or subcommittee for more than three consecutive terms, effective with the 104th Congress, and no Senate Republican may serve more than six years as chair and six years as ranking member of any standing committee, effective with the 105th Congress. Waivers can be granted.

Staff

Approximately 2,000 aides provide professional, administrative, and clerical support to committees. Their main job is to assist with writing, analyzing, amending, and recommending measures to the full chamber, as well as overseeing the executive branch's implementation of laws and the operation of programs. Pursuant to funding resolutions and other mechanisms, committees receive varying levels of operating funds for their expenses, including the hiring of staff. From these funds, each hires its own staff, and committees employ varying numbers of aides ranging from a few to dozens. (Committees may also fire staff.) Most staff and resources are controlled by the chair of a committee, although in general a portion must be shared with minority-party members. Further, some committees assign staff directly to their subcommittees, and give subcommittee leaders considerable authority in hiring and supervising subcommittee staff. Each committee sets staff pay levels within limits contained in chamber salary policies.

Oversight

Committees conduct oversight to assure that the policy intentions of legislators are carried out by those administering programs, and to assess the adequacy of programs for changing conditions. Some committees, especially in the House, establish separate oversight subcommittees to oversee the implementation of all programs within their jurisdiction. Also, each chamber has assigned to specific committees oversight responsibility for certain issues and programs that cut across committee jurisdictions, and each has a committee responsible for overseeing comprehensively the efficiency and economy of government activities.

Operations and Procedures

Referral

Each committee has nearly exclusive right to consider measures within its jurisdiction. In general, committees are not required to act on any measure, and a measure can not come to the floor for consideration unless through the action or at least concurrence of a committee. A procedure to discharge a committee from consideration is rarely successful.

Any introduced measure generally gets referred immediately to a committee. Especially in the House, some measures are referred to two or more panels, usually because policy subjects are split among committees. When more than one House committee receives a referral, a primary committee is usually designated. Other panels receive a sequential referral. In the Senate, referral is determined by the predominant subject matter in the legislation. Singly referred measures have been more likely than multiply referred ones to pass their chamber and to be enacted into law, in part because of the difficulty in coordinating the work of multiple panels.

Committees receive varying numbers of measures. Committees dispose of these measures as they please, selecting only a small percentage for action, for a number of reasons. For instance, a committee usually receives many proposals in each major policy area within its jurisdiction, but ultimately chooses one measure as its vehicle in each such area. While those measures not chosen usually receive no further congressional action, the idea, specific provisions, or entire text of some of these measures may be incorporated through the amendment process into others that the committees and chambers consider and that become law. Determining the fate of measures and, in effect, helping to set a chamber's agenda make committees very powerful.

Committees often send their measures to subcommittees for initial consideration, but only a full committee can report a measure to the floor for consideration. When a committee or a subcommittee considers a measure, it usually takes the four actions described below. This sequence assumes the committee favors a measure; but, at any time, action on a measure may be discontinued.

Executive Agency Comment

As a matter of practice and cooperation between the legislative and executive branches, a committee asks relevant executive agencies for written comments on measures it is studying.

Hearings

Committees frequently hold hearings to receive testimony from individuals not on the committee. Hearings may be for legislative, oversight, or investigative purposes. Legislative hearings are those addressing measures or policy issues before the committee, and they may address many measures on a given subject. Oversight hearings focus on the implementation and administration of programs created by law. Many committees perform oversight when preparing to reauthorize funds for a program, which may occur annually. Investigative hearings often address allegations of wrongdoing by public officials or private citizens, or seek the facts behind a major disaster or crisis. Oversight and investigative hearings may lead to the introduction of legislative proposals.

At hearings, committees gather information and views, identify problems, gauge support for and opposition to measures and proposals, and build a record of action on committee proposals. Some common elements of hearings include:

- Most, but not all, hearings are held in Washington, DC. Hearings held outside of Washington, DC, are called Field hearings.

- Committees invite experts (witnesses), including Members not on the committee, federal officials, representatives of interest groups, and private citizens to testify at hearings.

- Most witnesses testify willingly upon invitation by the chair or ranking minority member, and some request to testify. However, committees may summon individuals, as well as written materials, under a legal process (subpoena).

- Before testifying, witnesses generally are required to submit written statements, which they then summarize orally. Subsequently, committee members question witnesses.

- Committees generally must give at least one week public notice of the date, place, and subject of a hearing. The public usually may attend hearings and other committee meetings, and open hearings and meetings might be broadcast.

Markup

Following legislative hearings, a committee decides whether to attempt to report a measure, in which case it chooses a specific measure to mark up and then modifies it through amendment to clean up problems, and sometimes, to attract broader committee support. A business meeting for this purpose is called a markup. Both chambers require a minimum quorum of one-third of a committee's members to hold a markup session, and some committees establish a higher quorum.

- The procedures of each chamber for amending measures on the floor apply generally to its committees. In practice, the amending process may be formal for controversial measures and informal for ones less contentious.

- In leading a markup, a chair in practice generally chooses the legislative vehicle, and presents it for consideration and amendment. This vehicle may be an introduced bill, or another version prepared by committee staff at the direction of the chair.

- Senate committees may permit absent members to vote by proxy, by submitting their vote in writing in advance of the actual vote; proxy voting is banned in the House.

Report

A majority of committee members voting, with a majority quorum present, is needed to approve a measure and report it to the parent chamber. A committee rarely reports a measure without changes. Committees sometimes report measures with a series of changes in various sections, or with one large amendment as an entirely new text (called an amendment in the nature of a substitute). A committee may also set aside its amended measure and report a new one reflecting the amended text. In the House the new bill is called a *clean bill*; in the Senate, an *original bill*. Any committee amendments, and the entire measure, require a chamber's approval to be passed.

A reported measure usually is accompanied by a written document, called a report, describing the measure's purposes and provisions and telling Members of a chamber why this version has been reported and why it should be passed. The report reflects the views of a majority of the committee, but also may contain minority, supplemental, or additional views of committee members. It usually includes estimates of the legislation's cost should it become law, various statements of its impact and application, a section-by-section analysis, and a comparison with existing law. Officials of the executive and judicial branches of government use these reports as an aid to understanding the legislative history of a law and Congress's intent in enacting it.

Measures may reach the floor for consideration in ways other than by being formally reported. A measure may be called up and simultaneously extracted from a committee by unanimous consent, or, in the House, by suspension of the rules. These procedures, however, are seldom used without the consent of the committee of jurisdiction. By contrast, a measure may be extracted from a committee without its approval. For example, the House may agree to a motion to discharge a committee of consideration of a measure, and in general a Senator may offer the text of a measure before a committee as an amendment to a bill under consideration on the floor.

Committees and Chamber Action

The measure and its report are placed on a calendar of chamber business and scheduled for floor action by the majority-party leadership. In the House, the Committee on Rules works with the leadership to establish the terms and conditions for debating the more controversial or complex measures. These terms may include restrictions on offering and debating amendments. Other measures are considered under a few different procedures, where little or no debate and amendment is the norm.

In the Senate, noncontroversial measures ordinarily are called up by unanimous consent, and disposed of with little or no debate and no amendment. More controversial or complex measures may be considered under the provisions of a time agreement (or other unanimous consent agreement), which may restrict Senators' freedom of debate and amendment in part by establishing time limits on actions related to the measure. Alternatively, such a measure may require a motion to proceed to its consideration, which generally is debatable and must be agreed to by majority vote.

The influence of committees over measures extends to their consideration on the floor. The chair and ranking member of the committee or subcommittee that considered the measure (or their designees) normally manage floor debate for their respective parties. Managers guide measures through final disposition by the chamber, which includes planning parliamentary strategy, controlling time for debate, responding to questions from colleagues, warding off unwanted amendments, and building coalitions in favor of their positions. Especially in the House, committee members also have priority in recognition to offer floor amendments.

Committees' responsibilities extend beyond a measure's initial passage by the chambers to its enactment into law. If the chambers agree to different versions of a measure, the leaders of the reporting committees may facilitate its transmittal between the chambers to obtain agreement on one version. If, however, the chambers decide to reconcile their differences at a conference committee, members of the reporting committees will comprise most of the negotiators. In practice, the chambers rely on the chair and ranking member of the reporting committee to choose which of their party colleagues on a committees will serve as conferees. Finally, the chair and ranking member often head their chamber's delegations in conference.

Related CRS Reports

Brief fact sheets and long reports on aspects of the House and Senate committee system are included in the "CRS Guide to the Legislative and Budget Process," which is available online at http://www.crs.gov/products/guides/guidehome.shtml. Printed versions of the fact sheets and reports are also available from CRS.

Author Contact Information

Judy Schneider
Specialist on the Congress
jschneider@crs.loc.gov, 7-8664

Resources from TheCapitol.Net

Capitol Learning Audio Courses™

<www.CapitolLearning.com>

- Understanding the Path of Legislation, ISBN: 158733030X

- Congress, the Legislative Process, and the Fundamentals of Lawmaking,
  A Nine Course Series, ISBN: 1587331241

- Conference Committees: How the Work Gets Done, ISBN: 1587330210

Live Training

<www.CapitolHillTraining.com>

- Congress In A Nutshell: Understanding Congress *<www.CongressInANutshell.com>*

- Congressional Dynamics and the Legislative Process *<www.LegislaiveProcess.com>*

- Capitol Hill Workshop *<www.CapitolHillWorkshop.com>*

- Understanding Congressional Budgeting and Appropriations
  <www.CongressionalBudgeting.com>

- Advanced Federal Budget Process *<www.BudgetProcess.com>*

Publications

<www.AllOfOurBooks.com>

- Citizens Guide to Influencing Elected Officials *<www.tcncpg.com>*

- Congressional Directory *<www.CongressionalDirectory.com>*

- Congressional Deskbook: The Practical and Comprehensive Guide to Congress
  <www.CongressionalDeskbook.com>

- Legislative Drafter's Deskbook *<www.LegislativeDraftersDeskbook.com>*

- Lobbying and Advocacy *<www.LobbyingandAdvocacy.com>*

- Persuading Congress *<www.PersuadingCongress.com>*

- Pocket Constitution *<www.TCNConst.com>*

- Testifying Before Congress *<www.TestifyingBeforeCongress.com>*

703-739-3790 **303**

About TheCapitol.Net

We help you understand Washington and Congress.™

For over 30 years, TheCapitol.Net and its predecessor, Congressional Quarterly Executive Conferences, have been training professionals from government, military, business, and NGOs on the dynamics and operations of the legislative and executive branches and how to work with them.

Instruction includes topics on the legislative and budget process, congressional operations, public and foreign policy development, advocacy and media training, business etiquette and writing. All training includes course materials.

TheCapitol.Net encompasses a dynamic team of more than 150 faculty members and authors, all of whom are independent subject matter experts and veterans in their fields. Faculty and authors include senior government executives, former Members of Congress, Hill and agency staff, editors and journalists, lobbyists, lawyers, nonprofit executives and scholars.

We've worked with hundreds of clients across the country to develop and produce a wide variety of custom, on-site training. All courses, seminars and workshops can be tailored to align with your organization's educational objectives and presented on-site at your location.

Our practitioner books and publications are written by leading subject matter experts.

TheCapitol.Net has more than 2,000 clients representing congressional offices, federal and state agencies, military branches, corporations, associations, news media and NGOs nationwide.

Our blog: Hobnob Blog—hit or miss ... give or take ... this or that ...

Our recommended provider of government training in Brazil is PATRI/EDUCARE <www.patri.com>

TheCapitol.Net supports the T.C. Williams Debate Society, Scholarship Fund of Alexandria, and Sunlight Foundation

TheCapitol.Net

Non-partisan training and publications that show how Washington works.™

PO Box 25706, Alexandria, VA 22313-5706   703-739-3790   www.TheCapitol.Net

CPSIA information can be obtained at www.ICGtesting.com
Printed in the USA
BVOW06s0046210414

351145BV00001B/13/P